WHO IS ROGER CASEMENT?

WHO IS ROGER CASEMENT?

A NEW PERSPECTIVE

MICHAEL LAUBSCHER

There now steps upon our stage a man who is, perhaps, its most tragic figure. Look well on this man, because he carries in himself the whole story of Ireland. Learn the secret of this man and you have learnt the whole secret of Ireland.

Shaw Desmond, *The Drama of Sinn Féin*.

First published 2010

The History Press Ireland
119 Lower Baggot Street
Dublin 2
www.thehistorypress.ie

© Michael Laubscher, 2010

The right of Michael Laubscher to be identified as the Author
of this work has been asserted in accordance with the
Copyrights, Designs and Patents Act 1988.

British Library Cataloguing in Publication Data.
A catalogue record for this book is available from the British Library.

ISBN 978 1 8458 8972 2

Typesetting and origination by The History Press
Printed in Great Britain
Manufacturing managed by Jellyfish Print Solutions Ltd

CONTENTS

ACKNOWLEDGEMENTS

There has been, and continues to be, much scholarly interest in Roger Casement, and a number of outstanding books and articles have been published by eminent scholars in the field. In preparing this manuscript, I drew heavily upon the work that they have done in advancing our knowledge and understanding of this enigmatic humanitarian and revolutionary. *Who is Roger Casement?* is not intended to be a contribution to this growing body of scholarly literature, but a broader overview in a format that I hope will appeal to the general reading public. I have drawn extensively on the historical and biographical knowledge currently available, especially in the works listed in the bibliography, in generating an impression of Casement presented through the eyes of a fictitious journalist attempting to wrestle with the identity and motivations of a man with whom many outside England and Ireland were unfamiliar, even in 1916.

In keeping with the concept of journalistic dispatches as the presentational format, details that would not have been available to an American journalist covering the events of 1916 are often attributed to anonymous sources. In fact, much of that data has been based upon a reading of the biographies cited in the bibliography. I am indebted to those biographers for the wealth of information upon which I was able to draw, and I have tried to be as accurate as possible in capturing the history that they have so faithfully recorded. By casting myself in a role of a fictitious journalist attempting to make sense of the events for his readers, however, I often take the liberty of offering thoughts and reflections that are purely my own. Details about the arrest, trial and execution were drawn primarily from contemporary accounts in *The London Times* digital archives and from the trial transcript edited by George Knott. Historical details were drawn from a variety of sources.

I should also like to take this opportunity to express my appreciation to Stephanie Boner and the editorial staff at The History Press Ireland for taking an interest in my manuscript and for helping to turn an idea into a reality.

And most importantly, I want to acknowledge the support and encouragement of my wife Maria Esperanza, who never lost faith, and never allowed me to lose faith, in reaching closure on a project that has occupied me off and on for the past several years. Without that undying faith, I would never have persevered.

MONDAY 15 MAY 1916

In what may well prove to be the most improbable case of treason in the history of the British Empire, Sir Roger Casement was arraigned today at the Bow Street Police Court before Sir John Dickinson, Chief Magistrate for the Metropolitan Police, after being turned over to British authorities by the Royal Irish Constabulary on Easter Sunday.

Popular advocate of the oppressed, a veteran of almost twenty years in the British Consular Service, member of the Order of St Michael and St George, and Knight of the Realm, Casement is not one against whom a charge of treason can be easily entertained. Treason, after all, is one of the most heinous of political offences and would normally be associated with someone who, for whatever reason, had made a conscious and calculated decision to bring down his own government. Based on my coverage of British and Irish politics over the past decade, Sir Roger Casement simply does not fit the profile of a man who would turn against the very government to which he had dedicated his entire professional career. Indeed, the question of how a man with such impeccable credentials could become a traitor to the Crown is a question that intrigues even the most cynical of British observers.

Appearing before the court today in shackles, gaunt, stooped, and unkempt, the defendant impressed this observer as anything but the distinguished diplomat who had earned international acclaim for his humanitarian efforts in the Congo and the Amazon. His bedraggled appearance was more suggestive of a common criminal, although the charges against him are anything but 'common'. Conspiring with the enemy and fomenting revolution are allegations that have attracted the attention of politicians, legal scholars, and the general public in a way that far transcends any common criminal investigation. Had he been so inclined (and had British law permitted), the Chief Magistrate could have easily sold advance tickets for admission to today's proceedings. Given the attention it has received, one would never have guessed that this was merely a preliminary hearing. Assuming that the prosecution can indeed establish a *prima facie* case for a charge of treason, an arraignment, indictment, and formal trial before the King's Bench will still lie in the offing.

In an opening presentation that seemed almost at odds with his prosecutorial role, Archibald Bodkin, senior Counsel for the prosecution, summarised a career of stellar accomplishments, that went well beyond the norm in service to the Crown. His catalogue of Casement's awards and accomplishments began with the Queen's Medal for his service in southern Africa, during the confrontation sixteen years ago between Britain, and the Boers of the Orange Free State and the South African Republic. After a subsequent campaign against atrocities in King Leopold's Congo Free State, which culminated in a widely acclaimed but controversial public condemnation of the Belgian King's activities, he was made a Companion of St Michael and St George by King Edward. And after a similar campaign against atrocities in the Putumayo region of the Amazon, he was made a knight by King George in 1911, and awarded the Coronation Medal later that same year. Mr Bodkin's biographical résumé of the accused sounded more like a character reference for the defence, than an indictment by the prosecution, and could have easily left one wondering what this distinguished public servant was doing in the dock.

The prosecutor's tack was soon apparent, however, when he called his primary witness of the day. The testimony was in such marked contrast to Bodkin's introductory portrait that any loyal British subject could only recoil in outrage. Even before today's proceedings, the sentiments within governmental circles had already become openly hostile. One irate Member of Parliament demanded, in open session this week, to know why Casement, who is being charged not only with conspiring with Germany, with whom Britain has been at war now for almost two years, but also with masterminding the recent insurrection in Dublin, was being granted the privilege of a trial, when the other ringleaders of that uprising have already been tried, convicted, and executed by a military tribunal. Courts martial convened by General Sir John Maxwell, dispatched to put down the Irish rebellion shortly after returning from service as Commander-in-Chief of the Anglo-Egyptian armies, have thus far resulted in the execution of fifteen Irish dissidents over the course of just the past month.

The latest in the series of executions was carried out just three days ago at Kilmainham Gaol in Dublin, when Seán MacDiarmada and James Connolly were brought before firing squads. Both were among those taken into custody within days of the fall of the General Post Office, the rebel headquarters in Dublin, and proven, to the satisfaction of the military tribunals, to have been key participants in planning the insurrection. Mr Connolly, who reportedly had to be propped up in a chair to face the firing squad because of wounds sustained in the street fighting that raged for several days in mid-April, is actually believed to have been the commander of a ragtag group of revolutionary 'soldiers' known as the Irish Citizen Army. A witness to the execution has reported that in his final statement, Connolly referred to himself rather pompously as Commandant-General of the Dublin Division of the Army of the Irish Republic.

Public sentiment surrounding today's hearing at the Bow Street Police Court appears to echo the position taken by the indignant Member of Parliament: those Londoners queried by this reporter inevitably grew red in the face and fumed about this 'ungrateful Irish turncoat', who had taken advantage of Britain's preoccupation with the war on the continent to promote insurrection at home. His distinguished career with the Foreign Office seems to have fuelled, rather than mitigated, the outrage; Pádraig Pearse and James Connolly and the thirteen others executed in the aftermath of the Easter Rising are roundly condemned, as would be expected, but for Casement, the public outcry has been especially venomous, precisely because of his service record on behalf of the Crown. While the recent hostilities in Dublin may have elevated public awareness of historical tensions between England and its island province to the west, there was no concealing the fact that resentment among those interviewed for this article was not of recent origin; the general conviction expressed in no uncertain terms was that one should never have trusted an Irishman to serve in an official capacity with His Majesty's government in the first place. One especially irate citizen suggested that Casement had undoubtedly planned this all along, developing diplomatic connections with the German government during the course of his Consular career as part of a long-term clandestine intrigue to undermine the United Kingdom and sever its connection with Ireland.

During his opening address to the Court, Mr Bodkin added fuel to the fire of outrage by quoting from the defendant's letter to the Foreign Minister, Sir Edward Grey, upon occasion of being knighted five years ago, 'I find it very hard to choose the words with which to make acknowledgement of the honour done me by the King'. [1] Casement had stated in his letter:

> I am very deeply sensible of the honour done to me by his Majesty. I would beg that my humble duty might be presented to his Majesty, when you may do me the honour of conveying to him my deep appreciation of the honour he has been so graciously pleased to confer upon me.

Either Mr Casement was being disingenuous in his turgid expressions of appreciation to the Foreign Minister and the King in 1911, or his alleged collusion with Germany represents an especially invidious reversal of loyalties. In either case, Mr Casement's own words were resurrected today in a context that can only serve to discredit him.

Charged under the Defence of the Realm Act, a statute passed by the British Parliament in August of 1914 upon the outbreak of war with Germany, this erstwhile British hero now faces the possibility of being executed by the very government to which he devoted his entire professional life. In spite of the gravity of the situation, Casement appeared today to be calm and unruffled by the case being laid out before the court. Even the most myopic of observers could surely see that beneath the haggard appearance, the inevitable product of having spent the last few weeks in solitary confinement, there nevertheless appears the strength of character and nobility of bearing that one would expect from the image painted by the honourable Mr Bodkin in his opening remarks. He stood erect and apparently unmoved throughout the day's testimony, neither acknowledging nor challenging the evidence being presented. He spoke on only one occasion, at the very beginning of the day's proceedings, addressing the Court, not in his own defence but claiming, in a soft but firm voice, that the co-defendant appearing with him in the dock, Mr Daniel Julian Bailey, had been unjustly accused of complicity in the matter before them, and that he, Mr Casement, would provide for Mr Bailey's legal defence. It was a remarkable display of magnanimity, especially when seen in the light of Mr Bailey's subsequent testimony.

Indeed, the real drama of the day came with the interrogation of Mr Bailey, who had served with the Royal Irish Rifles as a part of the British army and who had been taken prisoner by the Germans. Bailey was arrested by the Royal Irish Constabulary on the same day and in the same general vicinity as Casement, on the coast of Kerry. According to his own testimony, Bailey had accompanied Casement from Germany to the coast of Ireland to help foment the rebellion that took place last month, and the two of them, along with a third conspirator named Monteith, had washed ashore on the coast of Kerry in the early morning hours of Good Friday after disembarking from a German submarine. Assuring the intrigued audience at today's hearing, that details of this preposterous escapade will emerge as the interrogation continues tomorrow, the prosecutor focused today's initial stages of the enquiry on the treasonous acts that occurred during the months leading up to their capture.

Mr Bodkin led the interrogation, although it seemed apparent from his frequent exchange of glances with Attorney General Frederick E. Smith that the latter was effectively guiding the course of the arraignment. It is unusual, to say the least, for such a high-level representative of the government to be present for a simple arraignment, which adds to the drama and intrigue surrounding the case. Mr Smith has a reputation for ruthlessness in his pursuit of 'justice', having ascended quickly from the House of Commons to Solicitor-General, just a year ago this month, and finally to the position of Attorney-General, this past October. While in charge of the Press Bureau at the outbreak of hostilities with Germany, he was instrumental in enforcing media censorship, in which capacity many of my journalistic colleagues found him to be heavy-handed to say the least. While his presence today may have been somewhat irregular in terms of judicial protocol, several of the columnists I know from the local press were not at all surprised by his personal interest in directing the course of the proceedings.

Under Mr Smith's intent gaze, Mr Bodkin led the defendant Bailey through an interrogation that proved him to be anything but a friend to his Irish compatriot. It can only be assumed that the witness must have struck some kind of deal with the prosecution, to gain leniency in his own behalf. The testimony was damning in the extreme, painting Casement as a vile traitor who conspired with the Empire of Germany, with whom Britain has now been engaged for almost two years in the most vicious war of attrition in the history of civilization. As part of that conspiracy, Casement allegedly tried to take advantage of their vulnerability, to coerce Irish soldiers being held as prisoners of war by the Germans to forsake their service to the Crown and join a brigade that would, with German support, exploit the wartime situation to forcefully remove Ireland from its historic place in the United Kingdom.

According to Bailey, Mr Casement appeared at a German POW camp in Limburg, where a number of Irish prisoners had been gathered together from various other camps throughout Germany, and had addressed the prisoners on numerous occasions in an attempt to recruit them for service in this Irish Brigade. Unfortunately for Mr Casement, he had been foolhardy enough to prepare a pamphlet for distribution among the assembled Irishmen, as a way of reinforcing his oral arguments. A copy of the pamphlet had come into the hands of the Court, providing it with documentary evidence to supplement the oral testimony that Mr Bodkin elicited during the course of the day's proceedings. The outraged prosecutor took obvious delight in being able to read from the document in open Court.

'My fellow Irishmen', he quoted with obvious sarcasm in his voice:

> … here is a chance for you to fight for Ireland. You have fought for
> England while England is your hereditary enemy. You have fought for
> Belgium in England's interest, though it was no more to you than the
> Fiji Islands. Are you willing to fight for your own true country?[2]

While the details defy credulity, the firsthand testimony from one who
personally witnessed Casement in action made for a powerful day of
melodrama in the London courtroom. Based on Bailey's account of the
events that led to his ultimate capture and arrest, it appears that during
the autumn of this past year, Casement conspired with the German
government to collect all those British soldiers of Irish descent who
were being held as prisoners of war in various detention facilities
across Germany, and assemble them in a single camp at Limburg an der
Lahn. They thus became a true captive audience for Casement's dia-
tribes about British oppression and Irish nationalism, as he attempted
to persuade them to join a brigade that would be freed from German
captivity, to fight for Irish independence. Germany was more than
happy to indulge his fantasies, of course, for if he could indeed convince enough men to participate in the endeavour, no matter how
hare-brained, it would certainly be an added distraction to an enemy
that was proving to be frustratingly tenacious.

Once again, drawing upon the pamphlet in his possession, Mr
Bodkin was able to use Casement's own words to support the charge
that the brigade was to be formed in collusion with England's enemy,
specifically for the purpose of fomenting insurrection within the
United Kingdom. 'With a view to securing the national freedom of
Ireland,' he read, his voice almost trembling with outrage:

> … with the moral and material assistance of the German Government,
> an Irish Brigade is being formed. The object of the Brigade shall be to
> fight for the cause of Ireland. The Brigade shall be formed and shall
> fight under the Irish flag: the men shall wear a special, distinctively
> Irish uniform and have Irish officers. The Brigade shall be clothed, fed,

and efficiently equipped with arms and ammunition by the German Government. It shall be stationed near Berlin and be treated as guests of the German Government.[3]

To Casement's dismay, according to Mr Bailey, the Irish soldiers proved to be less than receptive to his appeals. Casement apparently assumed that all true Irishmen would share his disdain for the British (a disdain that is still unexplained, given his lifetime of service to the Crown), as well as his passionate Irish nationalism. Not only were they uninterested, Bailey insisted during his testimony, the soldiers were openly hostile, to the point, on a couple of occasions, where German guards had to intervene to protect Casement from harm. Casement's appeals were, in Bailey's words, as eloquent as one would expect from an experienced diplomat, but he had obviously misjudged his audience, almost as badly as the insurrectionists themselves appear to have misjudged the willingness of the Irish population to support their uprising this past month in Dublin.

While the justice and efficacy of the cause may have been self-evident to Mr Casement, the Irish soldiers were not about to dismiss their own sacrifices on behalf of the Crown as misguided acts of stupidity. They had voluntarily and proudly enlisted to defend the United Kingdom, of which Ireland has been an integral part since the Act of Union in 1801, and according to Bailey, they were incensed and offended by this subversive appeal to their Irish heritage. As a result of a recent exchange of wounded prisoners, several of the former Irish prisoners of war were on hand in the courtroom today to support Mr Bailey's assertions. The wounds they had received while serving the Crown on the battlefield reinforced their outrage at the man who had tried to subvert their patriotism. While their testimony served the prosecutorial function of corroborating that of the main witness, their presence in the courtroom was obviously meant to have an emotional effect as well; one was missing an arm, another had a patch over a missing eye, a third had to be brought to the court in a wheelchair. Even for a 'neutral' observer, it was difficult to suppress at least a modicum of outrage over efforts to coerce such a group into forsaking the very cause for which they had sustained these grievous injuries.

Michael O'Connor, a corporal with the Royal Irish Regiment that had been a part of the British Expeditionary Force in France, was typical of the lot. Having lost an arm in combat, he was taken prisoner by the Germans in October and ultimately transferred to Limburg as a part of the collaborative effort between Casement and the German Government to form an Irish Brigade. Repatriated by Britain as a part of the recent prisoner exchange, he was more than happy to participate in the prosecutorial proceedings against the man they all roundly condemned as a traitor. He took special relish in recounting an incident when German guards had to intervene in Casement's defence; one of his fellow prisoners had become so enraged by Casement's attempt to pit the Irish against their British compatriots, that he shoved Casement against the wire fencing around the camp and was about to land a 'right cross to his bloody head' when a couple of guards seized the prisoner and dragged him away. 'If it weren't for those damned guards,' he insisted, 'we could have saved you all the bother of a trial.'

Several other wounded and disabled Irish veterans joined the chorus of complaints against Casement. John Cronin, formerly a private in the 2nd Battalion of the Royal Munster Fusiliers, was wounded at Etreux, taken prisoner, and transferred to Limburg. William Egan, a member of the Royal Irish Rifles, was wounded at Neuve Chapelle, spent three months in hospital in Cologne, then transferred to Limburg. Daniel O'Brien of the 19th Hussars was wounded in the retreat from Mons, captured and sent to Döberitz, then transferred to Limburg. James Wilson of the 2nd Royal Dublin Fusiliers lost his sight when a shell burst right next to him, was taken into captivity, and transferred to Limburg. All supported the allegation that between December and February, Mr Casement had repeatedly urged them to forsake their service to the Crown and enlist in the so-called Irish Brigade.

They also testified that, to add insult to injury, the effort to subvert their loyalty went beyond suasion and took the form of coercion. When it became apparent that the prisoners were not receptive to his arguments, according to the sworn testimony, Casement became complicit with the guards in arranging for various forms of punishment. Reduced rations, transfer to unheated barracks, additional work details, and threats of transfer to camps that were known to be 'less hospitable' – all were a part of the overall campaign to convince them that joining the Irish Brigade was in their best interest. As Mr Bodkin took pains to make clear through his line of questioning, the prisoners' resistance to this blatant coercion reflected a loyalty and patriotic fervour that was in marked contrast to the sentiments displayed by Mr Casement. According to those who took the stand today, neither persuasion nor coercion could sway the prisoners, virtually all of whom took pride in their service to the United Kingdom. While there is obviously no way of substantiating the estimate, Mr Bailey claimed that out of about 1,000 prisoners assembled at Limburg, only fifty or sixty actually agreed to join the Brigade – and there is no way of determining how many of those enlistments were the product of coercion as opposed to nationalistic principles. The former prisoners of war who took the stand today referred to a variety of ways in which the assembled prisoners had expressed their hostility toward Casement – jeers, catcalls, and the occasional attempt to silence him in the way soldiers inured to violence are often inclined to resort.

Unsurprisingly, there doesn't appear to have been much in the way of rational debate during the assemblages, although on one occasion someone apparently had the temerity to ask mockingly, what would happen when Germany lost the war. Mr Casement was obviously taken aback, according to Bailey, for he had apparently never even considered that as a plausible outcome. On another occasion, someone asked what would happen to the Brigade itself should the insurrection fail, irrespective of the fate of Germany. To the astonishment of the Court, Casement had actually negotiated a contingency plan for just such a possibility. Mr Bodkin was even able to use the pamphlet in his hands to substantiate that contingency, quoting that in the event that the insurrection should fail, 'the German Government will undertake to send each member of the Brigade who may so desire it to the United States of America, with necessary means to land'.[4]

The prosecution provided no background information about the prisoner exchange that made it possible for these witnesses to appear at today's hearing. It seems more than coincidental, to this reporter at least, that such an exchange would occur and include such valuable prosecutorial witnesses at precisely the most propitious time for the case against Mr Casement. It seems unlikely that the Crown could have been anticipating such a trial at the time it negotiated the exchange, so there is little reason to believe that the Foreign Office would have specifically sought to obtain these particular prisoners in exchange for the German POWs in its custody. It therefore begs the question, of why Germany would identify these particular prisoners for its side of the exchange, at the very time when the German government was providing Mr Casement with transportation to the coast of Kerry. Germany had to suspect that British intelligence had some inkling of the plot being hatched by Mr Casement and that his arrival in Ireland would be anticipated by Scotland Yard and the British Home Office. His arrest could therefore not have been a surprise to his German conspirators. Making these Irish POWs available to British authorities at this precise time would therefore appear to be part of an insidious betrayal by the German officials with whom Casement had conspired.

In the absence of documentary evidence, which will be difficult to obtain until the cessation of hostilities, if even then, one can only speculate as to German motives for such a betrayal. And among the foreign correspondents covering the arraignment hearing, speculation has been rife. It is not beyond the realm of possibility, for example, that the entire intrigue involving Mr Casement was part of a grand plan by Germany to lure Britain into a trap, with an unsuspecting Mr Casement duped into becoming the bait. Given his apparent sympathies with the German Empire and his belief in the prospects for a German–Irish alliance, Mr Casement would have naturally been vulnerable to such a ploy. The wild card in the ongoing war on the Continent is the role that the United States will ultimately play, and Germany and Britain are undoubtedly both involved in machinations to affect the US decision. While Germany has been seen as the aggressor nation in the US press, public relations are a fickle affair, and Germany could benefit immensely by drawing Britain into doing something rash. Publicly trying, and perhaps ultimately executing a humanitarian hero and knight of the realm, could be just the kind of rash public relations disaster that could benefit Germany among those who wield power and influence in the US capital. Setting Casement up for such a fate may be a cynical intrigue, but cynical manipulation of unsuspecting subjects is a staple of international affairs.

Whatever the background might be concerning the fate of these Irish prisoners of war, the fact remains that they proved to be a major factor in the prosecution's tactics at today's hearing in the Bow Street Police Court. Following their appearance, Mr Bodkin concluded his references to the notorious Casement pamphlet that was distributed at Limburg, by quoting the final appeal, 'Join the Irish Brigade and win Ireland's independence. Remember Bachelor's Walk. God save Ireland.'[5] As a final *coup de grace* in terms of appealing to Irish sentiments, the pamphlet's allusion to Bachelor's Walk was obviously intended to touch a nerve among the assembled prisoners, by reminding them of the incident two years ago, when the Dublin Metropolitan Police fired into an unarmed crowd, killing at least three and wounding more than thirty. Controversy still prevails about the true circumstances of the incident, with the police claiming that they were responding to threats of violence by the crowd as they attempted to apprehend members of the Irish Volunteers, who were running guns in from Howth.

I was on assignment in Dublin at the time, preparing an article about the machinations surrounding the Home Rule movement, so I was able to interview several of those involved on both sides. Whatever the truth behind the incident on Bachelor's Walk, it was perceived by those in the crowd to be an unprovoked massacre and quickly became a *cause célèbre* for the Irish Volunteers, who were determined, ultimately, to pursue the Home Rule movement to its logical conclusion, that being total independence for Ireland. There were even unsubstantiated rumours, at the time, that the same Roger Casement currently in the dock was the mastermind of the gun-running effort, purportedly in collusion with Erskine Childers, a former British artillery officer during the Boer War, and author of a fairly well-received spy novel called *The Riddle of the Sands*. According to reports at the time, the two of them recognised that a similar gun-running activity had already been undertaken by the Ulster Volunteer Force, which had made no secret of its intent to oppose Home Rule by whatever means necessary. The hostility of the UVF, including its preparation for armed opposition, constituted a grave threat to the Home Rule movement, and the Irish Volunteers, realising that a civil war was imminent, had made arrangements for its own illicit importation of arms. The subsequent events, including the tragic confrontation at Bachelor's Walk, have been a rallying cry for Irish nationalists ever since, and Casement obviously assumed that a reference to the 'massacre' would help incite the Irish prisoners at Limburg.

It was difficult to tell from the reaction in the courtroom whether the reference to Bachelor's Walk meant anything at all to those present at today's proceedings. The disdain with which Mr Bodkin quoted the passage in support of his case against Mr Casement, certainly suggests that he, at least, did not see any irony in using that passage to condemn the defendant's actions. Of even greater irony, perhaps, is the fact that Mr Smith, now the eminent Attorney General presiding over the prosecution of Mr Casement, was rumoured at the time to have been involved with Sir Edward Carson in the gun-running activities of the Ulster Volunteers as they prepared for armed opposition to Home Rule. Given the fact that Parliament had already passed Home Rule legislation at the time for the entirety of Ireland, it is possible, if not probable, that Mr Smith's participation with the UVF in preparing for armed resistance to implementation of the Home Rule Bill would have eventually led to his arrest for treason instead of Casement's, had events taken a different turn.

But treason is ultimately defined by historical circumstance, and with implementation of the Home Rule Bill postponed by the government upon the outbreak of hostilities with Germany, Mr Smith was able to abandon his pursuit of an armed insurrection, and the burden of resistance to government policy shifted to Mr Casement and the Irish Volunteers. The prosecution's use of Mr Bailey's account of the events to which he was privy in Germany leaves little room for doubt about the definition of treason in His Majesty's courtroom today. As Mr Casement's subaltern in Limburg, Mr Bailey presumably had first-hand knowledge about other negotiations that Casement had pursued with the German authorities to supplement the role of the Irish Brigade. This inside knowledge enabled the witness to provide additional insight into what transpired in the days and weeks leading up to the events of Easter weekend. According to Mr Bailey, Casement finally had to admit that the prospects for a viable Irish Brigade were nil, but he was unwilling to admit total failure in his effort to enlist the support of the German government. Although he had been out of direct contact with colleagues in Ireland for over a year, he was remotely aware of plans for a rising, and with funding from the Clan na Gael, with whose leadership he had met and negotiated while in the United States last summer, he sought to arrange for the smuggling of German arms and ammunition into Ireland for use by the rebels.

By this time, however, it seems that Mr Casement's credibility had suffered significantly in the eyes of his German contacts. Based on conversations with Casement during the course of their collaboration, Mr Bailey claimed on the stand that Casement had actually been able to meet and consult with Chancellor Bethmann-Hollweg sometime in December and had impressed the German leader with his ideas for an Irish Brigade. Casement apparently took great pride in convincing the Chancellor that German support for the oppressed peoples of this small island off the west coast of Britain would help offset the successes that the British had enjoyed in their public relations campaign to convince the world that they, the British, had championed the cause of small, oppressed countries by coming to the aid of Belgium against German 'aggression'. Even at this late date, with the adventure now in shambles, Mr Bailey himself still seemed personally impressed by the argument, and especially impressed by Casement's ability to pull it off in his consultations at the very highest level of the German government. He may be Casement's worst enemy at the moment, but the deferential tone of his testimony reflects the esteem that he must still harbour for the defendant.

But as Mr Bailey and his fellow witnesses attested to during the course of today's proceedings, Casement sorely overestimated his ability to carry out his side of the bargain. After three months of futile effort and with only about fifty or sixty recruits signed up for the Irish

Brigade, Mr Casement's stock with the German authorities had sunk considerably. And as Mr Bailey so cogently speculated, the Germans had lost faith, not only in Casement personally, but also in the level of Irish support that might be available for an insurrection. If only fifty or sixty out of the thousand or so prisoners were receptive to the idea of an insurrection, to what extent could Germany depend upon the Irish population generally, should Germany intervene in support of such an uprising? So Casement's failure to form a viable Irish Brigade had the additional consequence of undermining German faith in the overall enterprise.

Having failed to enlist the needed support for an Irish Brigade and losing credibility with and support from the German government, Casement apparently suffered a total collapse in January and had to be confined to a sanatorium in Munich. Mr Bailey obviously had no contact with him during this interlude, and it is unlikely, to say the least, that the German authorities will provide the Foreign Office with access to his medical records. So one can only speculate as to the depths of the depression and the extent of the soul-searching that must have plagued the defendant during his confinement. Disappointment with the response from his Irish compatriots in the Limburg camp, frustration with the level of support from the German government, the irreversible consequences of having left his homeland for enemy territory during a time of war, the prospect of a tainted legacy after a lifetime of achievement – the sudden accumulation of all these doubts and uncertainties at a time of maximum vulnerability had to have left him psychologically and emotionally crushed.

To survive that kind of overwhelming angst, and resume his clandestine activity on behalf of the Irish nationalists, he had to be driven by a passion that no one has yet been able to explain. But survive he did, for according to Mr Bailey, he was back in the Limburg camp by late winter, reconciled to the fact that the Irish Brigade was a stillborn concept but determined to press on with the effort to raise arms and ammunition for the planned rising in Ireland. In concluding his testimony today, Mr Bailey alluded to Robert Monteith, the third man arrested on the coast of Kerry this past Easter weekend, as the probable source of Casement's intelligence about the prospective rising. Monteith had apparently shown up in Limburg at about the time of Casement's return from hospital, allegedly dispatched by the Irish Volunteers to help Casement train the Irish Brigade that the plotters still assumed he was actively recruiting. Having just arrived from Ireland, Monteith would have certainly known enough details about the plot to advise Casement with regard to his role in acquiring the external support upon which the insurrection depended.

According to Mr Bailey, Casement was in a highly agitated state when he returned from the sanatorium, for he realised from Monteith that the plotters in Dublin were expecting the support of a Brigade that had never materialised, and a cache of arms and ammunition that Germany was not about to produce. So on top of all the other torments that had driven him to the outermost reaches of his sanity, he now faced the very real prospect that his personal failures in Germany were about to result in a catastrophe of monumental proportions in Ireland. Bailey described a man who, by this time, was driven by a frenzy that bordered on madness, as he tried desperately to salvage what he could of a chimera in which he had invested so much, and which now would undoubtedly cost him both his life and his reputation, and perhaps irreparably undermine the cause of Irish nationalism. In a last-ditch effort, he arranged for a shipment of arms to Ireland on a German cargo ship disguised as a Norwegian freighter; the German government also agreed to transport him, Bailey, and Monteith to Ireland via submarine. It is unclear from Bailey's testimony just what was to occur when they landed in Tralee. Without the Brigade that he had so optimistically anticipated and with only a token amount of munitions *en route*, it is difficult to fathom what Casement expected to accomplish upon arrival. He presumably kept Bailey in the dark about those details, but the witness certainly provided more than enough detail about their activities in Germany to support the prosecution's charge of treason.

After an exhaustive and, for this reporter at least, exhausting, day of testimony, the court adjourned in late afternoon, with Mr Bodkin's presentation of the prosecution's case to resume early tomorrow morning. Mr Casement stood erect in the dock throughout, projecting an air of quiet but firm dignity in spite of the cascade of evidence that he had colluded with the enemy and committed a heinous act of treason. One can only speculate as to what had to have been going through his mind as the case against him gained momentum.

While it is difficult to reconcile his record of service and accomplishments with the portrait that emerged from this day's proceedings, it is certainly easy to see why the British are so incensed by this case. Treason is arguably the most grievous of crimes, for it strikes at the very heart of the common weal, violating the social contract upon which every member of the polity depends for survival in a world of competing national interests. It is, in effect, the ultimate form of betrayal, with the perpetrator betraying the extended national family of which he has been a member and which has given him sustenance and security. It threatens the very fabric of the social order upon which the existence of that extended family depends. It is not surprising that Dante reserved a special place in Hell for those who betray their countries, relegating them to the Region of Antenora, named after the Trojan warrior who betrayed his nation to the Greeks, in the Ninth Circle of Hell, the frozen Pool of Cocytus where the condemned lie entombed in ice for eternity. Nor is it surprising that virtually every nation state, for its own protection, must treat treason as a capital offence. For someone as steeped in diplomacy, politics, and political philosophy as Roger Casement, the social contract concept is surely a familiar one, and violating that social contract had to have been motivated by a profound passion, which will hopefully be revealed during the course of these proceedings. Absent of such a passion, the treasonous behaviour of this otherwise noble man defies understanding, let alone common sense.

The focus of the Court during this first day of testimony has been on the facts surrounding the act of treason, rather than on the motivation underlying it. Efforts by this reporter to elicit comment on that question have thus far met with indifference; for the most part, those following the case have little interest in why Casement did what he did, they are only interested in the fact that he did it. Speaking on condition of anonymity, however, one former colleague of Casement's from the Foreign Office suggested that much of Casement's treasonous behaviour can ultimately be attributed to a sense of wounded vanity. According to this informant, Mr Casement harboured a profound resentment for the fact that his background and qualifications constrained him to service in the Consular rather than the Diplomatic Service. While he perceived himself to be performing diplomatic functions throughout his long and stellar career with the Consular Service, he was never accorded the esteem of being regarded as a member of the more prestigious and powerful Diplomatic Corps.

Furthermore, according to this former colleague, Casement was always at odds with the Foreign Office over what he perceived to be a less-than-aggressive follow-up to his exposés from the Congo and the Amazon. In this informant's opinion, Casement had an inflated sense of his own importance and felt that the Foreign Office did not take his reports seriously enough in dealing with the relevant Belgian and Peruvian authorities. Ironically, his impatience with the diplomatic dimension of the Foreign Office's response reflected not only his egotism, in the opinion of this source, but was also a perfect example of why he was unfit for the diplomatic corps to which he aspired.

A couple of the more sympathetic respondents have suggested that he basically became unhinged. Bailey's testimony about his confinement to a sanatorium, just a couple of months before his capture, would certainly support this hypothesis. While it may not excuse his behaviour in the minds of his accusers, it at least offers some explanation for what would appear to be a course of action that is totally at odds with his entire professional career. Such an explanation may not be inconsistent with the vanity theory; in fact, wounded pride may very well have festered for so long and reached such a fever pitch that his mental faculties might have been affected, according to those who expect an insanity defence. It is also possible that the stress of his experiences in Africa and South America may have had a delayed effect, leaving him vulnerable to a psychological malady that clouded his judgement and crippled his grasp of reality. Indeed, there are reports, thus far unconfirmed, that he spent a great deal of time on medical leave during his years with the foreign service; the nature of the illnesses might be revealing, when it comes to assessing the viability of an insanity plea.

And then, of course, there are those, like the irate respondent cited earlier, who sincerely believe that his collusion with Germany was the product of a long and carefully plotted scheme to undermine the historic relationship between Ireland and England, and to effectively tear Ireland from the fabric of the United Kingdom. His service to the Crown, according to this theory, was nothing more than a smokescreen to veil his subversion from within and to provide him with the contacts necessary to fulfil his objective. One of the adherents to this line of thought referred this reporter to an unpublished manuscript that Casement prepared, entitled 'The Crime Against Europe', in which he purportedly argues for the defeat of England by Germany in order to free Europe from what he alleges to be decades of economic tyranny. Several of my anonymous informants are helping me track down a copy of this manuscript, which hopefully will shed some light on the defendant's political thought. As further evidence of Casement's subversive efforts, this same informant referred contemptuously to articles that Casement published in the *Irish Independent* during the autumn of 1914, urging Irish men and women to refuse service in the British military during the war with Germany.

The atmosphere of the proceedings has been courteous and professional, as one would expect in a British police court, but there is no mistaking the determination of His Majesty's government to convict and execute their erstwhile knight in shining armour. While the honourable Mr Bodkin has taken the lead in presenting the prosecution's case, the presence of the Attorney General, the Honourable Mr Frederick E. Smith, throughout the course of the proceedings makes it quite clear how important this case is to the government. And Mr Smith's credentials as a staunch opponent of Home Rule in Ireland are surely not irrelevant to the case. As noted earlier, had it not been for the outbreak of war two years ago and the postponement of Home Rule for the duration of hostilities, it is entirely possible that Mr Smith himself would have taken up arms against the government. His militant opposition to Home Rule and his contempt for Sir Roger Casement's involvement with the Irish Volunteers are no secret.

In fact, during the years leading up to the war, when Ireland was engaged in an internecine struggle over the Home Rule movement,

Mr Smith and Mr Casement became sworn enemies, with Mr Smith advocating against Home Rule on behalf of the Unionists in Ulster and Mr Casement insisting that Home Rule be applied to Ireland as a whole – including the northern province of Ulster, where he spent his formative teen years near Ballymena in County Antrim. As noted earlier in connection with the incident on Bachelor's Walk, I had an opportunity to cover the struggle over Home Rule first-hand during those years immediately prior to the outbreak of hostilities with Germany, and I was therefore in a position to observe the opposing courses taken by these two unrepentant adversaries. Given the history of relations between them, one could easily conjecture that Mr Smith brings a bias to the court that could seriously affect his judgement. Under the circumstances, however, it is unlikely that anyone is going to question his role in these proceedings, especially given his official status as the sworn Attorney General for the realm. There is certainly no question that with him representing the Crown in this case, the prosecution will indeed be formidable.

Given the testimony and evidence thus far garnered by the prosecution, the outcome would almost appear to be a *fait accompli*. And with the public as well as the political pressure being brought to bear, that outcome will probably be expeditious. The defence has yet to present its side, of course, and this observer, at least, is looking forward with great anticipation to seeing how the defence will handle both the evidence and the public perceptions. There is more at stake for Mr Casement than a determination of guilt or innocence; his life and his reputation are both on the line. For a man who has devoted his life to humanitarian and political causes, the two are inseparable. With just one or two more days allotted for this preliminary hearing, a glimpse of the defence's strategy should soon be forthcoming.

Media coverage of the proceedings has raised an understandable furore among the British public. War news from abroad continues to dominate media attention: as noted in today's *Times*, this marks the 286th day of the second year in what has become a conflagration of unimagined proportions. Casualties continue to mount on all sides, atrocities of unspeakable horror have become almost commonplace, and the prospects for a resolution seem as remote now as they did twelve months ago. Speculation that President Wilson may make his good services available to broker a peace accord still finds its way into the occasional newspaper article, albeit in an increasingly subdued tone. After almost two years of war and the constant barrage of war-related news, however, cognitive fatigue threatens to dilute the effect of media coverage from the front.

The proceedings at the Bow Street Police Court have therefore provided a dramatic sidebar to those front-line reports, exciting public attention with a new twist on the threat to national security. Like the furore generated by the Military Service Act and the preoccupation with the war's impact on food prices at home, the Casement case lends the war news an immediacy that outweighs the statistics and military briefs coming back from places like Verdun and Riga and Erzrum and Kut. Outrage is a potent emotion which, when properly channelled, can reinvigorate the determination of the home front to support a long, drawn-out conflict that some have come to view as a virtual stalemate. The outrage inspired by this case could be a welcome spark for His Majesty's government.

TUESDAY 16 MAY 1916

Unconfirmed reports that Sir Roger Casement, presumably under the duress of interrogation, attempted suicide in the Tower of London by rubbing curare into an open wound have further fuelled public fascination with this increasingly bizarre case of alleged treason. Derived from the bark of a vine that grows in the Amazon rainforest, curare is a potent paralytic used by South American natives on the tips of their arrows and darts. The poison enters the bloodstream of the hunter's prey and attacks the central nervous system, causing paralysis and ultimately death through asphyxiation as the respiratory muscles cease to function. Casement would have undoubtedly had access to the substance during his work with the Putumayo. Sources within the intelligence community have been unable to explain how he could have gained possession of the poison while incarcerated in the Tower of London, especially since it has been almost five years since his last visit to the Amazon. It hardly seems likely that he would have retained a supply in anticipation of a moment such as this.

It is also unclear when the alleged suicide attempt occurred. He has been in the Tower of London since his transfer from Dublin just under a month ago, and his physical appearance in court this morning belied any suggestion that the attempt was recent. As with yesterday, he was led to the dock in shackles, but he showed no indication of having made an attempt to take his own life. If anything, he appeared to be more energetic and attentive than on the first day of the arraignment hearing, paying close attention to the testimony and making prodigious notes throughout the course of the day. As he took his place before the assembled officials and courtroom observers, he even seemed to nod an almost imperceptible but respectful greeting in the direction of his long-time adversary, the Honourable Attorney General. Mr Smith clearly ignored the greeting, assuming the same disdainful manner that was evident throughout the day yesterday.

Mr Bailey returned to the stand this morning to provide the final details of the collusion with Germany. Bailey admitted to being an active participant in the plot to foment insurrection in Ireland, although he claims that he was misled and manipulated by the defendant and insists that he played only a minor role, being kept mostly in the dark about many of the details. According to his sworn testimony this morning, his final days in Germany were spent being whisked from one place to another, including a brief stop with Mr Monteith for an introductory course on explosives in a suburb of Berlin. From there, the two of them were purportedly taken to Zossen where they remained for a week, receiving additional instruction on the use of various kinds of explosives. Mr Bailey seemed to have little appreciation for the inconsistency between his admitted training in explosives and his insistence that the role allotted to him was minor.

Around 11 or 12 March, according to Bailey's continued testimony, he and Mr Monteith were joined by Mr Casement in Berlin, where the three of them received train tickets from the German War Office to go to the port of Wilhemshaven for transportation to Ireland. While Mr Bailey claims that he was still not privy to how his training would ultimately be applied, it should certainly have been clear to him by this time that Sir Roger, having already arranged for the shipment of arms and ammunition to support the prospective insurrection, had also arranged for the three of them to participate in the planned rebellion. With the background that he had now acquired in the use of explosives, Mr Bailey was certainly not receiving military transport to Ireland as a tourist.

As astounding as it might seem, the transportation provided was by submarine rather than by surface vessel. The intent was obviously to avoid detection, but one can only wonder how three civilians with no prior naval experience must have reacted to the confines and unnatural environment of a submarine. Mr Bailey must surely have some lurid tales that he could have shared about that experience, but the prosecution had no time for the personal interest side of the story: Mr Bodkin's only objective was in the facts of the case, and the fact is that the German War Office provided the three revolutionaries with transportation on a German navy submarine.

Mr Bailey went on to testify that upon arriving just off the coast of Kerry, the submarine crew helped the three of them (Mr Bailey, Mr Monteith, and Mr Casement) load a number of pistols and several boxes of ammunition into an inflatable boat, in which they rowed to shore. Mr Bailey added further suspense to the already intriguing tale, by mentioning that the boat capsized in the rough seas as they approached the beach, forcing the three of them to wade the last several metres in waves that threatened to sweep them off their feet as they dragged the inflatable craft behind them. Exhausted, frightened, and still purportedly uninformed about what to expect, Mr Bailey helped bury the gear they had brought with them and struck off in the company of Mr Monteith, who supposedly knew where they were going, leaving Mr Casement behind on the beach for reasons unknown to Mr Bailey.

Mr Bailey's testimony then came to a rather abrupt conclusion with some tedious details about how he accompanied Mr Monteith to a shop in Tralee where they were met by several men who seemed to be expecting them. Two of the conspirators hustled Bailey and Monteith into a motor car and set off in search of someone named Rice, whom Bailey assumed was in command of whatever escapade it was in which they were involved. After a series of absurd mishaps, including a punctured tire and several failed attempts to reconnoitre with the mysterious Mr Rice, along with at least three encounters with suspicious police officials, Bailey was finally detained for questioning and subsequently brought to the Tower of London after revealing his connection with Mr Casement. Mr Monteith is still at large.

As a final *coup de grace* in terms of the charges being brought against Sir Roger, Mr Bailey ended his day and a half on the stand by observing that while on board the submarine, he had overheard discussions between Casement and members of the crew about a cache of arms being separately delivered for use in the insurrection – a cache of 20,000 rifles, a million rounds of ammunition, ten machine guns, and an untold number of bombs to be delivered on a Wilson liner disguised as a timber ship. How Germany came to be in possession of a Wilson liner was not revealed. Disclosing the nature of the cargo, however, was enough to generate an additional wave of outrage in those assembled before the presiding Magistrate, Sir John Dickinson. The accumulation of heinous villainies attached to the name of Roger Casement over the course of these last two days has rocked the normally staid British demeanour.

The remainder of today's testimony focused on the bizarre circumstances surrounding Mr Casement's capture and arrest on the coast of Kerry, marking the culmination of his conspiracy with Germany. For the reader unfamiliar with the geography of Ireland, Banna Strand is a six-mile stretch of hard-packed sandy shoreline in County Kerry of the south-western province of Munster, running along the coast from the village of Ballyheige at the northern end of the strand to the Barrow harbour at its southern end. It undoubtedly possesses some attraction for the vacationer interested in solitary walks along miles of isolated, windswept beach, but like much of the Irish coastline, it is remote, rugged, and forlorn. It is on this beach that Mr Casement, Mr Bailey, and Mr Monteith washed ashore late in the night of Thursday 20 April, or early in the morning of Good Friday, 21 April.

Following the conclusion of Mr Bailey's testimony, those in attendance at today's proceedings were treated to an hour of intriguing testimony by John McCarthy, the Irish peasant farmer who stumbled upon the abandoned boat on Good Friday morning and summoned police officials from the Ardfert Barracks. His testimony could have easily formed the basis of a melodrama from the London stage. Mr McCarthy is of indeterminate age, his facial features obscured by a full beard and marked by the wizening effects of years of exposure to the fierce weather that is so prevalent on the west coast of Ireland. His natural taciturnity, the product no doubt of a lifetime of limited opportunities for social intercourse in those remote south-western reaches of Munster, bestowed a droll quality upon the events that he described, complementing the overall impression that the Casement-led 'invasion' of Ireland was as much farce as melodrama. While his appearance in court might have offered a rare opportunity for this reclusive peasant to enjoy a bit of public attention, it was obvious from the quaver in his voice and the fixed stare upon his interrogator that he was not at all comfortable with the opportunity.

According to Mr McCarthy, he had gone out for a stroll along the strand in the wee hours of the morning on Good Friday. When pressed for clarification, he defined 'wee hours' as sometime between 2:00 and 2:30. Perhaps due to my journalistic inquisitiveness or simply to idle curiosity, I immediately wondered why anyone would be taking a stroll on such a disagreeable stretch of sand at that unseemly hour – insomnia bred from years of endless boredom perhaps, a falling out with the crone who shared his bed, or maybe a guilty conscience on this holiest of Christian holy days. Whatever the reason, it obviously had no relevance to the prosecutor's case, and Mr Bodkin wasn't about to be sidetracked by trivial matters. One cannot help but wonder, however, whether Mr McCarthy will ever again be able to enjoy a quiet stroll on the strand in the 'wee hours' of a Friday morning.

As he was returning from his stroll at about 4a.m., Mr McCarthy was taken aback by the appearance of an abandoned collapsible boat on the shore. Since he had not seen the boat there when he had passed that same spot on his way out some two hours earlier, he could only conclude that someone had come ashore behind him as he was walking the beach. It had to have been disconcerting for him to realise that if he had been just a bit faster or a bit slower, he might have actually encountered the boat's occupants when they made their landing. Or perhaps not: Mr McCarthy did not strike this reporter as being the type to ponder the capricious role of chance in life's mundane activities.

In any case, it must have been a disquieting experience for a man accustomed to the simple cycle of nature's day-to-day routine. Here he is, strolling along this barren stretch of beach, quietly contemplating whatever it is that propelled him into his 'wee hour' ramble, and in the uncertain light cast by the sinking moon, he spies a boat that had obviously come ashore behind him and been abandoned by whoever had ridden it in with the tide. He must have surely cast an uneasy glace across the shimmering waves, surveying the horizon for the boat's origin: it's a small, fragile craft that couldn't have come from very far. After a moment of uncertainty, curiosity overcomes his initial trepidation and he approaches the boat, now turning his uneasy glances from the waves to the distant dunes, wondering whether he himself is being observed by some evil intruder.

Upon closer examination, he discovers that whoever abandoned the boat has left behind a dagger and a tin box filled with small calibre cartridges. In the sand he is able to see footprints left by at least two, perhaps three, men, leading away from the boat and toward those distant dunes. The extraordinary nature of the scene, along with the ghostly atmosphere of the early morning moonlight, would have been enough to spark even the dullest of imaginations, and while Mr McCarthy is a simple man, he is obviously not a dullard. The flickering shadows cast by the moon around those distant dunes suggest the presence of a lurking malevolence that he prefers not to encounter by himself, and with his heart undoubtedly pounding like never before, his early morning stroll becomes a mad dash for Curragh, the little village where he and his family maintain their humble abode.

Imagine the overwhelming surge of panic, when he suddenly realises that his dash toward Curragh and home is running parallel to the footprints that he noticed leading away from the boat. By this time the courtroom had become hushed in anticipation as Mr Bodkin urged his witness to continue this incredible tale about the events of that morning. With a growing sense of imminent doom, McCarthy follows the footprints right into and through his own yard, passing within metres of where his family lay sleeping at the time the intruders passed. At this point Mr McCarthy, beside himself with apprehension and uncertainty, summons a neighbour named Driscoll to help him decide what to do, and together they return to the shore upon which the abandoned boat is resting.

By now, the sun has begun to rise and to his amazement, as well as that of the incredulous courtroom, Mr McCarthy realises that he is no longer the only one who had taken to the solitary beach of Banna Strand in those 'wee hours' of Good Friday morn. According to Mr

McCarthy's sworn testimony, he and Driscoll arrive at the scene of the covert landing and find, as astonishing as it may seem, Mr McCarthy's own seven-year-old daughter digging around in the sand not far from the collapsible boat. Again, this reporter's journalistic inquisitiveness and idle curiosity cry out for more detail, but Mr Bodkin is no more interested in how the little girl came to be on the beach, alone, at sunrise, than he was in why Mr McCarthy was out wandering around at such an ungodly hour in the first place. Perhaps she, too, is plagued with insomnia or by a guilty conscience on this Christian holy day. Or perhaps she is just an unruly child who is accustomed to taking off on her own while her parents presumably lie sleeping in the next room.

In any case, McCarthy and Driscoll are less alarmed by her unexpected appearance on this deserted beach than by what she has unearthed as a result of her excavating activities. To their dismay, she is playing with a fully loaded Mauser revolver. In short order, they discover two more revolvers buried just beneath the surface of the sand and three life vests cast alongside the boat. It is now apparent to both McCarthy and Driscoll that something is seriously amiss. After taking the revolvers back to McCarthy's house for safekeeping (as well as to keep them out of the hands of his wayward daughter, no doubt), they rush off to the local constabulary in Ardfert for assistance.

The excitement is now becoming contagious, as this hulking peasant farmer and his companion barge into the ramshackle police barracks at Ardfert. Having dozed away the hours of a typically uneventful night in this quiet little village, the constables on duty must have been both alarmed and shaken by this intrusion upon their somnolent preparations for the morning shift change. It isn't difficult to imagine a warm room redolent of the heavy aroma generated by a boiling pot of tea, the only sound an occasional attempt to muffle a snore. And suddenly the door bursts open and a savage apparition storms across the threshold, dumping into their laps an adventure that they sense will change their lives forever.

At this point in the day's proceedings, Mr McCarthy had had his hour in the limelight, bringing the Good Friday drama to its second act with the entrance of Police Sergeant Thomas Hearn and Constable Bernard

Riley from the Ardfert barracks of the Royal Irish Constabulary. Under Mr Bodkin's guidance, they pick up where Mr McCarthy left off in relating the events of that fateful day. Armed with a shotgun, a carbine and a couple of shillelaghs, they accompany McCarthy and Driscoll to a scene that has now attracted the attention of most of the Curragh residents, whose morning chores have been interrupted by all the commotion. For a group of farm labourers who have probably never witnessed anything more dramatic than the occasional bar-room brawl, this has to be a striking way to start the Good Friday holiday. Rumours are rampant when Hearn and Riley arrive, as the villagers outdo each other in imagining how this boat and its ominous contents came to rest on their stretch of beach on Good Friday, of all days. With all the news from the continent, it isn't difficult for them to conclude that this is surely the harbinger of an all-out German invasion, with the abandoned boat a sure sign that scouts have already disembarked to map out the landing points for the flotilla that is undoubtedly approaching the horizon at that very moment.

According to the testimony of the two police officials, they immediately set off in search of the unknown subjects, following the tracks that fortunately hadn't been obliterated by the milling crowd. The tracks lead them to the ruins of an old, circular earthen fort – a rath, in local parlance – the type of which was common throughout Medieval Ireland as the locus for an extended family's farmstead. Known among the locals as McKenna's Fort, undoubtedly after the family whose ancestors once occupied the fort, it is there that they discover a dishevelled and somewhat distraught stranger, since identified as the defendant Sir Roger Casement. Challenged by Constable Riley to surrender himself, the stranger has the marvellous aplomb to chastise him by cavalierly commenting, 'That's a nice way to treat an innocent English traveller.'

Not to be so easily put off, Riley insists that the subject identify himself, to which the stranger responds with astonishing presence of mind that he is an author named Richard Morten and that he has been doing local research for a biography of St Brendan, a sixth-century Irish monk known among the Irish as Brendan the Voyager in honour of his seven-year quest for the fabled Land of Promise. To come up with such a tale on the spur of the moment, Casement obviously had to have had intimate knowledge of the area around Tralee, for Brendan is in fact the patron saint of the region and is reputed to have established monastic cells around the village of Ardfert itself between the years 512 and 530. There is even a mountain peak named after him just across Tralee Bay. Given the circumstances, confronted by an armed official after what must have been a harrowing night on this remote and desolate stretch of beach, Casement's ability to immediately offer a plausible and germane explanation for such a bizarre state of affairs is a testimony to his extraordinary equanimity. While he is understandably reluctant to admit it on the stand, Riley must have been at least momentarily stymied by the subject's composure and ready responses.

By this time, however, Sergeant Hearn had arrived on the scene and together they concluded that further investigation was warranted, a conclusion that was reinforced when they searched the prisoner and discovered an itinerary in German, along with a cancelled railroad ticket from Berlin to Wilhelmshaven. In addition, they found in his possession a piece of paper that appeared to be a communication between the prisoner and an unknown conspirator with ominous import, containing references to the need for arms, ammunition and explosives as well as an unspecified landing plan and its co-ordination with forces that were presumably already in place.

Their suspicions were raised further when a young lad named Martin Collins came forward with another piece of paper that he claimed to have seen the prisoner roll up and drop intentionally behind him upon being taken into custody. Mr Bodkin introduced the latter document into evidence, pointing out that German linguists have suggested that it appears to be a code for deciphering clandestine communications. While Sergeant Hearn and Constable Riley admittedly had no way of assessing its meaning or its significance at the time, they were able to generate a bit of levity during an otherwise sombre day of testimony by insisting on their ability to at least recognise that the document was not written in Irish – or in English, for that matter. Taking everything into account, the two policemen were sufficiently alarmed to hold the prisoner incommunicado and to contact higher headquarters for further instruction.

From the testimony provided by Sergeant Hearn and Constable Riley, it is apparent that their 'higher headquarters' staff must have recognised the possibility that the Ardfert police had stumbled upon a major conspiracy involving national security. It is this reporter's understanding that the Foreign Office had been tracking Casement's activities abroad for some time and had been providing intelligence reports to the Special Branch of Scotland Yard in anticipation of just this kind of eventuality. Based on those intelligence reports, it is likely that Scotland Yard had alerted the various police forces throughout the land to be on alert for a possible incursion. In light of those alerts, one can easily appreciate the sense of urgency that must have been generated by the report from Ardfert. According to Sergeant Hearn, it didn't take long for the authorities to respond: on 23 April, just two days after Casement's arrest, Sergeant Thomas Brechin of the Military Foot Police arrived to take custody of the prisoner and to escort the erstwhile hero and knight of the realm to Euston Station, where he was turned over in chains to London's Metropolitan Police.

Mr Bodkin concluded the day's proceedings by turning his attention to the cache of arms that Mr Bailey alleged were being smuggled into Ireland at a time to coincide with Casement's arrival, these being the arms that he had heard being discussed on the U-19 while *en route* from Germany to Ireland. As the first witness to help establish the facts surrounding the matter of the smuggled arms, Mr Bodkin called Sidney Ray Waghorn, chief signalman of HMS *Bluebell*, a Royal Navy sloop that was patrolling off the coast of Ireland on the night of 21 April. According to Mr Waghorn, he sighted a freighter bearing Norwegian colours at about 6p.m. that evening and in accordance with his standing orders for such a situation, he signalled the standard request for identification. The vessel identified itself as the *Aud en route* from Bergen to Genoa. While the crew of the *Bluebell* had no knowledge at this point of any plot to smuggle arms into Ireland, the commander of the sloop was nevertheless suspicious of the freighter's true identity and intentions, so he ordered it to follow the *Bluebell* into Queenstown Harbour for further investigation.

All seemed to be going well, according to Mr Waghorn, until they reached a point just off Daunt's Rock lighthouse, at which time the *Aud* unexpectedly shut down all its engines and the crew began to abandon ship. The crew of the *Bluebell* were momentarily befuddled by this astonishing turn of events, but Mr Waghorn testified that he soon noticed smoke coming from the starboard side of the freighter and that two German ensigns were now evident at the ship's masthead. The *Aud*'s crew, now clearly wearing German naval uniforms, attempted nothing hostile, according to the witness; they simply rowed over to the *Bluebell* and peacefully surrendered. Unfortunately, it was too late to save the *Aud* for a follow-up investigation: the crew had successfully completed its efforts to scuttle the vessel before taking to the lifeboats and the burning ship quickly sank beneath the waves. The crew of the *Bluebell* marked the site with a buoy and proceeded to port with their prisoners.

Mr Bodkin then called John Dempsey, an Admiralty diver who testified that he was dispatched to the site of the sunken vessel just five days ago. It appears that the two incidents – Mr Casement's capture on the coast of Kerry and the confrontation between the *Bluebell* and the *Aud* – were not immediately connected. It was only after the interrogation of Mr Bailey that the authorities suspected a connection and sent Mr Dempsey to investigate. Upon descending to the seabed, he found the scuttled freighter and its contents, which turned out to be, in fact, the rifles and ammunition that Mr Bailey had alleged were *en route* from Germany. As evidence of his discovery, Mr Dempsey brought back a rusty rifle and a cartridge clip, both of which he had retrieved from the sunken vessel. According to Mr Dempsey, additional divers have now been dispatched to salvage as much of the cargo as possible.

In concluding the day's proceedings, Mr Bodkin called Colonel Nicholas Belaiev of the Russian army, who was able to identify the rifle introduced into evidence as one of Russian manufacture, produced at the Russian Imperial Toula Rifle Works in 1905. The significance of this identification is not yet apparent, at least not to this reporter. Regardless of its origin, the most damning fact is that the rifle was being made available by a nation with which the Commonwealth has been at war, for use in an insurrection against the Commonwealth.

And while the connection between the *Aud* and Mr Casement's landing in Kerry is to this point purely circumstantial, Mr Bailey's earlier testimony about Casement's discussions in Germany and the overheard conversations on board the U-19 make it difficult to dismiss the connection. It is surely not coincidental that a shipment of arms on a German vessel just happens to appear off the coast of Ireland on the same night that Casement and his co-conspirators arrive on board a German navy submarine. Mr Bodkin's clear intent is to establish that Mr Casement was in fact delivering arms to support the insurrection that ultimately began on Monday 23 April, just two days after the arrival of Mr Casement and the appearance of the *Aud* and its military cargo.

While the defence has yet to present its side of the case, the preponderance of the evidence suggests that an indictment for treason is inevitable. There seems to be no doubt that Mr Casement conspired with the enemy to form an Irish Brigade in support of an insurrection against the Crown, negotiated an arrangement for the enemy of the Crown to support that insurrection through the provision of arms and ammunition and perhaps even through the eventual deployment of military force, and landed on Irish territory to personally participate in that insurrection. The facts of the case seem irrefutable, making it difficult to appreciate how Mr Casement has been able to maintain such profound composure throughout these two days of testimony. He must either have a defence that is not yet evident, or he is simply resigned before what appears to be the inevitable. Or, in what would be the ultimate outrage to the Crown and its loyal subjects, rather than denying the charges or defending himself against them, perhaps he actually takes pride in what he has allegedly done.

Given Mr Casement's stature and his connections in the diplomatic world, the prosecution will undoubtedly make the further case that Mr Casement was not just a participant in planning the insurrection, but more than likely the ringleader. Mr Pearse and Mr Connolly, and the others executed over the course of this past month, have been convicted as major conspirators, but none had the expertise, the background, and the political resources that Casement possessed. It is unlikely that any one of them could have provided the kind of leadership that Casement would have brought to the undertaking.

His landing on the coast of Ireland just two days before the actual rising took place, lends credence to this theory. While he was physically absent from his homeland for almost two years, it is obvious from the evidence presented that he was not out of touch by any stretch of the imagination. As a matter of fact, the evidence clearly indicates that he spent much of that time engaged in negotiations on behalf of Ireland with the highest levels of the German government, and before that, he apparently engaged in mustering support, both financial and political, from Irish expatriates in America. Given that kind of commitment and involvement at the international level, it is inconceivable that he was a mere supernumerary in the gang of conspirators. His role was obviously critical if not central to the entire affair, and given his proven leadership qualities during a stellar career in the Foreign Service, it shouldn't be difficult for the prosecutor to convince an obviously receptive court that he was the key to the entire uprising.

The case against the defendant seems to have already been well enough established to warrant an indictment, at least. The prosecution has obviously been working hard to amass the overwhelming evidence that has been presented before the Lord Chief Magistrate over these past two days. One could almost characterise the proceedings as a mini-trial rather than an arraignment, with an indictment the virtual equivalent of a guilty verdict. The resources brought to bear by the Home Office and the Attorney General in amassing this evidence so quickly makes it abundantly clear how determined the British government is in pursuing the case against Mr Casement. The sheer speed of its response to Casement's arrest suggests that much of the evidence must have already been in the pipeline, just waiting the opportune moment for it to be brought to the surface. After all, it has been less than a month since Mr Casement's ill-fated landing on Banna Strand. Even for an efficient staff working at fever pitch, putting together such an exhaustive case would seem to this reporter to be a rather stellar prosecutorial achievement.

The honourable Mr Bodkin suggested at the end of today's proceedings that the prosecutor's presentation will finish in a timely fashion tomorrow. It remains to be seen what, if anything, the defence might present at that point. After two days of damning evidence that will surely result in an indictment anyway, it may be strategically advisable for the defence to avoid tipping its hand and simply wait until the actual trial to present its side of the case. Given the government's interest in an expeditious resolution of the matter, that opportunity should not be long delayed. Legal consultants seem unanimous in their projections that such a trial will probably come within weeks, not months. It is likely that Mr Casement's fate, for good or ill, will be determined before this summer passes into the history books.

THURSDAY 18 MAY 1916

As anticipated, the inquiry into the charges against Sir Roger Casement concluded yesterday at the Bow Street Police Court with the defendant being bound over for adjudication in civil court. The formal charge lodged against him alleges that 'on the 1st day of November, 1915, and on divers days thereafter, and between that day and the 21st day of April, 1916, he unlawfully, maliciously, and traitorously did commit high treason without the realm of England in contempt of our Sovereign Lord the King and his laws'.[6] If he is indicted, tried and convicted, which appears likely at this point, Casement could face the gallows. Given the highly politicised atmosphere that will be prevalent at trial, the prospect of Mr Casement surviving the summer will ultimately depend on a number of factors, not the least of which will be what His Majesty's government perceives to be in its own best interest.

The proceedings on the third and last day of the hearing lacked the drama and the intrigue that characterised the first two days of testimony. Mr Bodkin was true to his promise that the prosecution would complete its presentation in short order on the third day, leaving most of that day for the defence. Unfortunately, those of us in the media who were hoping to catch a glimpse of the defence's strategy were sorely disappointed; as I correctly predicted in my last dispatch, the defence recognised the inevitability of an indictment and chose to keep its strategy under wraps until the actual trial. Its only contribution to yesterday's proceedings was a futile attempt to dismiss some of the testimony introduced into evidence by Mr Bailey.

Mr Artemus Jones, who led the defence's effort to squash a portion of that damning testimony, tried to undermine its credibility by suggesting that Mr Bailey was either coerced or misled during his initial interrogation by the Royal Irish Constabulary at its Abbeydorney Police Barracks, where Bailey had been held over the weekend following his capture on Good Friday. Two of the police officers present at the interrogation, a Sergeant Restrick and District Inspector Frederick Britten, testified under direct examination by the prosecution that Mr Bailey, known to them at the time by the alias David Mulcahy, offered to provide important information relative to national security in exchange for protection and release from custody. While they acknowledged offering Bailey the protection he requested, they were adamant in denying that they had offered to set him free in exchange for his information.

Despite a strenuous cross-examination by Mr Jones, the two officers did not budge from their insistence that Mr Bailey offered his information freely. Mr Jones asked them specifically if they had threatened him in any way or taken advantage of his expressed need for protection, playing upon his fears in order to wrest and manipulate information. The officers remained steadfast in their denials, with Inspector Britten claiming that even after repeated requests by the prisoner for a guarantee against punishment, the interrogating officers impressed upon him that while they could and would guarantee protection, they could not guarantee that he would not be punished. Inspector Britten claimed further that in spite of his efforts, he was never able to get a clear-cut answer from the prisoner as to why or from whom he needed protection; he simply assumed that Mr Bailey had reason to fear those who would be implicated by the information he was offering.

In spite of Mr Jones's vociferous insinuations to the contrary, Inspector Britten remained firm in his testimony that Bailey finally divulged his information without coercion, pressure, or false guarantees. According to Inspector Britten, that information included details about the clandestine arms shipment from Germany and its timing to coincide with the planned insurrection. It was when Bailey mentioned that he had arrived on the coast of Kerry via German submarine in the company of Roger Casement that Inspector Britten, recognising the name of the fugitive consul for whom alerts had been circulating from Scotland Yard, realised that he was indeed on to something of major import. Mr Jones then tried to imply that Inspector Britten had actually known about Casement's capture before interrogating Mr Bailey and that he had intentionally led Bailey into naming him as a co-conspirator. Inspector Britten denied that he had any knowledge of Casement's capture before initiating the interrogation and pointed out that even if he had known, the fact remains that it was Mr Bailey himself who brought up the consul's name.

Mr Jones's motion of inadmissibility was an obviously futile attempt to cast a shadow over the prosecution's case. Chief Magistrate Sir John Dickinson dismissed the motion out of hand and concluded the police court hearing, laying the foundation for the civil court to follow up – which it is certain to do quite promptly. Mr Casement was led from the room in chains, his demeanour pretty much the same as when the proceedings began on Monday. Attorney-General Smith, on the other hand, had a great deal of difficulty concealing his smug sense of satisfaction with the outcome. There was even the slightest hint of a sneer on his face as Mr Casement passed almost within touching distance on his way to the cell that will hold him until the Grand Jury convenes.

The obvious disdain that the Honourable Attorney General harbours toward the defendant has piqued the curiosity of this incorrigibly curious reporter, and since there were still several hours left in the day, I made a point of interviewing a few of the subordinate members of his legal staff. Most of them were naturally reluctant to share inside information about the past relationship between Mr Casement and Mr Smith, but one young solicitor seemed especially eager to seize the journalistic limelight for a few moments – on condition of anonymity, of course. Anonymous sources are usually motivated by a personal agenda, and for that reason their input must be regarded with a certain degree of scepticism. Without those sources, however, we in the journalistic profession would be denied access to information that often casts a light on factors that would otherwise forever remain in the shadows.

The information that I was able to glean from this solicitor seems entirely plausible, given my own exposure to, and coverage of, the events alluded to in an earlier dispatch about the Home Rule movement. Assuming the information's veracity, the light cast upon Mr Smith's attitude in the police court would seem to dispel a great deal of the shadow that obscures what is going on beneath the surface of these proceedings. Based upon the solicitor's input, it seems safe to say that Mr Smith not only has a long-standing and deep-seated animosity toward the defendant, but if historical circumstance had taken a different turn, he could very well have found himself in the dock that Mr Casement now occupies.

According to my eager informant, that animosity and the treason that Smith was able to sidestep through an accident of history, had their roots in the Irish Home Rule movement. To fully appreciate the implications of this informant's input, it would probably be helpful to have some context for the allegations. Toward that end, let me take the liberty of providing a quick survey of that Home Rule movement. Readers interested in more detailed coverage of the movement can refer to the series of dispatches that I wrote while on assignment in Dublin three years ago – a series that was picked up by the Associated Press wire services and carried by a number of American newspapers.

Daniel O'Connell, known affectionately among his Irish compatriots as The Liberator, because of the overriding passion of his political life, dedicated his professional career to the cause of Irish 'liberation' by seeking a repeal of the 1801 Act of Union, which provided the legal basis for integrating Ireland into the United Kingdom. His failure to achieve that objective prompted subsequent Irish politicians to focus on the more limited prospect of Home Rule as their only recourse in gaining some degree of national sovereignty. Charles Stewart Parnell, the leader of the Irish Parliamentary Party at Westminster from its inception as the Home Rule League in 1875 until his fall from grace due to an affair with Kitty O'Shea, the wife of a fellow Member of Parliament, made Home Rule a central issue in his political agenda. He received much-needed support from the idealistic Liberal Prime Minister William Gladstone, who took it upon himself to introduce Home Rule legislation in the House of Commons for the first time on 8 April 1886. That Bill, proposing the formation of an Irish Assembly that would have jurisdiction over clearly defined domestic areas to the exclusion of defence, treaties, trade and coinage, all of which would still fall under the purview of Westminster, was defeated by the House of Commons in June of the same year after just two months of debate.

Undaunted by his initial failure and convinced that Irish Home Rule was eventually going to materialise one way or another, Gladstone was determined to see Parliament take the initiative in offering Home Rule to Ireland rather than waiting for Ireland to make demands that might be less acceptable and more difficult to deal with. He therefore tried again with a second Home Rule Bill in 1893. This time he was able to garner enough votes to get the Bill through the House of Commons, only to have it vetoed overwhelmingly by the conservative House of Lords in a resounding 419 to 41 vote. Mr Gladstone retired from government soon thereafter, his efforts ostensibly doomed to be forever frustrated by the opposition of the upper house in Parliament.

It was the third Home Rule Bill, according to my informant, that brought Mr Casement and Mr Smith into irreconcilable conflict with each other. Known formally as the Government of Ireland Act, this legislation provided for a bicameral House of Parliament in Dublin with jurisdiction over affairs that pertained exclusively to Ireland. The island would remain a part of the United Kingdom with Irish representation in the central Parliament at Westminster provided by the Irish Parliamentary Party. Westminster would retain jurisdiction over all other matters, including foreign policy, defence, trade and any other affairs bearing on the Commonwealth as a whole. The Bill was initially introduced in the House of Commons on 11 April 1912, where it was passed by a slim majority but again resoundingly defeated by the House of Lords.

As is often the case in politics, however, a deal had been struck behind the scenes to make this apparent defeat the first step in a subtle manoeuvre toward ultimate approval. The new Prime Minister, Herbert Asquith, had served as Home Secretary during the final years of William Gladstone's premiership, during which time he had become fully committed to the Liberal agenda that Gladstone had pursued.

Among the passions that he and Gladstone shared was abhorrence for what they perceived to be unbridled self-interest among the privileged members of the House of Lords. From their perspective, the aristocrats in the upper house of Parliament were more concerned about protecting their own vested interests, than in promoting the greater good of society as a whole. With that ideological premise to guide him, Asquith ascended to the premiership determined to limit the historical power wielded by the House of Lords.

As a tactical manoeuvre towards that end, he had negotiated a deal with John Redmond, the head of the Irish Parliamentary Party at Westminster, agreeing to support the passage of an Irish Home Rule Bill in exchange for Redmond's support of a Bill that Asquith would introduce called the Parliament Act of 1911. This Act, entitled 'An Act to make provision with respect to the powers of the House of Lords in relation to those of the House of Commons', was, in fact, precipitated by a clash between the two Houses over tax legislation that had generated an apparently insurmountable level of opposition from landowners in the House of Lords. To limit that House's ability to continue wielding its self-serving power at the expense of what Asquith and his fellow Liberals perceived to be in the national interest, the coalition forged by Asquith and Redmond between the Liberals and the Irish Parliamentary Party provided sufficient support to get the Act through Parliament. The key provision of the Act gave the House of Commons authority to overrule a House of Lords veto, if the vetoed legislation could be passed by the House of Commons in three successive years.

Therein lay the weapon that would be wielded in making Irish Home Rule a reality. Keeping his promise to Redmond, Asquith followed the 1912 defeat of the Home Rule Bill with its introduction again in 1913, when, as anticipated, it was once again passed by the House of Commons only to meet the same veto in the House of Lords. He introduced it for a third time in 1914, when it was passed by the House of Commons on 25 May, after which any vote in the House of Lords was now moot under the Parliament Act of 1911. The conservative members of Parliament were naturally outraged, but Asquith and Redmond had outflanked them.

The years leading up to the Bill's ultimate passage were tumultuous ones in Ireland, where support varied significantly between the Catholic-dominated southern counties and the Protestant-dominated northern ones of Ulster. The Protestants in Ulster recognised that in a democratically elected Irish Parliament, their minority status could leave them at the mercy of a government dominated by the Catholic constituency in the south. Furthermore, there was a long-standing and mutually beneficial economic link between Ulster and Great Britain, with Belfast, the largest city not only in Ulster but in all of Ireland, forming the keystone in that link. To think that Ulster's privileged position could suddenly be subordinated to a Parliament in Dublin was outrageous to those who had benefited from the intimate affiliation with Britain.

And then, of course, there was the implacable historical legacy of the Plantation programme that dated all the way back to the seventeenth century, when Britain enlisted planters from Scotland and the north of England to displace native Irish landholders in the area now encompassed by the province of Ulster. The privileged status afforded the beneficiaries of this 'plantation' of faithful subjects from England and Scotland into the northern regions of Ireland, guaranteed an Ulster population loyal to the Crown. With the power of the Crown behind them, the transplanted subjects became the dominant political force in Ulster, forging through their descendants another dimension of the close link that persists to this day between Ulster and Britain.

To galvanize that incipient Ulster opposition to any severance of the Irish-British confederation, Sir Edward Carson, a Crown prosecutor and conservative Member of Parliament, became the leader of a new Irish Unionist Parliamentary Party dedicated to opposing any kind of political devolution. He was joined in that effort by his political and judicial protégé, the very Frederick E. Smith who is now presiding over the Casement prosecution as Attorney General. The Unionists under Carson and Smith saw the privileged status of Ulster threatened by the insidious collaboration of British Liberals and Irish Parliamentarians in producing the linked Parliament Act/Home Rule legislation. Following the lead of Carson and Smith, the Unionists made it eminently clear that they would resort to any means at their disposal to prevent the implementation of a Home Rule Bill.

Thus was born the adversarial relationship that has been so apparent this week at the Bow Street Police Court between Sir Roger Casement and the Honourable Mr Frederick E. Smith. According to my anonymous source, the young solicitor on Mr Smith's staff, Mr Casement had by this time become actively engaged in the movement toward Irish independence. As an experienced diplomat and eloquent advocate, he spearheaded the Nationalist campaign during these years of increasing unrest, bringing him into direct and often virulent conflict with Mr Smith, who was leading just as vigorous a campaign on behalf of the Unionists. The campaign grew increasingly hostile as it became apparent that the product of the Redmond-Asquith deal was leading toward ultimate passage of the Home Rule Bill.

Unfortunately, the hostile rhetoric evolved into the potential for armed conflict as the Bill's passage became imminent. Recognising the inevitability of Home Rule and an Irish Parliament in Dublin, the Unionists finally adopted the position that the six counties of Ulster should simply be excluded from the purview of the Bill. If anything, according to my informant, this exacerbated rather than mollified the hostility between Smith and Casement, for Casement, who has a strong family attachment to Ulster and was therefore passionately committed to a united Ireland, took even greater umbrage to this position, which would effectively divide the island into separate bodies. On New Year's Day of 1913, Carson even went so far as to propose an official amendment to the Home Rule Bill, providing that if Home Rule were to be implemented, Ireland should be legally partitioned into northern and southern political entities with Ulster specifically excluded from the domain of any Irish Parliament that might be established in Dublin. The introduction of this amendment naturally cemented the irreconcilable lines that had been drawn between the Unionist and Nationalist constituencies.

As passions became increasingly inflamed over the issue, the Unionists under Carson and Smith became more and more militant, threatening outright civil war. In 1912, they organised the Ulster Volunteer Force, now known simply as the UVF, to become the military arm of the anti-Home Rule movement, arming it with guns and ammunition smuggled in from abroad. In effect, as my anonymous source emphatically pointed out, Carson and Smith were laying the foundation for treason as they prepared for armed insurrection in response to legislation that had been duly and legitimately enacted by the British government.

Reinforcing rumours that abounded at the time, many of which I was cognizant while covering the Home Rule movement, my anonymous source of today insists that Mr Casement responded in kind, participating in the formation of a group called the Irish Volunteers and seeking to arm them with smuggled weapons. My source also asserts that while the UVF gun-running activities were conveniently overlooked by the British authorities, similar efforts by the Irish Volunteers were interdicted and suppressed, as exemplified by the tragic events of Bachelor's Walk to which I alluded in a dispatch earlier this week. The adversarial relationship between Casement and Smith was thus firmly ensconced, carrying forward to this very day and into the precincts of the Bow Street Police Court.

As for the treasonous activity upon which Mr Smith had embarked, my informant sarcastically noted that an accident of history intervened to spare him the need for armed resistance: on 28 June two years ago, a disgruntled Serb student shot and killed Archduke Franz Ferdinand, the heir to the Austro-Hungarian throne, precipitating the conflagration in which Britain has now been embroiled for what seems to many like an eternity. The rapidly unfolding events that followed Ferdinand's assassination quickly led to Germany's invasion of Belgium in August of 1914, at which point Britain entered the conflict in Belgium's defence. Recognising that they would need to enlist a huge number of young men into military service, including Irishmen who were still officially citizens of the United Kingdom, the British government elected to postpone implementation of the Home Rule Bill until after the cessation of hostilities, thus temporarily eliminating the point of contention between the Nationalists and the Unionists. Mr Smith not only sidestepped an act of treason but even managed to succeed his mentor, Sir Edward Carson, as Attorney General, acceding to that post just seven months ago in October of 1915 – at the very time when his political adversary Mr Casement was in Germany recruiting an Irish Brigade.

As noted earlier, anonymous sources always have personal agendas and the tenor of my interview yesterday with the staff solicitor certainly suggests a hostile one *vis-à-vis* his current employer. The information nevertheless seems plausible and consistent with both the events and unsubstantiated reports that emerged during the course of those events. While some degree of scepticism may be warranted in assessing the motives, sympathies, and attitudes of the personalities involved, the facts as related by my anonymous source appear to be sound and credible. The report certainly casts the Police Court proceedings in a different light. As has been apparent to this reporter from the opening moments of the hearing, Mr Bodkin may be conducting the interrogation of witnesses, but Mr Smith is clearly orchestrating the performance. Given the background provided by this anonymous informant, the expenditure of resources in developing such an exhaustive case so quickly, and the sheer determination within official circles to make an example of the defendant, may be as much the product of personal motives as political. This drama within a drama may prove as fascinating as the main plot as we approach what appears to be an inevitable political trial.

In related news, the Royal Commission appointed eight days ago to enquire into the causes of the Easter insurrection in which Casement was an alleged participant if not a ringleader, met today in the Royal Commissions House at Westminster. Members of the Commission include Lord Charles Hardinge of Penshurst, who recently returned to his post as Permanent Under-Secretary at the Foreign Office after serving for six years as the Viceroy of India and is presiding over the activities of the Commission; Sir Montague Shearman, a distinguished judge and member of the Bar; and Sir Mackenzie Chalmers, a one-time legal adviser on the Viceroy's Council in India and recently retired Under-Secretary in the Home Office. With Casement's Police Court hearing concluded as of yesterday, I was free to attend today's session of the investigative Commission.

Today's session focused on that portion of the Commission's charge concerning 'the conduct and degree of responsibility of the civil and military executive in Ireland'. Sir Matthew Nathan, who served within the Home Office as the Under-Secretary for Ireland for the last two years and who shared responsibility for government administration in Ireland with Sir Augustine Birrell, the Chief Secretary for Ireland since 1908, appeared before that Commission today. In a testimony that shocked the Commission as well as the general public, he revealed that German sources had provided the government with advance knowledge of the preparations being made for the rebellion that occurred this past Easter Monday. He read from a lengthy prepared statement in which he attempted to trace the background that led to the insurrection, emphasising the role of the Home Rule controversy and placing much of the responsibility on a small but militant cadre within the Irish Volunteers who were intent upon secession and an independent national government for Ireland.

In defence of his perceived failure to respond to the intelligence acquired from the government's German sources, Mr Nathan argued that too forceful an intervention could have alienated the loyal majority, reminding the Commission that there are more than 25,000 Irish Catholics currently serving in the army against the German Empire. He insisted, however, that he and his colleagues were nevertheless preparing arrest warrants for a number of the ringleaders when the insurrection pre-empted them. He did admit, however, to having grossly underestimated the potential strength of the armed revolutionaries, mistakenly believing, even in light of the German intelligence, that the Royal Irish Constabulary would be perfectly capable of handling any eventuality.

In his testimony today, Mr Nathan further argued that in his judgement, fear that the Military Service Act would be applied in Ireland was a significant factor in contributing to the rapid rise in militancy in recent months, as hostilities on the continent have escalated over the past year in both magnitude and ferocity. The prospect of conscription into the British army for service against German aggression has been like a Damocles sword hanging over all young men in the Commonwealth, and those in the secessionist movement had launched an aggressive public relations campaign to convince the young men of

Ireland that they owed no allegiance to the Crown in this particular fight. His remarks echoed testimony in the Bow Street Police Court hearing about Mr Casement's letters to the *Irish Independent* newspaper, urging Irishmen to refuse service in a cause that, according to him, had nothing to do with Ireland.

Mr Nathan also testified that the revolutionary movement had received a great deal of financial support from Irish expatriates in the United States, with at least £15,000 known to have been funnelled through British banks into the coffers of the Irish Volunteers and Sinn Féin between September of 1914 and April of 1915, after which British intelligence was no longer able to trace the flow of funds. With these funds, according to Mr Nathan, the revolutionaries were able to amass what intelligence authorities estimated to be a collection of about 1,800 firearms of varying kinds, which he and his colleagues did not feel represented a level of force with which the Royal Irish Constabulary could not contend. In essence, Mr Nathan seemed to be attributing the failure to take more aggressive action, to a miscalculation rather than to malfeasance or negligence.

In a clear link between the Commission's enquiry and the Bow Street Police Court proceedings that concluded yesterday, Mr Nathan referred to a memorandum that was ultimately recovered from one of the arrested leaders of the insurrection (*viz*. Mr Casement) suggesting that a German offensive would be co-ordinated with the rising. While the government's German sources had provided advance information about preparations for the revolt, this particular fact was apparently a surprise. Had there been any reason to suspect an alliance with the enemy of the Crown, Mr Nathan insisted, more aggressive action would have been both warranted and taken.

The reference to German sources has once again raised a question in this reporter's mind about the role that the German government was playing behind the scenes. It is apparent from the testimony thus far introduced into evidence, at both the Casement hearing and the Commission enquiry, that Germany was actively involved in preparations for the Irish rebellion. Witnesses' testimony and documentary evidence are supported by the recovery of arms from the scuttled *Aud* and by the very fact that Casement and his co-conspirators arrived on the coast of Kerry via German submarine. There is little doubt that the insurrection was receiving support from the German War Department. And yet, at the same time, German 'sources' were providing the British authorities in Dublin Castle with intelligence that could have allowed them, if they had been sufficiently attentive, to forestall that very rebellion. It begs the same question that I raised in an earlier dispatch about what Germany was actually doing and what it hoped to accomplish, both in providing the advance intelligence to which Mr Nathan alluded and in repatriating Irish POWs who could support the government's case against Sir Roger Casement.

Mr Nathan was followed by Mr Birrell in testifying before the Commission today. Mr Birrell offered little in the way of substantive amplification, although he was able to fill in a few details here and there. He noted, for example, that with the strong endorsement of John Redmond and his Irish Parliamentary Party, most Irish citizens of the Commonwealth were resolute in their patriotic support of the military's engagement against German aggression, and that the nationalistic movement was a fringe activity that did not at first seem to constitute a major threat to national security. Until the eruption of hostilities on 24 April, his administration in Dublin Castle had no reason to believe that this small cadre of revolutionary-minded zealots could not be effectively suppressed by the Royal Irish Constabulary.

In spite of his estimates of the threat, Mr Birrell contended that he nevertheless took that threat seriously enough to consult with Generals Kitchener and French in March about the possibility of dispatching British troops to Dublin, just as a show of force. Understandably, the generals felt that they could not afford to divert personnel from the war effort to simply provide a 'show of force' in response to what Mr Birrell admittedly considered a fringe element. In response to a direct question from Mr Shearman of the Commission, Mr Birrell pointed out that, while hindsight is often useful in assessing blame, it served no useful purpose to speculate about missed opportunities and that furthermore it was impossible ever to know for sure whether such a 'show of force' might have headed off the insurrection.

Mr Birrell was obviously intent upon defending his reputation as an effective Chief Secretary responsible for administering official matters on behalf of the government in Ireland. While the Commission was respectful of his position and his exemplary government service, the Commission representatives appeared to be just as obviously determined to find a scapegoat for what transpired last month in Dublin. At one point during the course of the interrogation, Mr Shearman suggested that Mr Birrell never spent enough time in Ireland to effectively fulfil his responsibilities as Chief Secretary, nor to keep his finger on the pulse of Irish sentiment, which might have enabled him to anticipate the magnitude of the hostilities precipitated on 24 April. Mr Birrell was noticeably offended by the insinuation, explaining that his responsibilities required him to represent Ireland at frequent Cabinet meetings in Westminster. With thinly veiled anger in his response, Mr Birrell suggested furthermore that given the abysmal level of official concern about Ireland in recent months, 'a jackdaw or a magpie could do just as well as the Chief Secretary to cry out "Ireland!"'[7] when Bills were being discussed by the Cabinet. The clear implication was that it wasn't him but the Cabinet that was remiss in matters related to Ireland.

The official enquiry has also raised questions about the appropriateness of the response engineered by General Sir John Maxwell. Based on feedback from sources who were present in Dublin when the armed revolutionaries took to the streets, it would appear that Mr Birrell was correct in suggesting that the insurrection was the product of a small but zealous fringe group; most Dubliners were as taken aback by the events as the British authorities, and contrary to what the secessionists must surely have expected or at least hoped for, there was no general rallying of the population behind them. As a matter of fact, most peace-loving Dubliners roundly condemned the action during its early stages and directed their anger not at the British but at the armed militants who had turned their beloved city into a battleground.

That disapproval may have lingered, had it not been for the violent nature of General Maxwell's response. Many in Parliament and the Royal Commission fear that the general may have accomplished what the rebels failed to accomplish: to galvanize popular support behind the movement and against the British. The enquiry that began today at Westminster's Royal Commissions House will certainly be making that a central issue in their investigation. Of particular concern is the secrecy that has shrouded the courts martial of those identified as comprising the central leadership of the rising and the summary nature of their extra-judicial executions.

A total of fifteen revolutionaries have been shot to date. With the exception of Thomas Kent, who was executed at the Cork detention barracks, all have been carried out by firing squad in total obscurity behind the walls of Kilmainham Gaol in Dublin. No transcripts of the court-martial proceedings have yet been made public, generating enormous suspicion about the fairness of the tribunals, nor has there been any explanation or justification given for precipitate executions that many in the Home Office fear will be characterised by the press as atrocities. In addition to Mr Kent, those executed thus far include Pádraig Pearse, Thomas Clarke, and Thomas MacDonagh on 3 May, less than a week after their capture; Joseph Plunkett, Edward Daly, Michael O'Hanrahan, and Willie Pearse the very next day; John MacBride on the 5 May; Eamonn Ceannt, Michael Mallin, Sean Heuston, and Con Colbert on 8 May; and Seán MacDiarmada and James Connolly just last week on the twelfth. Several of my anonymous sources in Dublin have indicated that outrage at the Connolly execution has been especially intense, given the fact that he had to be dragged out and propped up in a chair to face the firing squad because of the severity of his wounds.

Mr Casement may very well be the next to be executed, but the very public proceedings against him are in marked contrast to the secret courts martial of the other participants. One cannot argue that the handling of his case reflects lessons learned from General Maxwell's approach, for Mr Casement was whisked away from Ireland and delivered to the authorities in London even before the other participants were being hustled into the confines of Kilmainham Gaol. From the very beginning, Casement was singled out for special treatment. It seems safe to assume that his former position in the Foreign Office had much to do with that decision. Given his trusted role in government circles and the royal decorations bestowed upon him, his alignment with armed insurrection against the Crown is perceived as especially egregious by the government and the public alike. As suggested in an earlier dispatch, the British public is in sore need of an issue that will revitalise their flagging spirits after almost two years of debilitating warfare on the continent. By conspiring with the enemy during a time of war, Mr Casement may very well have provided them with that issue.

With the Police Court hearing now concluded, the case against Mr Bailey and Mr Casement is now being bound over for trial. The first formal step will be the convening of a Grand Jury to consider bills of indictment. Speaking on behalf of the Attorney General and the prosecution team at the conclusion of yesterday's proceedings, Mr Travers Humphreys urged an expeditious handling of the case. In response, Mr Artemus Jones pointed out that he had not been engaged to represent the defendant until just this past week, and had not even had an opportunity to consult with him until just before the police court hearing. While proclaiming sympathy with the defence counsel's burden, the court nevertheless made it clear that a Grand Jury will convene during the current term, which means that it will have to meet within the next week to ten days, allowing the Lord Chief Justice the opportunity to schedule a trial for early next month. As Sir John Dickinson pointed out in his ruling, that will allow the defence a full three weeks to prepare!

SATURDAY 20 MAY 1916

The entire city of London, indeed the entire British Empire, is gripped by the ongoing saga of the now infamous Sir Roger Casement. While his name may not be common place among this reporter's readers in the United States, he has been widely recognised and highly regarded throughout Britain for over a decade. He first achieved prominence in 1904, with the publication of an investigative report about alleged atrocities in the Congo Free State. It was on the basis of that report that King Edward VII honoured him with an appointment to the Order of St Michael and St George, one of the highest orders of chivalry in the United Kingdom, reserved for those who have made especially notable contributions in their service to the Commonwealth. As specified in its criteria, the Order was established to honour those 'who hold high and confidential offices within Her Majesty's colonial possessions and in reward for services rendered to the Crown in relation to the foreign affairs of the Empire'. Ironically, the current reigning monarch, King George V, under whom Casement has allegedly perpetrated the crime of treason, was the Grand Master of the Order at the time of Casement's appointment honouring his foreign service.

The prominence being given to the current proceedings by British authorities and its potential impact upon international relations have made the case a matter of more than passing interest to all concerned Americans, who view with alarm the deteriorating situation in Europe.

There is a growing sense that the United States, in spite of all efforts to the contrary, will inevitably be drawn into the growing conflict. The Casement case is revealing new dimensions to the relationship between Britain and its neighbours both east and west, and thus casting various new shades of light on the background of the current conflict. It may ultimately prove to be nothing more than a passing melodrama generated by a disgruntled former consul in the British Foreign Service, but the insights it affords could also prove invaluable in assessing Britain's role as a major participant in the events that have led to the current situation in Europe.

The apolitical reader will also find much of interest in following the case, for the defendant holds a fascinating appeal that transcends whatever role he might have played in Britain's conflict with Germany and in the Irish insurrection. How an internationally honoured humanitarian could end up in the dock accused of high treason is an intriguing question that defies explanation. With the arraignment hearing now concluded, there is a temporary lull in the official proceedings, allowing us to explore a bit of the background of this fascinating figure before his trial convenes. In an effort to gain some appreciation for that background, I obtained a copy of the 1904 investigative report that propelled Casement to the forefront of humanitarian interventionism. It not only provides a devastating indictment of colonialism and the commercial exploitation of indigenous societies, but also affords the careful reader a great deal of insight into Casement's character. I was also fortunate to find a member of the entourage who accompanied Casement on that fact-finding mission. While understandably insisting on anonymity to avoid being drawn into the current high-profile legal intrigue, this informant was able to provide me with some valuable personal observations about that expedition into the depths of human depravity.

Before reviewing Casement's involvement in that mission, however, a bit of historical background might be helpful for those American readers who are unfamiliar with the *fin de siècle* European colonial activities that comprised the context for his investigation and his subsequent report. Now known as the Belgian Congo, following its annexation by Belgium in 1908, the Congo Free State was internationally recognised as a sovereign entity in 1884. Until then, of course, central Africa was a vast, unexplored and untamed area in which there had been little interest among the nations of Europe and America. As explorers from Europe began to penetrate this wild and hostile environment, it became increasingly clear that the region had untapped resources that could be exploited, if properly developed by the more advanced European societies. Among those who recognised the commercial potential was King Leopold II of Belgium, who became intrigued by reports emanating from Henry Morton Stanley's expedition to the Congo River basin in 1874.

Eager to take the initiative in this heretofore undeveloped region of the world, Leopold hosted an International Geographical Conference in Brussels in 1876. Purporting to be motivated by humanitarian concerns for the indigenous societies that Stanley described in his reports from the Congo expedition, Leopold used this forum to propose the establishment of an international benevolent committee that would be devoted to 'civilizing' this primitive region through scientific exploration and legalised trade, as well as the suppression of an Arabic slave trade that had been savaging the indigenous peoples for decades. In lofty language that had to impress the conference participants, Leopold proposed a crusade to 'pierce the darkness which hangs over entire peoples' and to bring the blessings of modern civilization to this backward region of the world. An organisation known as the International African Association grew out of the conference's proceedings, and in recognition of his purported commitment to the Association's goals, King Leopold was named its President.

As a first step toward 'civilizing' the native population, Leopold commissioned Stanley to return to the Congo in 1879 as an employee of the newly formed International African Association with responsibility for establishing a caravan route up the river to Stanley Pool, the lake that had already taken its name from this intrepid explorer. Stanley established a number of commercial outposts during the course of this expedition, providing a network of trading posts that terminated at Stanley Pool, where the last of the outposts was named Leopoldville in honour of the Association's President. By the time Stanley returned to Europe in 1884, the International African Association, the benevolent and humanitarian organisation to which the International Geographic Conference had given birth, had metamorphosed into the International Association of the Congo, a purely commercial enterprise with Leopold as the sole stockholder.

Recognising Leopold's bold headstart in establishing an infrastructure upon which to build a commercial enterprise in Africa, a variety of other European nations felt compelled to intervene in an effort to control the future direction of African colonisation. Otto Von Bismarck, Chancellor of the newly confederated German Empire, was eager for his fledgling new Empire to assume what he perceived to be its rightful place among the world's colonial powers, and as a first step toward that goal, he took the lead in the European intervention by convening a conference of fourteen nations in Berlin that lasted from November 1884 to February 1885. France, Germany, Great Britain, and Portugal, all of whom had already taken an interest in establishing a colonial presence in Africa, were especially interested in negotiating an agreement to regulate commercial development. Sir Edward Malet, Britain's ambassador in Berlin, represented the United Kingdom at the conference, which culminated in the General Act of Berlin signed by the conference participants on 26 February 1885. This act distributed spheres of influence among the major colonisers but specified clearly that free trade and improved conditions for the indigenous populations would be the hallmarks of the agreement. As stipulated in Article 6 of that convention, the signatories committed themselves, 'to watch over the preservation of the native tribes, and to care for their moral and material well-being',[8] in the furtherance of which they would support, 'all religious, scientific or charitable institutions and undertakings created for the above ends or which aim at instructing the natives and bringing them home to the blessings of civilization'.

In view of the investment that Leopold had already personally made in the Congo River basin, the conference participants agreed that his International Association of the Congo would be charged with administering that particular 'sphere of influence'. Renamed the Congo Free

State, the area encompassed by Henry Morton Stanley's network of commercial outposts became Leopold's personal domain. In keeping with the spirit of the agreement, Leopold pledged that there would be no restriction on the exercise of free trade and that his organisation would be firmly committed to improving both the moral and the material lot of the indigenous peoples. In effect, he cast himself in the role of a modern-day messiah, bringing Christian civilization and its benefits to the deprived natives who subsisted in sub-human conditions deep in the darkest heart of Africa.

Over the course of the next decade, rumours began to emerge suggesting that Leopold's idealistic pronouncements had either been a smokescreen for greed, or had been subverted by the forces of commercialism. Horrible tales of wide-scale atrocities began to appear regularly in the *West African Mail*, the newspaper that Edmond D. Morel began publishing specifically to expose mistreatment of natives on the African continent and to provide a medium for public advocacy on their behalf. As a signatory to the General Act of Berlin, Britain naturally had a vested interest in ensuring that the accord was duly followed, not only to protect the rights of the native population but also to promote its own commercial interests in maintaining free trade throughout the Congo region, especially given the emerging demands for rubber in the new automobile industry. Reports of atrocities therefore attracted the attention of Parliament as well as members of both the Home Office and the Foreign Office. In May of 1902, Sir Charles Dilke, a Member of both Parliament and the Privy Council, even suggested that the Berlin conferees reconvene to address the issue.

While that proposal never attracted sufficient international support to become viable, the widespread concern within government circles prompted Herbert Samuel to raise the matter in the House of Commons just a year later, in May of 1903. Armed with graphic descriptions of floggings and beatings and mutilations and murder, Samuel made an impassioned plea for governmental intervention in the Congo Free State. With Morel's continued appeals to public sentiment and Parliament's demands for an official government response, pressure on the Foreign Office became too great to resist further action, and the decision was taken to launch a formal investigation into the administration of the Congo Free State. The Foreign Office needed to tread softly in order to preserve its good relations with Belgium, where Leopold was still the reigning monarch, but at the same time it had to sponsor a credible enquiry into the African activities of that nation's sovereign.

It was into this volatile atmosphere that Casement was propelled in the spring of 1903. His official position at the time and prior experience in Africa, combined to make him the ideal candidate to head up the investigation on behalf of the Foreign Office. In the spring of 1903, he was the British Consul in Boma, the administrative centre or capital of Leopold's domain, where he had consular responsibility for the Congo Free State along with Portuguese West Africa and the French Congo. He had even met personally with Leopold while *en route* to his consular assignment almost three years earlier, when Leopold had made a point of trying to disabuse this new British consular representative of the allegations that had by then become widespread.

Prior to assuming his responsibilities in Boma, Casement had served the Foreign Office in various capacities in Lourenço Marques, St Paul de Loanda, and Cape Town, and before that he had apparently acquired extensive personal and professional experience in Africa through private employment. I am now in the process of researching his background during those earlier years and will hopefully be able to supplement these reports at a later date with additional information about Casement's initial exposure to this vast and mysterious continent. It is the Congo Report of April 1903, however, that catapulted him into international prominence and earned him the accolades that make his current situation so implausible and bizarre. Given the imminence of a Grand Jury hearing, which will probably occur sometime within the next several days, it is therefore of more immediate interest to focus on what that 1903 expedition reveals about the character of the accused.

It is difficult to assess from this distance and in the absence of first-hand informants just what kind of relationship Casement enjoyed with the Foreign Office in the early years of his government service, prior to the 1903 assignment. It is probably safe to assume that he and the Foreign Office were both feeling their way during those early years, testing the waters, so to speak, in an effort to determine just what kind of long-term relationship, if any, might lie in store. There is no doubt, however, that during the course of those initial years of service, his superiors must have acquired tremendous confidence in his abilities; trusting a man with only eight years of professional experience in the consular corps to lead an investigation of such international import was no mean leap of faith. In researching future articles for this series, I hope to gain some insight into the basis of that confidence, rooted, no doubt, in the prior African experience alluded to earlier. The fact is, however, the Foreign Office did indeed delegate to this hereto-fore unknown consular official full responsibility for determining the veracity of allegations that bore directly on a major foreign policy and commercial issue that would have far-reaching implications for the Commonwealth.

It is also safe to assume that this relatively unknown consular official must have welcomed the challenge as a way not only to demonstrate that the government's confidence was not misplaced, but also to advance his own career within the Foreign Service. Informants with whom I have had the good fortune to become acquainted, have consistently alluded to Casement's indomitable vanity. He apparently believed that he was blessed with a superior intellect and with abilities that made him uniquely suited to every assignment – personal qualities that obviously did not endear him to the informants whom I interviewed. According to those informants, he seemed able, throughout his career, to position himself, whether by design or by coincidence, to be not just the obvious choice for a particular assignment, but the only logical choice. Based on the input received from those informants, it is not difficult to imagine him accepting the Congo charge from his superiors with a certain degree of impudence, indulging the conviction that they really had nowhere else to turn if they seriously expected the mission to be regarded with any degree of credibility. All things considered, it would appear that he was virtually made for the assignment, and with the benefit of hindsight, it is obvious that he made the most of it.

Based on an exhaustive study of government archives, a reading of the Congo Report that was published by the Foreign Office, interviews with a number of Foreign Office officials, and input from the anonymous informant who accompanied him up the Congo, I have attempted to reconstruct most of the events that led to Casement's June 1905 royal recognition as a Companion in the Order of St Michael and St George. Drawing heavily on all those sources, the account that follows may not be accurate in all respects but should hopefully capture the essence of what transpired over the course of those fateful three months. It all began on the 5 June 1903, when he travelled upriver to Leopoldville on Stanley Pool.

From the very beginning, he tried to keep his official role low-key to facilitate access to local informants and to avoid drawing the attention of officials representing the Congo Free State. In spite of his right, as a consular representative, to an official escort, for example, he chose to commission the use of a private river steamer, the *Henry Reed*, from the American Baptist Missionary Union, thus enabling him to avoid dependence on and manipulation by the State authorities. To the fullest extent possible, he travelled incognito throughout the region for the next several months, making personal observations, conducting extensive interviews, and collecting archival evidence in a determined effort to ferret out the truth of what was going on in this 'heart of darkness'. As is true for any enterprise, however, every decision can be a two-edged sword, and his decision to avail himself of the services afforded by the American Baptist Missionary Union, an understandable and reasonable way of avoiding interference by the authorities of the Congo Free State, would later make him vulnerable to the accusation that his report was unduly influenced by the biased perspectives of critical Christian missionaries.

His basic itinerary can be summarised in short order. He spent the first month of his investigation in Leopoldville, after which he travelled to a number of villages with names that will be completely unfamiliar to most readers of these dispatches. Chumbiri, Bolobo, Lukolela, Ikoko, and Coquilhatville are a few examples of the strange and exotic way stations that drew his attention while travelling upriver. He spent a total of fifteen weeks navigating among these remote outposts of civilization, returning to Leopoldville on 15 September. In many respects, Casement's Congo Report might be seen as a documentary parallel to the Joseph Conrad novella that appeared just a year before Casement drafted his findings. Many of my readers are no doubt familiar with that fictionalised *Heart of Darkness*, either through the book that appeared in 1902 or through the serialised version that appeared in *Blackwood's Magazine* a couple of years earlier. Indeed, according to my informant from Casement's 1903 voyage into the real-life heart of darkness, Casement and Conrad actually knew each other, having spent several weeks together in Matadi at the mouth of the Congo during Casement's initial exposure to the continent. As noted earlier, I am attempting to learn more about those early years in Casement's experience and will hopefully be able to provide some background information about the relationship between Casement and Conrad in a later dispatch.

Along the way upriver, during that summer of 1903, Casement received the support of several missionary organizations – the British Baptist Missionary Society, the American Baptist Missionary Union already alluded to, the Congo Balolo Mission, and the American Disciples of Christ. These missionary societies were the only organised alternatives to governmental and commercial enterprises when it came to the logistical support he needed. While he therefore turned to them as a way of insulating himself from interference in the conduct of his investigation, critics have been quick to cite the relationship as evidence that his judgement was influenced by their worldview, and by their natural inclination to focus on any perceived mistreatment of the indigenous people, to whom they had become sentimentally attached. It is certainly not unreasonable to assume that Casement may have approached the assignment with a personal affinity for that worldview. The official records clearly indicate that the missionaries had a history of advocacy, revealing sentiments that might have influenced their selection of sites to visit and informants to interview.

In fact, many of the reports that had made their way into Morel's *West African Mail* had originated with disaffected missionaries, most of whom had acted clandestinely in order to draw attention to the plight of the native population without precipitating retribution from the government and commercial authorities. One can imagine how eager they must have been to meet personally with this official government representative who had finally been dispatched to investigate – the first tangible indication that their pleas had not been falling on deaf ears. Ellsworth Faris, Edward Layton, and Robert Eldred from the Disciples of Christ, and Arthur Billington, Joseph Clark, Elizabeth Clark, and Lena Clark from the American Baptist Missionary are a few examples of the authoritative sources who provided the kind of first-hand, credible input upon which Casement was able to base his final report. They had spent years ministering to the spiritual, and often the physical, needs of the native population, and as has been the case with missionaries throughout the ages, they had become as attached to their charges as they would have been to members of their own families. According to my informant from the Casement entourage, the passion and graphic detail that imbued the missionaries' testimonies was not only moving but convincing. Outside critics may question the objectivity of their input and of Casement's judgement, but according to this informant, the first-hand testimony left no doubt that atrocities had occurred.

A reading of the official investigative account has certainly given me a much more direct sense of Casement's investigative methods, his frame of reference, and the bases of his conclusions. It is replete with detail, making it a bit tedious to read, but the result is an accumulation of evidence that is at once overwhelming and shocking. The first and most obvious impression that alerted Casement to the existence of a major calamity, based on his own knowledge and experience from his prior exposure to the region, was the stark absence of native peoples in areas with which he had become familiar during his private employment years earlier. As he noted in the section of his report dealing with Chumbiri:

> I had visited this place in August of 1887 when the line of villages comprising the Settlement contained from 4,000 to 5,000 people. Most of these villages today are entirely deserted, the forest having grown over the abandoned sites, and the entire community at the present date cannot number more than 500 souls.[9]

The same unsettling observation marked his progress through the remaining sites on his itinerary. In the section on Bolobo, he reported that this area:

> ... used to be one of the most important Settlements along the south bank of the Upper Congo, and the population in the early days of civilized rule numbered fully 40,000 people, chiefly of the Bobangi tribe. Today the population is believed to be not more than 7,000 to 8,000 souls.[10]

In speaking of Lukolela he noted that, 'This district had, when I visited it in 1887, numbered fully 5,000 people; today the population is given, after a careful enumeration, at less than 600.'[11] And with regard to the area around Lake Mantumba he observed that, 'The population of the lakeside towns would seem to have diminished within the last ten years by 60 or 70 percent.'[12]

The impression had to have been deeply unnerving. A thriving and vibrant native presence had ceased to exist; erstwhile settlements, now buried under jungle growth, and their inhabitants simply gone. The evidence would have been lost on an investigator who lacked the personal experience that Casement brought with him as a result of his earlier exposure to the area. The effect had to have been especially traumatic for a man like Casement. My Foreign Office informants were unanimous in claiming that while Casement's personality and temperament might have raised their hackles, none of them doubted the sincerity of his philosophical conviction that the civilizing influence of European societies would be a blessing to the primitive populations of the world. Seeing evidence that European intervention had been a curse rather than a blessing had to have been profoundly disillusioning for someone so philosophically convinced not only of the moral rectitude but indeed of the moral obligation to bring 'civilization' to the backward societies of central Africa.

Casement acknowledges in his report that there was always the possibility that the Congolese had been the victims of a natural disaster: sleeping sickness was endemic to the area and smallpox had become a plague to those who lacked any natural immunity. Armed conflict among warring tribes could also have contributed to the population decline. But supplemental evidence collected along the way strongly suggested otherwise. Joseph Clark, one of the missionary informants who had lived among the natives since Casement's prior visit, was among those who testified that the extent of the decimation could not be adequately explained by anything other than the measures being taken by government and commercial authorities to exploit the native population. Such a conclusion had to have been devastating to one who firmly believed in a civilized and civilizing European commitment to the less advanced societies of the world.

Another of the initial impressions that he recorded in the report, and which immediately coloured his perception of subsequent events, was the condition of the native hospital in Leopoldville, which he was able to observe shortly after arriving at the start of his investigation in June. Unlike the outpost's clean, modern hospital for Europeans in the employ of the State, the native hospital consisted of three dilapidated mud huts, completely lacking in the basics of medical hygiene. With ill-concealed disapproval, he observed in his report that when he visited the native hospital he had found, 'seventeen sleeping sickness patients, male and female, lying about in the utmost dirt,'[13] with most of them 'lying on the bare ground'. His detailed description of one case in particular bordered on the pathetic: a woman in the terminal stages of sleeping sickness had actually fallen into an open cooking fire and had been left lying out on the open ground in front of the hospital hut. Adding to the macabre nature of the incident, Casement went on to point out that when he attempted to speak with her, she 'upset a pot of scalding water over her shoulder,'[14] prompting him to leave her in her abject misery before worse could unfold. In contrast to the conditions in the native hospital, he observed that even the government workshop for repairing its steamers, a 'hospital' of sorts, for the State's material possessions, was a paragon of 'brightness, care, order, and activity'.[15]

It was also in Leopoldville that he gained his initial exposure to suspect labour contracts and the practice of levying questionable and burdensome requisitions upon the native population for the support of the State and its employees. Upon learning of his visit, a number of native workers brought copies of their contracts to him, asking him simply to let them know how much time was left on their period of service. While reading the contracts in order to answer their questions, none of which was put forward in the form of a complaint but simply as an innocent query, Casement discovered evidence of alterations and other suspicious conditions, leading him to believe that the workers had been coerced or at best misled into providing the authorities with a legal document that effectively reduced them to a form of slavery with an open-ended commitment. In classical bureaucratic indirection, a rhetorical device to which he resorted frequently throughout the report, Casement made the observation that a majority of the workers in Leopoldville had been brought in from the Upper Congo to 'serve the authorities not primarily at their own seeking'.[16]

Requisitions levied upon the native population for the benefit of the European interlopers also became an issue that surfaced immediately in Leopoldville and continued to be an issue at each subsequent stop along his itinerary. Food requisitions were a case in point. The root of the cassava plant, steeped, boiled, and made up into loaves or puddings called *kwanga*, is the staple food upon which all inhabitants of the Congo depend. As cited in his report, 'The natives of the districts around Leopoldville are forced to provide a fixed quantity each week of this form of food, which is levied by requisitions on all the surrounding villages. The European Government staff is also mainly dependent upon food supplies obtained from the natives of the neighbourhood in a similar manner.'[17] The hardship of being compelled to support the presence of a foreign population was further exacerbated by the fact that the native population itself was 'yearly decreasing, while the demands made upon them remain fixed or tend even to increase'.[18]

Forced labour and various forms of 'requisition' became the norms that Casement found at each stop along the way. As the basic subsistence item, *kwanga* was commonly requisitioned throughout the territories. Depending upon location and availability, other foodstuffs could also be requisitioned, like fowls and goats in Chumbiri, hippopotamus meat in the Belobo region, and fish from the riverside dwellers of Lukolela. In all cases the government made a pretence of reimbursing the natives, but in no case were they relieved of the quotas imposed upon them, even when those quotas obviously exceeded their available resources or deprived them of the wherewithal to meet their own basic needs, and their 'remuneration' was anything but just.

Complaints that quota demands were 'in excess of their means of supply and out of proportion to the value received in exchange'[19] were commonplace among the natives that Casement interviewed. As one example among many, the residents of a small village named Litimba informed him that 'when short of cassava from their own fields' to meet their weekly quota of *kwanga*, they had to buy the root 'in the local market and had to pay for it in the raw state just twice what they received for the prepared and cooked product they delivered to the government post'.[20] As one native informant in a small Chumbiri village lamented, 'How can we possibly plant and weed our gardens, seek and prepare and boil the cassava, make it into portable shape, and then carry it nearly a day's journey to the post?'[21] With a total population of only ten, this village was required to submit over 200 pounds of *kwanga* per week to the closest government outpost! This informant went on to state that failure to meet the quota could result in a beating or in detention of the male villagers for several days to cut firewood for the government post.

In addition to a variety of foodstuffs, labour could also be compulsorily requisitioned. Casement cited one especially egregious example in the Bolobo region, where native labourers were forced to build a wooden pier to accommodate government vessels coming upriver. As Casement learned, no remuneration was made to any of the native labourers, 'They were ordered, they said, to do it as a public service.'[22] To add insult to injury, the labourers that he interviewed pointed out that 'the pier was being so badly put up that when finished it would be quite useless, and all their work would thus be thrown away'.[23] As a 'public service,' natives were routinely ordered to cut firewood for the steamers, clear brush from the telegraph lines, and perform whatever other tasks might require manual labour – all with little or no remuneration.

And then, of course, there was always the insatiable demand for rubber, the *raison d'être* for the Congo Free State's very existence. And it was to meet this demand that labour was provided under the terms of the suspect contracts into which the natives had been coerced. Through the ruthless administration of his Congo Free State, Leopold sought to exploit the exponential increase in the demand for rubber to meet various industrial needs and especially to support the rapidly growing automobile industry. The collection of rubber in the Congo was especially inhumane to begin with; lacking the requisite knowledge and technology for extracting this raw material, the natives frequently resorted to slashing the vines and lathering their bodies with the residue, allowing the latex to harden so they could transport it from the bush on their own bodies then scrape it off, usually along with several layers of skin, for submission to the weighing officials. The quotas imposed became increasingly impossible to meet, as the government and commercial authorities both sought to maximise their profits at the expense of a native population that was perceived to be nothing more than ignorant beasts of burden.

As noted earlier, the former colleagues whom I interviewed for this report tended to be critical of his vanity and egotism, but they invariably tempered the hostility generated by his personality with praise for his unflagging confidence in the efficacy of what they called the 'three Cs' (Christianity, commerce, and civilization) as agents for transforming primitive societies. According to my Foreign Office informants, his early service in Africa was distinguished by his firm belief that Britain and the other advanced societies of Europe would be the saviours of that dark continent. By introducing Christian values and free enterprise to this deprived and neglected mass of humanity, European settlers would be doing God's good work in promoting the Africans' advance from barbarism to civilization.

Therefore, he had to have been appalled and grossly disillusioned by what he was finding as he proceeded upriver. The evidence was incontestable; explaining the evidence was more difficult. For a man as confident as my informants suggested in the 'three Cs', the central philosophical question for Casement had to be whether the Congo of 1903 was an aberration in the 'three C' paradigm – or an unsettling but exemplary reflection of some inherent defect in that paradigm.

Whatever the case, Casement had to have been outraged by what he was finding. And while subtle in expression, that outrage becomes apparent as one reads through the report. The exploitation for economic gain was bad enough; the diabolical nature of the physical abuse attendant upon that exploitation was beyond Casement's most lurid nightmares. It is to that abuse that we will turn in my next dispatch.

MONDAY 22 MAY 1916

Moving expeditiously to ensure the earliest possible trial date, the prosecution in the case against Sir Roger Casement will present a formal bill of indictment to the Grand Jury that has now been scheduled to convene on Thursday of this week, 25 May. Under the judicial procedures governing the legal process for a trial at Bar, the Lord Chief Justice has appointed a Grand Jury consisting of twenty-three members to hear the prosecution's evidence. To issue a bill of indictment, at least twelve of them must concur that a *prima facie* case has been established to support the charge of high treason. Should that occur, which appears most likely at this point, the Lord Chief Justice will then set a trial date. By scheduling the Grand Jury presentation for as early as this week, it will still be possible to include such a trial in the current session of the Bar, thus virtually guaranteeing a trial within the next three or four weeks.

The defence has naturally expressed dismay with the sense of urgency that is being generated by the prosecution. With both public and official passions at such a fever pitch, it is certainly in the prosecution's best interest to move quickly, and it is apparent that the honourable Attorney General will employ every legal tactic available to avoid a cooling-off period before the trial commences. While Mr Smith can use the old adage that 'justice delayed is justice denied' to sanction his haste, the defence has good reason to insinuate that there are ulterior motives behind his haste, especially given the history of hostility between Mr Smith and Mr Casement. No matter how well insulated the Bar might be from outside pressure, the presiding justices are human and understandably sensitive to the social and political climate that will prevail in the immediate weeks ahead. Mr Smith can obviously use this to advantage by pressing for an early trial.

Mr Casement continues to be held incommunicado, granted access only to his defence counsel. All attempts by the press to obtain interviews have been turned aside. We in the media have had no direct contact with the accused since his arrest, and are therefore only able to speculate about his version of events. Anonymous sources within the Irish independence movement are understandably outraged, not only by the prosecutor's determination to make an example of this former national hero, but more especially, by the hasty courts martial and executions that have occurred in Dublin since the suppression of last month's uprising. Those sources have been able to offer little substantive input in our effort to gain some insight into Casement's involvement in that uprising. If anything, they appear to be remarkably in the dark themselves, seemingly as mystified as the press by the prosecution's allegations of Casement's central role in leading the rebellion. Among those insiders with whom I've been able to consult, Pádraig Pearse and James Connolly are generally regarded as the organisers and leaders of the rebellion. Sympathisers are naturally furious about the summary executions in Kilmainham Gaol, and while there is certainly outrage about the handing of Mr Casement, his prosecution has not generated the same kind of anger. The mixed reactions seem to reflect not only puzzlement about his alleged role in the rising but also a noticeable ambivalence toward his identification with the 'cause', given his long-time service to the Crown.

With the current lull in the legal proceedings, I shall continue to seek informants who might cast some light on both his involvement in the rebellion and his motives. In the meantime, however, the examination begun in my last dispatch will hopefully provide valuable background in helping us understand what ultimately brought Casement to the dock. If nothing else, his mission to the Congo thirteen years ago and the much-heralded investigative report that brought him royal accolades should provide some context for all that has transpired over the past decade. His accomplishments during the fulfilment of that assignment are what propelled him into international prominence and gained him recognition as a dedicated representative of His Majesty's government. Unfortunately, according to my inside informant from the entourage that accompanied him, the experience also left him severely traumatised and disillusioned.

As noted in my last dispatch, Casement's 1904 report provided extensive documentary evidence of commercial exploitation by King Leopold II in his administration of the Congo Free State. Under the guise of bringing the benefits of modern civilization to the indigenous peoples of the Congo, Leopold allegedly created a personal fiefdom that violated both the commercial and the humanitarian terms of the 1885 General Act of Berlin. In that last dispatch, I discussed the evidence that Casement reported in support of those allegations, which won him both international acclaim and royal honours. The exploitation was just the tip of the iceberg, however; it was the atrocities that Casement documented in support of that exploitation that generated the greatest outrage and cemented his reputation in humanitarian circles. It is to those atrocities that we must now turn.

While the labour demands and material requisitions that he uncovered were in themselves sufficiently shocking to the civilized sensibilities of Parliament and the British public, it was the enforcement mechanisms that truly galvanized outrage and scandalised the world when the report was released. By substantiating the allegations of atrocities that had been appearing in Morel's *West African Mail*, Casement's report increased the pressure on the Foreign Office to take some kind of action. Flogging with the *chicotte*, an especially harsh form of punishment with a whip made of hippopotamus hide, was the most common form of abuse that was cited repeatedly throughout his investigative journey. Failure to meet a requisition quota, lagging behind the demanded pace on a work project, inadequate deference to authority, perceived lack of co-operation, complaints about mistreatment – any number of 'offences' could result in being stretched naked between two poles and flogged viciously with the *chicotte*.

77

Natives up and down the Congo were able to show him the scars of repeated flogging. One village chief in the Lake Mantumba region told Casement of a case involving a canoe that had been requisitioned by the local authorities and never returned to its rightful native owner. When Casement urged the chief to seek reimbursement, 'he pulled up his loin cloth and, pointing to where he had been flogged with a *chicotte*, said, "If I complained I should only get more of these."'[24] On another occasion, upon enlisting the service of a half dozen natives in Ikoko to help the crew of the *Henry Reed* with some repairs, Casement was perplexed by the reaction of the local chieftain, who objected strongly to Casement's hiring of local villagers. When he approached the chieftain for an explanation, he was told:

> I am responsible each week for 600 rations of fish which must be delivered to Bikoro. If it fails, I am held responsible and will be punished. I have been flogged more than once for a failure in the fish supply and will not run any risks. If these men go, I shall be short-handed, therefore they must stay to help in getting the weekly tax.[25]

Recognising the man's plight but still needing the help, Casement not only paid the labourers for their work, but also reimbursed the chieftain for releasing them, allowing the chieftain to hire replacements to ensure that the village's quota could be met.

While no one in Casement's entourage was able personally to witness a flogging, the evidence and native testimony made it clear that the practice was ubiquitous, flagrant, and absolutely vicious. The informant whom I was able to interview from Casement's group reported that virtually every native with whom they interacted, including children in their early teens, had grotesque scars on their bodies, some so widespread that they appeared to have been flayed to the point of losing not only the outer layer of skin but also a layer of underlying muscle. As described by those who had been subjected to such punishment, the victim would be stripped naked, then stretched out on the ground between two fixed poles or tree roots, lying on his belly with his wrists bound to one pole and his ankles to the other. The enforcer would then attack them viciously, flaying the bare back, buttocks, and thighs, with blood and skin erupting from the prone and immobilised body. The mere sight of the infamous *chicotte* in the hands of those who led the work gangs could terrorise natives into meek submission.

Forced labour with the threat of a flogging for resistance was another enforcement mechanism to which the local authorities frequently resorted. Should one of the natives fail to meet a requisition quota, he could be taken into custody and forced to provide free (i.e. slave) labour as recompense for the shortfall on his quota. While in Bongandanga, for example, Casement personally observed that a group of natives were under guard by armed sentries. Upon inquiring, he was informed that, 'If the rubber brought by its native vendor was found on the weighing machine to be seriously under the required weight, the defaulting individual was detained to be dealt with in the *maison des otages*, or local prison.'[26] Upon visiting the prison enclosure, he:

> ... counted fifteen men and youths who were being guarded while they worked at mat-making for the use of the station buildings. These men, I was then told, were some of the defaulters of the previous market day, who were being kept as compulsory workmen to make good the deficiency in their rubber quota.[27]

The quasi-legal 'quota', given legal status by the contracts that the natives had been either coerced or tricked into signing, was thus being used as a justification for legalised slavery, compelling the 'offenders' to perform a service that was in no way related to their contractual obligation to provide rubber.

But what perhaps generated the greatest outrage, were the reports of murder and mutilation. In desperation, natives had begun to flee the region *en masse* to escape the abuse to which they were being subjected for commercial ends. While visiting a group from the Basengili tribe that had fled into the jungles near Bolobo, Casement noted in his report that:

> They went on to declare, when asked why they had fled, that they had endured such ill-treatment at the hands of the government officials and

the Government soldiers in their own country that life had become intolerable, that nothing remained for them at home but to be killed for failure to bring in a certain amount of rubber or to die from starvation or exposure in their attempts to satisfy the demands made upon them.[28]

The government and the commercial enterprises that had received trade concessions from the central administration could not tolerate this, of course: natives who fled not only deprived the authorities of slave labour but also, if left unpunished, provided encouragement for others to follow suit. In response, therefore, the *Force Publique*, an armed force of native militiamen established under the command of European officers specifically to enforce the 'slave' contracts, would hunt down and kill those who had the temerity to seek an escape. The members of this militia, men who were brutal by nature and who had become accustomed to savagery in the service of their superiors, had no compunction about killing under orders of their European commanders. As though murder were not enough, however, Casement learned that these militiamen were under further orders to sever and turn in the hands of their victims in order to provide proof of having fulfilled their mission and to intimidate anyone else who might be considering flight.

This savage practice led to several examples of collateral atrocities that fuelled the outrage even further. Casement was curious to learn why a number of living informants had missing hands, when the mutilating practice was presumably applied to those who had been slain. He was informed that in the chaos of mopping up after a massacre, the assailants often mistook unconscious victims for dead, or simply neglected to finish off wounded victims, and would inadvertently cut off the hands of survivors, thinking they had already been killed. Casement cited the case of a woman named Eyeka who had fled into the forest with a panic-stricken group that included her young son. During the mayhem, she fainted upon seeing her son shot to death, and as she was regaining consciousness she 'felt her hand being cut off, but made no sign. When all was quiet and the soldiers had gone, she found her son's dead body beside her with one hand cut off and her own also taken away.'[29]

On another occasion in Bokoti, he interviewed a young boy whom he estimated to be about twelve years of age and who claimed that his hand had been severed a couple of years before, which would have been when he was no more than ten. During the flight of his family, he witnessed the killing of his mother and father and was himself shot and presumed dead (Casement was able to examine the scar where the bullet had struck him a grazing blow in the back of the head). The child claimed that he 'came to his senses while his hand was being hacked off at the wrist'.[30] Casement was naturally sceptical and asked how he could have endured that without crying out. His simple but horrifying response was 'that he felt the cutting, but was afraid to move, knowing that he would be killed if he showed any sign of life'.[31]

The example that received the greatest notoriety seems to have been that of a young boy named Epondo, whose case drew the most attention because the victim in this case was able to personally identify the assailant, a sentry by the name of Kelengo who had a local reputation in the little village of Bonginda as being especially brutal. As with the case cited just above, Epondo had fled the village with his family, and during the subsequent pursuit by the *Force Publique*, he was wounded and presumed dead, at which point Kelengo allegedly severed his hand in accordance with the routine practice for verifying the disposition of fugitives. Outraged by the slaughter of a neighbouring family and the mutilation of a child they all knew well, a number of the villagers in Bonginda testified personally against Kelengo during Casement's enquiry. My informant from Casement's entourage mentioned how fearful the entire scene had been, with the emotions of the Bonginda natives approaching mass hysteria, their courage to confront Kelengo ratcheted up at least temporarily by the presence of outsiders who could presumably take action against the man who had been brutalising them.

Armed with a transcript of the villagers' testimony and an affidavit of the transcript's accuracy sworn to by William Armstrong and D.J. Danielson, two of the local missionaries, Casement took the boy back with him to Coquilhatville and filed formal charges against Kelengo. With Epondo in tow as witness and victim, Casement presented the case to the Government Commandant in Coquilhatville, then sent the boy back home while he himself resumed his journey, assuming that justice would run its course. My informant was loath to criticize a man for whom he obviously felt respect bordering on reverence, but in sending the boy back home and trusting to local justice, he felt that Casement had either succumbed to an irrational degree of naiveté or had grimly placed expediency ahead of his concern for Epondo. There is no record of what happened in terms of any follow-up to Casement's charges, but my informant left little doubt about his conviction that Epondo and the residents of Bonginda were sacrificed to Casement's need for a documented case that he could use to enhance the credibility of his report.

The Epondo case achieved special notoriety following the publication of Casement's report, when King Leopold elected to make that particular case an issue in his attack upon the report's credibility. It was the only case in which formal charges had been brought before an official of the Congo Free State, making it impossible to ignore, and Leopold was determined to cast a shadow over Casement's entire report by raising as much doubt as possible about the accuracy of the charge. Leopold was able to find enough locals who were willing to testify that the boy's hand 'had been bitten off by a wild pig' to enable him to suggest a logical alternative to the charge that had been filed in Coquilhatville. Convinced that he had raised a reasonable degree of doubt about the charge, he went on to argue that, 'It is only natural to conclude that if the rest of the evidence in the consul's report is of the same value as that furnished to him in this particular case, it cannot possibly be regarded as conclusive.'[32] Ultimately, the efficacy of the case rested on the credibility of the opposing versions of the story, although Casement was able to bolster his version with physical evidence that the boy had also been shot, suggesting that his fate had been similar to those described earlier.

During the course of Casement's exhaustive investigation, it became apparent that Leopold had violated both of the basic tenets of the Berlin Accord – guarantees of free trade and regard for the rights and welfare of the indigenous peoples. Contrary to the spirit of free trade, Leopold had divided the area encompassed by the Congo Free State into three commercial regions, reserving one region exclusively for exploitation by the government itself (called the *Domaine de la Couronne*) and leasing the other two regions to private commercial concessions – the Anglo-Belgian India-Rubber Company (the ABIR) and the smaller La Lulanga Company. The ABIR operated in the basins of the Lopori and Maringa Rivers with its headquarters in Bassankusu; the La Lulanga Company operated along the Lulongo River below Bassankusu. The Government of the Congo Free State regulated the operation of both companies by requiring them to obtain official licenses, and reserved the rest of the State's territory as its own exclusive domain. No other outside entities, including the signatories of the Berlin Accord, had access to the Congo market.

While Casement made due note of this violation of the free trade agreement, his report focused primarily on the atrocities that he uncovered. And it was apparent to this reader, at least, that he was not only outraged, but personally distressed by what he found. My informant from his entourage reinforces that reading of the report: he could almost see a physical depression settling over the man like a blanket as they proceeded deeper and deeper into a realm where human empathy and morality had been ruthlessly subordinated to sheer greed. Casement may have begun the investigation with career ambitions in mind, intent upon establishing a reputation for himself both within the Foreign Office and on the international stage, but the bureaucratic language that he necessarily employed in preparing an official government report fails to conceal the passion that gradually overcame him during the course of the investigation. Objective reportage and dry statistical data gradually give way to a more critical and disparaging presentation of concrete incidents, as he works his way through the report.

Whatever empathy he may have developed toward the natives during his earlier exposure to the Congo was resurrected and reinforced by seeing what his fellow Europeans had done to them. Based on input from the various informants who knew him at the time, the philosophical disillusionment must have been as traumatic as the emotional agony that he experienced. Colleagues in the Foreign Office may not have liked him much because of his vain and brittle temperament, but they were in total agreement about his unmitigated belief that European intervention in primitive societies would have a civilizing influence upon the native populations and would redound to their physical as well as spiritual well-being. For such an idealist, that trip up the Congo in the summer of 1903 had to have been heartbreaking.

My informant pointed out that, upon returning to England, at the beginning of December 1903, Casement worked feverishly to prepare a report that would accurately capture the essence of what he had discovered and would thus galvanize the kind of response that he felt was critical in rectifying an enormous wrong. That assessment was confirmed by other sources I had the opportunity to interview within the Foreign Office, who claimed that he was like a man possessed, sequestering himself virtually from dawn to dusk with pen and paper and the voluminous notes that he had taken while in Africa. The Foreign Office was naturally eager to see the product of his efforts, and pressed him relentlessly for the initial draft, which finally went forward to Lord Lansdowne, the Foreign Secretary, on 12 December. While it was being reviewed, he continued to work on the attachments that would accompany the final version of the report.

According to my sources, it was while working on the attachments for the final draft that Casement made the personal acquaintance of Edmond Morel, the journalist who had been conducting an aggressive media campaign in his *West African Mail* on behalf of indigenous societies, and who had been openly critical of the Foreign Office for failing to take a stronger position in support of decolonisation in Africa. Given their mutual interest in the Congo and its native population, it was inevitable that they would eventually come together in common cause. My informants tell me that Morel had been looking forward with great anticipation to Casement's return: having never met the consul before, he had no idea how sympathetic this official government representative might be toward the plight of the Congolese natives. And the advance prominence given to Casement's investigation made it obvious that the report he was about to produce would be a critical turning point, one way or the other, in both public and government perception of the data that Morel himself had been publishing in his newspaper.

The two were apparently drawn to each other from the moment they met, each of them recognising a kindred spirit in the other. Reports are that they conversed for hours, comparing notes and impressions and discussing strategies for reform. Even before the report's release, Morel had to know from these conversations that he had a formidable ally in his campaign to initiate reform. And Casement must have been equally quick to recognise not only that he had made a lifelong friend, but that he had also stumbled upon an associate who could be instrumental in developing a strategy to complement whatever official government action might be forthcoming.

This complementary strategy that grew out of their association offers additional insight into Casement's character. It is my understanding that Casement took the initiative in encouraging Morel to found a private organisation called the Congo Reform Association for the purpose of leading advocacy efforts on behalf of reform in the Congo Free State. Casement reportedly even drew upon his own personal resources, limited though they might have been, to provide the financial wherewithal for Morel to establish and maintain the Association. Because of his official capacity within the Foreign Office, Casement was unable to assume a personal role in this new non-governmental Association, but he was apparently indefatigable in working behind the scenes to ensure its success. The extent of his involvement with the Association reflects the level of his personal commitment to reform, and his empathy toward the native population; clearly the investigation and the follow-up report were more than just stepping stones toward career advancement, however much ambition might have been a part of his original motivation in accepting the assignment. Whether the direct result of his exposure to the atrocities occurring under Leopold's Congo Free State or the end product of a long evolutionary process, there is no doubt that by the winter of 1903/04, Casement was a dedicated advocate of the oppressed and the downtrodden.

His involvement with the Association would also appear to reflect a certain distrust of organisations over which he had limited influence. One would assume that having just completed an official investigation for the government, his first inclination should have been to allow the

Foreign Office to exercise its authority in the international arena. By aggressively pursuing the establishment of a non-governmental body directed toward achieving the same end, he was surely revealing a basic distrust in the very agency with which he was employed. And even then, there was already a private philanthropic organisation in place to which he could have turned, that being the Aborigines Protection Society under the direction of H.R. Fox Bourne. He obviously did not have faith in that organisation, either. It is tempting to speculate that such distrust may have been directly related to the personal vanity to which so many of his colleagues have alluded; anything that did not bear Casement's personal imprint was suspect in his eyes. In other words, to put it crassly, he felt that he knew better than anyone else how best to proceed in the matter.

Whatever distrust he may have harboured toward the Foreign Office had to have been exacerbated by the controversial handling of his report. Apparently loath to undermine its diplomatic relations with Belgium and King Leopold, the government was wary about releasing such an inflammatory product and was reportedly inclined, at first, to find some way to legitimately suppress the report or at least limit its circulation. Recognising early on that this would have disastrous consequences in terms of public relations, both at home and abroad, the Foreign Office quickly rallied behind the report, and set to work preparing it for submission to Parliament. Casement had to have known about the machinations within his own agency, and never one to be patient with the niceties of international diplomacy, he must surely have developed even greater scepticism about the prospect of achieving reforms through government channels.

It was while working on the final revisions of his report with Sir Francis Villiers, the Assistant Under-Secretary of State for Foreign Affairs, and Harry Farnall, the Foreign Office official in charge of the Congo desk, that tensions appear to have heightened dramatically between Casement and his colleagues in the Foreign Office. While Casement was reportedly agreeable to the idea of excising the names of Congo Free State officials whom he had interviewed, a consensus grew within the Foreign Office that it would be wise to exclude all names – not only those of State authorities but also those of native informants, missionaries, concession officials, and even the names of the villages visited – and replace them with alphanumeric symbols to maintain anonymity. The purported intent was to preclude use of the report as a way of identifying parties for retribution.

According to sources with whom I had the opportunity to discuss the preparation of the final draft, Casement was irate. His rationale was that nothing would be gained by deleting names, since the identities were self-evident from the context of the report. Casement's argument was that anyone sufficiently impugned by the report to seek retribution could easily replace letters and symbols with names based on their own knowledge of places, events, and individuals. In contrast, much would be lost, for in Casement's judgement, removing the names of individuals who had demonstrated extraordinary courage in coming forward and offering substantive testimony would dilute the effect of the report. Furthermore, the resulting lack of specificity in the report's details would make the entire document vulnerable to attack by King Leopold and his minions.

The latter indeed proved to be the case; Leopold was able not only to accuse Casement of vague generalisation, but also to suggest that without the corroboration of named individuals, there was no reason to believe that any of the alleged atrocities had ever really occurred. The official version of the report was published by the Foreign Office and forwarded to Parliament in February of 1904 under the imposing title of *Correspondence and Report from His Majesty's Consul at Boma Respecting the Administration of the Independent State of the Congo*. In spite of Casement's strenuous objections, the final draft appeared with alphabetical letters substituted for all names, presumably with the tacit approval of Lord Lansdowne, the Secretary of State for Foreign Affairs, and Lord Salisbury, his Under-Secretary of State for Foreign Affairs. Based on interviews with a number of Casement's associates, it seems fair to say that he felt betrayed by his colleagues and believed that the bastardised version of his report might actually be counterproductive and redound to the detriment of reform efforts. His backing of Edmond Morel and the Congo Reform Association, as an alternative to government action, was undoubtedly reinforced by this falling out with the Foreign Office. Casement reportedly even went so far as to threaten resignation, but for reasons that I have not yet been able to determine, he obviously elected not to follow through.

The government's follow-up to the report would seem to have exacerbated Casement's ire and distrust even further. Following its publication, of course, King Leopold found himself in a position where he had to take an aggressive stance against its allegations. He immediately took the offensive by questioning the overall credibility of the report, suggesting alternative explanations for some of the documented findings, pointing out, for example, that depopulation could have been the result of the sleeping-sickness epidemic that had raged through the Congo, and even trying to claim, contrary to accepted anthropological opinion, that mutilation could have been the product of traditional native customs. Where atrocities might have occurred, he insisted that they were isolated incidents, carried out by rogue employees of the State or the Concessions. Public opinion was not to be assuaged, however, given the plethora of evidence that had been accumulating from other sources, as well. Recognising the need to change course in his tactics, Leopold became more conciliatory, offering to appoint an official Commission of Inquiry to identify and prosecute wrongdoers and to recommend appropriate reform measures.

My sources in the Foreign Office agree that the diplomatic corps welcomed this as a face-saving way for both sides to move forward. Casement, however, was reportedly apoplectic. He accused the Foreign Office of being weak and insipid, pointing out that any 'Commission of Inquiry' would simply be repeating what he had already accomplished, thus wasting time, and that this particular 'Commission of Inquiry', under the charge of King Leopold himself, would obviously lack the objectivity necessary to conduct an unbiased investigation. Exhausted by months of intensive labour on the investigation and the report, disheartened by what he perceived to be an anaemic response on the part of the Foreign Office, and weakened by illness that he had contracted while in the Congo, Casement went into seclusion in Ireland for the next year and a half.

To the amazement of all, Leopold's own Commission of Inquiry ulti-mately vindicated Casement, releasing its report in November of 1905, almost two years after the publication of Casement's report. Based on its own independent investigation, it declared that Casement's findings were both accurate and just. While King Leopold was thus pilloried by what were now accepted as indisputable facts, he had nevertheless managed successfully to delay any concrete action toward reform, just as Casement had disconsolately predicted when the Foreign Office had accepted Leopold's offer at face value.

Following the release of this report from the Commission of Inquiry, Leopold boldly launched another delaying tactic by appointing a sepa-rate Commission for Reform, apparently assuming that he could still maintain his long-standing façade of magnanimity toward the welfare of indigenous societies. Mired in diplomatic concerns about the role that Leopold's Belgium might play *vis-à-vis* the perceived escalation of Germany's threat to continental stability, His Majesty's government was once again prepared to welcome a face-saving alternative to direct confrontation and announced its support of the reform commission. By this time, however, the barrage of testimonials from the Congo had finally begun to erode Leopold's political base at home, and in 1908 Belgium formally annexed the territory known heretofore as the Congo Free State and renamed it the Belgian Congo, significantly reducing Leopold's role in the administration of what had now been converted from a private personal domain to membership in the gov-ernment's network of foreign colonies.

By this time, Casement had long since removed himself from the fray. In spite of any rancour that existed between him and the Foreign Office, however, His Majesty's government found it expedient to honour what had to be acknowledged as a significant contribution to the enhancement of Britain's moral stature in the eyes of the interna-tional community. While there had been tempestuous differences over what constituted appropriate diplomatic initiatives, the fact remained that it was Casement's investigative work and advocacy that had laid the basis for Britain to take the lead in publicly pressuring King Leopold for reform. It was therefore appropriate that as one of his first official acts after assuming office in 1905, the new Foreign Secretary, Sir Edward Grey, had the pleasure of informing Casement that King Edward VII had appointed him to the rank of Companion in the Order of St Michael and St George.

Whether generated by vanity, by a dispassionate assessment of the circumstances, or by a sense of professional principle, it would appear, in retrospect, that Casement's reaction to the Foreign Office's treatment of his report may very well have been a harbinger of things to come in his relations with that office. Far be it from this reporter to suggest that the seeds of treason were sown in the dust-up following publication of Casement's Congo Report nor that the subsequent relationship might have anything to do with his treatment at trial in the current proceedings against him. There are unsubstantiated rumours, however, that when Casement formally severed his ties with the Foreign Office and the British government last year, he returned the credentials for his appointment to the Order of St Michael and St George unopened: the investiture had apparently been laid aside upon receipt and disregarded for all those years. To spurn such an honour, at that early stage in his consular career, surely speaks volumes about the value he placed on service to the Crown.

It has been exactly eleven years this month since the announcement of that singular honour. Obviously, much has transpired to bring him from that elevated status to his current ignominy. Even as far back as April 1903, during his official investigation of the Congo Free State and the preparation of his follow-up report, it is apparent that the relationship between him and the Foreign Office was tempestuous at best. But strained relations and wounded vanity are not the seeds of treason. And while Casement may be temperamentally volatile, he does not strike this reporter as the type to make an impetuous decision that would forever brand him a traitor. The clue to that decision has to lie hidden in the evolution of his political sentiments over the course of those eleven years. Once discovered, that clue should help us not only understand the enigma of this humanitarian turned revolutionary, but perhaps gain some insight into the current tensions between Britain and the Emerald Isle as well.

Presumably, much will be revealed during the course of the upcoming trial, which will mark the climax to this very public display of British pique toward its erstwhile hero. I am also making every effort, through personal interviews and archival research, to plumb the depths of these past eleven years in the life of Sir Roger Casement. Interested readers can expect regular dispatches over the course of the coming weeks. As noted earlier in this article, his assignment to the Congo investigation was based on a prior history of involvement with African affairs. As a prologue to my enquiry into the course of events over these past eleven years, I have been interviewing a number of his colleagues and associates who knew him during that initial exposure to the Dark Continent. I hope in my next dispatch to be able to supplement my coverage of his Congo mission with some details about those earlier years in Africa.

It was obvious from his Congo Report, and from my interviews with his Foreign Office colleagues that his investigation into the atrocities of the Congo Free State left him severely traumatised and disillusioned. In the aftermath of that disillusionment, he was not satisfied simply to fulfil his official responsibility within the Foreign Office: in working behind the scenes to launch the Congo Reform Association and in pressing the Foreign Office constantly for more aggressive response, he clearly demonstrated that he had launched himself upon a personal mission that may have had its roots in his consular role but far transcended the scope of those official responsibilities. By examining his involvement with Africa during the decade that preceded his Congo Report, I hope in my next dispatch to provide some context for the disillusionment that led to the adoption of this personal mission – a mission that eventually extended beyond the indigenous peoples of Africa, as evidenced by his later activities in the Amazon, and which may have, in fact, brought him ultimately to the coast of Kerry and to the dock in London.

THURSDAY 25 MAY 1916

As anticipated, the Grand Jury hearing the case against Sir Roger Casement returned a true Bill of Indictment yesterday at the High Court, needing only an hour of deliberation to convince itself of the charge's merits. In his public reading of the indictment, Lord Chief Justice Rufus Isaacs, the Marquess of Reading, made note of the fact that this is the first indictment for high treason under the Indictments Act of 1915, which became effective just last April the first. According to the legal informants with whom I have been able to consult, the significance of that statement from the Lord Chief Justice is simply that the 1915 Indictments Act was introduced to facilitate the articulation of charges, by eliminating the use of the archaic Norman language that had been a tradition in the High Court. The actual charge against Mr Casement, according to those informants, is based on a statute that dates back to the realm of King Edward III in 1351. This is merely the first time that a formal charge of high treason under that fourteenth-century statute has been formulated in lay terms as specified by the Indictments Act.

The 1351 statute was apparently an attempt at the time to legally codify all recognised forms of treason into a single governing statute and thus provide a clearly articulated legal definition of what actually constitutes the crime. Until then, the definition was at the sole discretion of the King and his judges, which meant that at best the definition would vary according to who happened to be in power; at worst, of course, the definition until then could be construed by the reigning monarch in whatever way best suited his whim or fancy. The statute's jurisdiction was eventually extended to include Ireland with the passage of Poynings' Law in 1495, the parliamentary Act initiated by Sir Edward Poynings, the British Viceroy to Ireland, to effectively make Ireland subject to the laws of England. And with the 1801 Act of Union, the Irish accepted citizenship in the United Kingdom of Great Britain and Ireland, thus eliminating any doubt about the jurisdiction of British law. My sources within the Irish independence movement will undoubtedly have a different perspective on the extent to which Ireland has been a willing participant in the historical process that produced these legal bonds between Britain and Ireland, but the court would certainly seem to have a sound legal basis for applying the 1351 statute in the case involving Sir Roger Casement.

One of my legal sources was able to provide me with a copy of that statute, which lists a number of specific acts that come under the definition of treason, among them any attempt, whether planned or actually carried out, to murder the King, his wife, or his eldest son and heir; violation of the King's wife, his eldest unmarried daughter, or the wife of the King's eldest son and heir; and murder of the Chancellor or Treasurer or any of the King's Justices. The relevant clause in the charge against Mr Casement is that it would be considered an act of high treason 'if a man do levy war against our Lord the King in his realm, or be adherent to the King's enemies in his realm, giving to them aid and comfort in the realm or elsewhere'[33] ('*si h me leve de guerre contre n e dit Seign' le Roi en son Roialme, ou soit aherdant as enemys n e Seign' le Roi en le Roialme, donant a eux eid ou confort en son Roialme ou p aillours'* in the vernacular of the time).

While this 565-year-old statute may not be frequently invoked, it is still the authoritative basis for charges of high treason. The most recent case adjudicated under the statute was just thirteen years ago when Arthur Lynch was brought before the Bar on charges of high treason, for his activities on behalf of the Boers during the British war in South Africa. Mr Lynch translated his sympathies for the Boer cause into concrete action, by forming a brigade of fellow Irish sympathisers to fight against the British on the side of the enemy. At the end of the war, Mr Lynch had the good sense not to return to England, but he couldn't resist standing for election *in absentia* to represent Galway in the House of Commons. In spite of his exile in Paris, he had the good fortune (or perhaps ill fortune, depending on one's point of view) to actually win the election, at which point he brazenly returned to London and was promptly arrested. On 23 January 1903, he was found guilty of treason under the statute of 1351 and was sentenced to be hanged. The subsequent details of his case merit a separate article onto itself (remarkable as it may seem, he was ultimately pardoned and is currently serving at Westminster as a Member of Parliament from West Clare); for purposes of this dispatch, however, suffice it to say that his case reflects the ongoing relevance of this archaic fourteenth-century statute and the government's willingness to apply it to contemporary events.

While the recently enacted Indictments Act provides for the use of more understandable language in the charges levelled against an alleged traitor, the language of the formal charges against Mr Casement makes one wonder whether the court would have been just as well served by retaining the language of the original 1351 statue. The basic charge of the indictment as presented to the Grand Jury by Lord Reading is as follows:

> Sir Roger David Casement, otherwise known as Sir Roger Casement, Knight, on the 1st day of December, 1914, and on divers other days thereafter, and between that day and the 21st April, 1916, being then, to wit, on the said several days a British subject, and whilst on the said several days an open and public war was being prosecuted and carried on by the German Emperor and his subjects against our Lord the King and his subjects, then and on the said several days traitorously contriving and intending to aid and assist the said enemies of our Lord the King against our Lord the King and his subjects, did traitorously adhere to and aid and comfort the said enemies in parts beyond the seas without this realm of England, to wit, in the Empire of Germany.[34]

In presenting the document to the Grand Jury, Lord Reading highlighted the fact that Mr Casement was, as specified in the charge, a British subject at the time of the alleged acts and therefore legally culpable under the definition of treason. My sources within the Irish independence movement have suggested that this may, in fact, become an issue at trial as a question of sovereignty and national allegiance. Technically, of course, the government will argue that Casement was indeed a subject of the Crown and that legally, any acts committed by him to 'aid and assist' the enemy during a time of war are therefore acts of treason by definition. While Casement's own lifetime of dedicated service will make it difficult for him to credibly dispute the object of his national allegiance, my sources have raised, what they consider to be, a legitimate point *vis-à-vis* the relationship between England and Ireland, in that Ireland has been a subject colony, rather than a willing member of the British Empire and that 'allegiance' to the Crown has been imposed rather than adopted. From their perspective, the acts of which Mr Casement has been accused are therefore seen as acts of war rather than acts of treason.

This sentiment will surely resonate with many of my American readers. Technically, all fifty-six signers the American Declaration of Independence, including the second and third presidents, could have been tried by the British and executed for treason under the aegis of the same statute. With 140 years of hindsight, it is unlikely that anyone in the current government of His Majesty the King would retrospectively argue that the likes of John Adams and Thomas Jefferson and Benjamin Franklin should have been executed. Representatives of the Crown will no doubt argue, however, that the analogy is inappropriate, pointing out that contrary to the position taken by my sources in the Irish independence movement, colonial status does not apply in the case of Ireland, whose national parliament voluntarily joined with the Parliament of Great Britain to approve the 1801 Act of Union, creating the United Kingdom of Great Britain and Ireland.

It will nevertheless be interesting to see how this argument plays out over the course of the next several weeks as the Casement case approaches trial. Mr Jones and his defence team have not yet given any hint of their legal strategy. Pleading innocent does not appear to be a part of that strategy, since Mr Casement has never denied the allegations levelled against him. Despite the position taken by the Irish dissidents, the sovereignty argument does not appear to be a viable legal defence, given the relationship clearly established under the Act of Union. It seems apparent that legally speaking, Mr Casement was indeed a British subject who owed allegiance to the Crown and that aiding and assisting the German Empire was therefore an act of treason rather than an act of war.

Perhaps the Lord Chief Justice himself offered an opening to the defence, when he stressed the concept of intent in his charge to the Grand Jury. In reference to the charge that Casement 'traitorously' provided aid and assistance to the enemy, Lord Reading explained to the Grand Jury that the word 'traitorously' implied the intent to support Germany in waging war against Britain (as opposed, for example, to providing humanitarian aid and assistance to Germany). To what extent the defence can construe Casement's intentions in a way that will be favourable to his case remains to be seen. As Lord Reading amplified in his charge to the Grand Jury, intent can only be inferred from one's actions, and in the main body of the indictment that followed, the prosecution cited six specific acts from which it 'inferred' traitorous intent.

In presenting the six specific acts from the bill of indictment, Lord Reading pointed out that they fell into two general time frames – a period of time in Germany when Casement allegedly interacted with Irish prisoners of war, and a period of time in Ireland immediately preceding Casement's capture. He then read the six counts of the indictment to those assembled as a necessary legal formality before dismissing the jury for its deliberations. The following is a direct citation of the first of those six counts:

> That on or about the 31st of December 1914, the accused solicited, incited and endeavoured to persuade certain persons, being British subjects and members of the military forces of our Lord the King, and being prisoners of war then imprisoned at Limburg Lahn Camp in the Empire of Germany – to wit, Michael O'Connor and others whose names are unknown – to forsake their duty and allegiance to our Lord the King and to join the armed forces of his said enemies and to fight against our Lord the King and his subjects in the said war.[35]

Counts two and three of the indictment employ exactly the same language, making it superfluous to include them here. They simply add to the catalogue of specific incidents that the prosecution has characterised as treasonous by citing two more dates (6 January and 19 February 1915) on which the accused allegedly 'solicited, incited and endeavoured to persuade'[36] Irish prisoners of war 'to forsake their duty and allegiance to our Lord the King and to join the armed forces of his said enemies'. The names of several more plaintiffs are also cited in those counts, indicating the availability of additional witnesses who can attest to the veracity of the allegations – John Robinson and John Cronin who will apparently claim that they were approached by the accused on January 6 and William Egan, Daniel O'Brien, and James Wilson on February 19. While counts two and three may appear to be redundant and a mere effort by the prosecution to embellish the scope of the allegations against Mr Casement, they are a necessary component of any legal procedure in providing specific evidence as opposed to general charges.

The fourth count of the indictment addresses the matter of the leaflet that Mr Casement allegedly distributed among the prisoners at Limburg to supplement his attempt at recruiting them for an Irish Brigade. Once again I shall take the liberty of quoting the article verbatim for the record:

> That in or about the months of January and February 1915, at Limburg Lahn Camp in the Empire of Germany, the accused had circulated and distributed to and amongst certain persons, being British subjects and members of the military forces of our Lord the King, and being prisoners of war then imprisoned at Limburg Lahn Camp aforesaid – to wit, Michael O'Connor, John Robinson, John Cronin, William Egan, Daniel O'Brien, James Wilson and divers others whose names are unknown – a certain leaflet with the intent to solicit, incite, and persuade the said British subjects, being Irishmen, to forsake their duty and allegiance to our Lord the King and to aid and assist his enemies in the prosecution of the said war against our Lord the King and his subjects.[37]

As my readers will no doubt recall, Mr Bodkin took great delight in quoting directly from that leaflet during the arraignment hearing at the Bow Street Police Court, less than two weeks ago. He must, no doubt, have taken equal delight in being able to attach the text of that leaflet to the indictment as a supplement to count four. Rather than summarise the text, I shall take the liberty of quoting that document verbatim, as well; it speaks for itself in a way that no summary could possibly capture:

> Irishmen, here is a chance for you to fight for Ireland. You have fought for England, your country's hereditary enemy. You have fought for Belgium in England's interest, though it was no more to you than the Fiji Islands. Are you willing to fight for your own country with a view to securing the national freedom of Ireland? With the moral and material assistance of the German Government, an Irish Brigade is being formed. The object of the Irish Brigade shall be to fight solely for the cause of Ireland and under no circumstances shall it be directed to any German end. The Irish Brigade shall be formed and shall fight under the Irish flag alone; the men shall wear a special distinctively Irish uniform and have Irish officers. The Irish Brigade shall be clothed, fed, and efficiently equipped with arms and ammunition by the German Government. It will be stationed near Berlin and be treated as guests of the German Government. At the end of the war the German Government undertakes to send each member of the Brigade who may so desire it to the United States of America with necessary means to land. The Irishmen in America are collecting money for the Brigade. Those men who do not join the Irish Brigade will be removed from Limburg and distributed to other camps. If interested, see your company commanders. Join the Irish Brigade and win Ireland's independence! Remember Bachelor's Walk! God save Ireland![38]

While counts one to four catalogued Casement's advances upon the Irish prisoners at Limburg, the fifth count deals with the Irish Brigade that actually materialised from his efforts, meagre as it might have been. This may be the most difficult count to prove in court, given the more generalised nature of the charge, and the fact that only one concrete witness appears available to substantiate it (others are cited, but the vague nature of the citations makes it clear that they are the product of hearsay, probably from Mr Bailey). It is, however, the most damning of the articles of indictment since it explicitly charges Casement with organising a combat brigade to side with Germany in its war against the United Kingdom:

> That on or about the 31st of December 1914, and on divers days thereafter in the months of January and February, 1915, the accused had persuaded and procured certain persons being members of the military forces of our Lord the King – to wit Daniel Julian Bailey, one Quinless, one O'Callaghan, one Keogh, one Cavanagh, one Greer, and one Scanlan and divers others whose names are unknown – to the number of about fifty, the said persons being prisoners of war then imprisoned at Limburg Lahn Camp, in the Empire of Germany, to forsake their allegiance to our Lord the King and to join the armed forces of his said enemies with a view to fight against our Lord the King and his subjects in the said war.[39]

And in the sixth and final count of the indictment, the prosecution cites Mr Casement's clandestine arrival in Ireland last month, allegedly to deliver arms and ammunition for the rebellion:

> That on or about the 12th day of April 1916, the accused set forth from the Empire of Germany as a member of a warlike and hostile expedition undertaken and equipped by the said enemies of our Lord the King, having as its object the introduction into and landing on the coast of Ireland of arms and ammunition intended for use in the prosecution of the said war by the said enemies against our Lord the King and his subjects.[40]

In concluding his charge to the Grand Jury, Lord Reading reminded them that they were not trying the accused but were simply determining whether the evidence presented at the Bow Street Police Court arraignment was sufficient to support a *prima facie* case against him. Should the evidence be strong enough, in their judgement, to justify a formal trial, then, as the Lord Chief Justice made eminently clear, they were obligated to return a true bill, which, as noted earlier, they were able to do after just an hour of deliberation. Lord Reading thanked them for their service, emphasising the gravity of the case in a way that will obviously foreshadow the tenor of the trial itself, and immediately fixed 26 June for the commencement of that trial.

Mr George Gavan Duffy, a member of the Irish Bar representing Mr Casement at the Grand Jury proceeding, then requested that the Lord Chief Justice appoint Mr Alexander Sullivan to be the primary defence counsel. Mr Sullivan is a Sergeant-at-Law of the Irish Bar, the highest order of barristers in that august legal body, and a recently recognised member of the English Bar. To assist him, Mr Duffy requested that Mr Artemus Jones serve as co-counsel. Both had represented Mr Casement at his arraignment before the Bow Street Police Court. Mr Duffy further recommended that Mr John Hartman Morgan, a professor of constitutional law at University College, be made available as a legal adviser and that he himself be retained as a solicitor for the defence. Lord Reading pointed out that since the law stipulated that he could only appoint two official counsels for the defence, he would honour Mr Duffy's request on behalf of Messrs Sullivan and Jones while allowing Messrs Morgan and Duffy to serve in an unofficial capacity for the defence. Criticism of Lord Reading's decision has already begun to circulate, questioning why he is going out of his way to accommodate the defence. Given the legal stipulation as regards defence counsel, he would have been perfectly justified in denying the request that Messrs Morgan and Duffy be included on the defence team. The consensus of opinion, however, is that he is simply foreclosing any later attempt on the part of the defence to claim that Casement was inadequately represented.

Mr Sullivan immediately took advantage of his official appointment as the chief defence counsel, to challenge the trial date, requesting that it not commence until at least 10 July. He argued vehemently that he had been placed at a great disadvantage from the very beginning, having been denied access to the accused until the middle of May, and pointed out that he would need to collect evidence in both Ireland and the United States, including the service and advice of a US attorney who could not arrive in England in time to be of any real value before the beginning of July. Mr Duffy joined in arguing inadequate time for preparation, pointing out that no one on the defence team had access to Mr Casement until at least 17 May and that even then, he was in no condition to assist in his own defence for several days. Sir George Cave, the Solicitor General representing the prosecution, insisted that the time granted the defence for consultation with its client was in no way atypical for this kind of case.

The Lord Chief Justice dismissed both bases for the defence's appeal, showing as little patience with the first argument as Mr Cave and questioning the relevance of the second, since nothing in the indictment had anything to do with the United States. Mr Sullivan assured the court that the relevance would become evident at trial but that divulging details in advance would place his defence strategy at risk. This certainly piqued the interest and curiosity of all those in attendance, but Lord Reading was not persuaded, insisting that in the absence of any convincing evidence to support the need for input from the US, there was no reason to delay.

Mr Sullivan's allusion to evidence from the United States is an intriguing one, which I will attempt to explore. Several of the informants that I interviewed during the Police Court hearing made repeated references to preliminary consultations in the United States, when speaking of Mr Casement's activities in Germany. I did not have the time to follow up then, but will do so as soon as possible. Those consultations purportedly took place with Mr John Devoy, a one-time Fenian organiser who was convicted of treason himself and exiled to the United States, where he became a journalist with the *New York Herald* and a leader of Clan na Gael. For those readers who are unfamiliar with that organization, it is comprised of Irish expatriates in America who are devoted to assisting the Irish Republican Brotherhood in separating Ireland from the United Kingdom. Given Mr Casement's involvement in the Irish uprising last month, it is not beyond the realm of plausibility that he might have had some interaction with Mr Devoy. That is a subject that will be explored and reported upon at a later date.

In related news, the Royal Commission inquiring into the events of last month's insurrection in Ireland met again today, calling the heads of the Royal Irish Constabulary and the Dublin Metropolitan Police to testify. Sir Neville Chamberlain, the Inspector General of the Royal Irish Constabulary, was the first to appear, insisting that he regularly provided Sir Matthew Nathan, the Crown's Under-Secretary for Irish Affairs in Dublin Castle, with intelligence information that should have alerted him and his government colleagues to the imminence of armed confrontations. He argued further that just this past January, three months before the rising, he had drawn the Under-Secretary's attention to intelligence suggesting that extremists were coming into possession of explosives and had urged the implementation of stricter controls over their acquisition and distribution.

He also pointed out that he had urged the same action with regard to the possession and carrying of firearms, recommending at that time that anyone not serving in an official capacity for the Crown should be required to obtain a permit for the possession of rifles, shotguns, and pistols. He insisted that as early as May 1914, two years ago, he had warned the government representatives in Ireland that the Ulster Volunteer Force and the Irish Volunteers were both aggressively arming themselves and that soon they would both have trained armies that would outnumber the police. His testimony clearly suggested that there had been gross negligence in Dublin Castle, leaving the Commission with the distinct impression that if his warnings and recommendations had been heeded, the tragic events of last month could have been avoided.

During the course of his testimony, Mr Chamberlain made specific reference to Sir Roger Casement by name, alleging that he had been involved in the formation of the Irish Volunteers, from its inception as a separatist militia, and that he had capitalised upon the German contacts, nurtured during his diplomatic career, to obtain weapons for that militia. The intelligence upon which Mr Chamberlain based his allegations will no doubt be of great value to the honourable Attorney General during the forthcoming trial, establishing the fact that Mr Casement had been collaborating with Germany even before the outbreak of war. It remains to be seen whether Mr Chamberlain himself will be called to testify against Mr Casement.

Colonel E. Johnston, Chief Commissioner of the Dublin Metropolitan Police, followed Mr Chamberlain in testifying at today's session of the Royal Commission. Mr Justice Shearman of the Commission expressed dismay at the standing instructions Colonel Johnston described with respect to political activists: according to Colonel Johnston, he had the full authority as police commissioner to act upon evidence of any criminal offence – except in the case of known political activists, like members of Sinn Féin. In those cases, he had first to consult with Dublin Castle before initiating action. In amplifying upon the import of that testimony, he pointed out, for example, that even with solid intelligence in hand, he could not search a house for known weapons cachés without consulting the Under-Secretary, if the house belonged to a member of Sinn Féin.

According to Colonel Johnston, the standing regulations under which he operated, also applied to gun-running activities, and in the first known official acknowledgement that the Ulster Volunteer Force and the Irish Volunteers were treated differently, he confirmed that since gun-running activities were covered by the same standing orders that applied to all other criminal offences involving political activism, his police could not interfere with those activities before consulting officials in Dublin Castle. In the case of arms smuggling, he was usually directed to intervene only if it was known that the delivery was for the Irish Volunteers. This astonishing testimony from a high-level police official would certainly seem to validate the rumours to which I alluded in an earlier dispatch, about the circumstances that led to the tragedy on Bachelor's Walk and about Mr Casement's involvement in gun-running through Howth. It is certain to raise alarming questions about the stance taken by the authorities in Dublin Castle concerning Mr Nathan and the Chief Secretary, Augustine Birrell. Today's witnesses cast a much different light on the testimony provided by Messrs Nathan and Birrell at the first meeting of the Commission (see my dispatch of 18 May). Confirmation of different policies in Dublin Castle relative to the Ulster Volunteer Force and the Irish Volunteers could conceivably offer Mr Casement's defence team a mitigating factor in dealing with any testimony that might be offered at trial about his gun-running activities on behalf of the Irish Volunteers.

SATURDAY 27 MAY 1916

With a four-week interlude now pending between this week's indictment and the commencement of trial, there is likely to be little in the way of news concerning the plight of Sir Roger Casement, the British knight and decorated humanitarian who has been accused of treason for colluding with Germany against the Crown during a time of war. The prosecution has already presented a substantial case against him during the preliminary hearings, and the defence is presumably mounting an exhaustive effort to prepare for what will undoubtedly be an international spectacle. Unfortunately for those of us in the media, a solid curtain of absolute secrecy has descended over the preparations of the defence team, making it impossible to anticipate their strategy or to ferret out leads for pre-trial dispatches. In the absence of hardcore news, however, this is a welcome opportunity to continue accumulating background information about Mr Casement and his career, to provide the context within which the trial will take place. In my dispatches of 20 and 22 May, I documented some of the details behind the 1903 Congo investigation that catapulted Mr Casement onto the world stage. In this dispatch, I shall attempt to summarise Mr Casement's African experience prior to that investigation – a formative period that laid both the professional and the philosophical foundations for his eventual engagement with the nether world that King Leopold had created in the heart of Africa.

Based on feedback from those who knew him at the time, Mr Casement's initial exposure to Africa left him ill-prepared for the trauma of his return in 1903. Fresh out of school, and full of youthful enthusiasm for adventure, he took advantage of his uncle's affiliation with the Elder Dempster shipping company to obtain a purser's position on the SS *Bonny*, one of the company's commercial vessels, with which he made three round-trip trading visits to the new Congo Free State in 1883 and 1884. He was reportedly an astute observer of contemporary world affairs, so he would have been fully aware of the humanitarian objectives articulated in the mission statement published by King Leopold's International African Association, which by 1884, had become the International Association of the Congo, charged with administrative responsibility for the Congo Free State to which the SS *Bonny* carried the company's young recruit. Those objectives were perfectly consistent with the perception that Britain had of its own imperial role, bringing the benefits of western civilization to the far reaches of the world as it engaged in commercial development that would complement that civilizing outreach. Mr Casement's formal education at Ballymena High School in County Antrim, along with the informal education that he received at the hands of his uncle Edward Bannister, the Elder Dempster executive who was also a serving British Consul and who had apparently assumed the role of surrogate father upon the death of Casement's parents, instilled in the young man a firm conviction that Britain was indeed serving the interests of God and civilization through its imperial outreach. According to those business associates whom I have been able to interview for this series of dispatches, Mr Casement was eager to be a part of this noble enterprise when he signed on with Elder Dempster.

But those same associates soon recognised that Mr Casement's personal ambitions were not compatible with the mundane duties of a ship's purser. As later colleagues in the Foreign Office would maintain, his blossoming ego was always way out in front of his actual status, and he was forever seeking to elevate himself to a role greater than the supporting part into which he had been cast. That consuming ambition, in conjunction with his insatiable appetite for adventure, led him to resign his position with Elder Dempster after only two years and to accept an assignment with the Sanford expedition that King Leopold had commissioned to lay the foundation for a commercial network in the Congo Free State. Given his age and relative inexperience, that assignment – to oversee the expedition's receipt and distribution of supplies through Matadi – did not entail a level of responsibility much greater than that with which he had become disenchanted as the *Bonny*'s purser, but it did bring him into direct and constant contact with the native population, for whom he was rapidly developing a profound affection.

I was unable to find any members of that 1886 Sanford expedition to interview, but a couple of Casement's former Elder Dempster associates were able to pick up bits and pieces of information about his subsequent career from contacts they made during their continued commercial visits to the region. The feedback to which they were privy suggested that Mr Casement, while occupying a modest if not lowly position in the administrative hierarchy of the expedition, was rapidly acquiring a reputation for diligence, integrity and professional competence in his handling of the responsibilities assigned to him. More importantly, he was building a collateral reputation for fairness and sensitivity in his dealings with the natives. Unlike most of those associated with the commercial interests of King Leopold's Association, he approached the natives as human beings worthy of respect and understanding rather than a sub-human species to be looked down upon with condescension and contempt. Mr Casement's capacity for empathy and reputation for fairness endeared him to the native population, while at the same time making him an asset to those whose commercial enterprises depended upon the services of the natives. This early work with the International Association of the Congo obviously prepared him for all that was to come, although my sources have given no indication that he had any inkling of the association's potential for the kinds of atrocities that came to light during his 1903 investigation.

It soon became apparent to my Elder Dempster informants that King Leopold was intent upon monopolising the rubber trade with the Congo, and to that end he began freezing out competitors by issuing concessions for commercial development to agencies like the Anglo-Belgian India-Rubber Company and the La Lulanga Company (see my dispatch of 22 May). And to shroud the association's activities from outside observers, he also began replacing foreign employees attached to the expedition's activities, which led inevitably to Mr Casement's detachment from the project after just a year of employment. By that time, however, he had apparently acquired a reputation that lent recognition to his name when he subsequently applied for work with a Christian mission station run by the noted missionary W. Holman Bentley. Once again, the responsibilities that Mr Casement assumed, this time on behalf of a religious mission, did not tap the full range of his talents, but the job kept him in the Congo and in touch with the native population. If anything, the interaction with the natives was even more rewarding, for there was no longer any commercial veneer to the venture. And while he did not have the training of an ordained cleric, Revd Bentley was apparently impressed by the positive impact that his relationship with the natives had on the mission's efforts to spread the Christian Word. While I have been unable to find anyone among my informants who could vouch for a strong religious dimension to Casement's personality, it is probably safe to assume that there was at least a degree of consonance between his world view and that of the Christian missionaries, *vis-à-vis* the relationship between western civilization and the indigenous populations of the less developed world.

The interview data that I have collected from various sources throughout Mr Casement's career suggests that his commitment to a cause often conflicted with his need to make a living, and that seems to have been what ultimately led to his decision to leave Revd Bentley's mission. My sources are not entirely sure how he managed it, but from the middle of 1890 to the middle of 1891 he was actually able to return to gainful employment in the Congo, in spite of King Leopold's stricture on foreign employees: someone apparently intervened on his behalf in order to capitalise upon his prior surveying experience to help get things moving with the construction of a railway from Matadi to Stanley Pool. My Elder Dempster informants lost track of him when he left the Congo in 1891: while they had not made a special point of following his career when he had left the company seven years earlier, they nevertheless heard about him occasionally as they pursued their commercial interests in Africa, and it is on the basis of that occasional feedback that I have been able to summarise his first seven or eight years on that continent. Input about his subsequent experiences in Africa has come exclusively from sources in the Foreign Office, which he joined in the autumn of 1895.

Between his departure from the Congo Free State in 1891 and his appointment to the Foreign Office in 1895, he was apparently able to draw upon surveying skills that he had acquired in the Congo to gain employment with a British company that had been commissioned to establish a commercial infrastructure in the Niger Coast Protectorate. I learned this indirectly from my Foreign Office informants, who alluded to Mr Casement's 'surveying' experience in unequivocally condescending terms, obviously harbouring resentment over the fact that Mr Casement had been excused from the standard examination requirements for civil-service employment when he received his appointment in 1895. I suspect that his reputation for dealing with African natives, along with more than ten years of direct practical experience on this forbidding continent had more to do with that decision than his 'surveying' experience; the posting for which he had been hired, after all, was with the Africa Department, charged with the responsibility for dealing with the challenges of a region with which few junior officers in the foreign service had any experience, or interest. This was not the last time, however, that I was to encounter this kind of resentment on the part of Foreign Office associates.

Those informants within the Foreign Office have enabled me to gain some insight into Mr Casement's consular career, from the time he joined the Foreign Service in 1895 until he was dispatched to investigate the Congo atrocities in 1903 (see my dispatches of 20 and 22 May for details about the latter). The first of several assignments on the continent was as Her Majesty's Consul to Portuguese East Africa, posted in Lourenço Marques. Ostensibly, his role was to protect the interests of British subjects in the Portuguese colony. Already resentful about his exceptional *entrée* into the Foreign Service, my informants were quick to point out that Mr Casement actually found it demeaning to have to deal with the mundane daily complaints that came to his desk from British residents who were inconvenienced in various and sundry ways by the Portuguese administrative authorities. As they sarcastically suggested, he preferred to deal with 'loftier' policy issues regarding the relationship between Britain and Portugal.

Those 'loftier' concerns may have sewn the first seeds of the discontent that seems to have affected his attitude toward the Foreign Office for the rest of his career. One of my informants, also assigned to Lourenço Marques at the time, spoke about an obscure incident involving a local chieftain named Gungunhana, the native leader of a small territory called Gazaland. According to this informant, Britain and Portugal were engaged in a dispute about jurisdiction over this rather insignificant territory, and in what he perceived to be the best interests of his people, Chief Gungunhana elected to ally his people with Britain, helping to bolster the British claims. Unfortunately for him, obscure diplomatic considerations outweighed the significance of suzerainty over the disputed territory, leading Britain ultimately to concede jurisdiction to Portugal – after having acknowledged the alliance with Chief Gungunhana. With little diplomatic leverage left at its disposal, after having ceded jurisdictional authority, the Foreign Office found itself in a position where it could only file a verbal protest when the Portuguese retaliated against the Chief and his family, subjecting them to various forms of public humiliation as they reasserted Portuguese authority and domination. As a junior officer on site, Mr Casement had to be careful about expressing disapproval, but my informant maintains that he was transparently unhappy about what he felt was a betrayal of trust on the part of the British government in its dealings with the indigenous population.

While protecting the interests of British subjects was the official responsibility of the consular position, several of my informants acknowledge that it soon became evident that Mr Casement had a more clandestine assignment, as well. Fourteen years before his arrival in southeast Africa, Britain had settled a dispute with the Boers of the Transvaal, conceding a limited form of self-government in return for recognition of the Queen's sovereignty. Britain had maintained a colonial presence in southern Africa since acquiring the Cape of Good Hope from the Dutch in 1815 and establishing the Cape Colony to control trade routes to India and the Far East. The Boers, descendants of the original Dutch settlers, had begun to distance themselves from British control by migrating from the Cape Colony into adjacent areas, establishing the two Boer republics of the Transvaal and the Orange Free State.

Fiercely independent farmers, who felt that they owed allegiance to no one other than themselves, they resisted British efforts to extend their colonial interests beyond the immediate environs of the Cape region. In 1877, however, the British physically annexed the Transvaal to their colonial domain as the South African Republic. For a couple of years thereafter, the Boers and the British were allied in a common cause, to thwart an uprising of the Zulu nation that threatened the very existence of the Transvaal. Once that uprising was quelled, the Boers, under the leadership of one Paul Kruger, began an armed resistance to British control. The conflict was brief, with a formal truce signed in 1881 between the government of William Gladstone and the Transvaal Boers under Paul Kruger. The truce proved to be fragile, at best, and with the discovery of a vast lode of gold at the Witwatersrand in 1886, Britain took a much more aggressive interest in maintaining sovereignty over the entire region. By the time of Mr Casement's arrival in 1895, the tension had escalated to the point where armed conflict seemed to be inevitable.

While they did not elaborate, my informants maintain that a number of incidents had led Britain to believe that Lourenço Marques was the main transit point for the smuggling of German arms to the Boers in the Transvaal, and they needed someone to conduct an investigation into the matter – in effect to become a spy on their behalf. Whatever the character traits might be that qualify one for the craft of espionage, the Foreign Office must have seen them in their young new consul. And given his propensity for adventure, Mr Casement was apparently not averse to supplementing his 'official' responsibilities with the task of ferreting out evidence of gun smuggling to an insurrectionist group. The Crown's judgement of Casement's potential for espionage apparently proved to be justified; he was able to submit a report to the Home Office in June of 1896 to the effect that a number of containers with hundreds of rifles and Maxim guns, along with several million rounds of ammunition, had arrived in Delagoa Bay under the rubric of 'Government Goods' and had been transported via rail to Pretoria. How he came up with that information is still a mystery to those Foreign Office associates who were stationed with him in Lourenço Marques, but the rumours at the time held that he had bribed an official in the harbour customs office.

With obvious relish at the prospect of Casement's total fall from grace, those same FO sources who provided me with this information were quick to point out the ironic reversal of roles twenty-one years later, with Mr Casement's own smuggling of German arms, just two months ago, to another insurrectionist group, this time closer to home. The sentiments represented by the contrasting behaviours are certainly revealing. In 1895, Mr Casement was obviously a loyal supporter of the Crown's colonial ambitions, fully committed to suppressing armed insurrection by a group that the Crown considered its rightful subjects. And by drawing upon Mr Casement's intelligence-gathering skills, Lord Salisbury's Foreign Office was fully aware of the nascent insurrection in the South African Republic.

Unfortunately for the government, the Foreign Office was unable to make effective use of Mr Casement's intelligence at the time. Its ability to respond militarily to the arming of the Boers was temporarily on hold, because of the lingering after-effects of what, my FO informants all agree, was a completely bungled paramilitary operation just six months prior to Mr Casement's report. With the covert approval of Cecil Rhodes, the Cape Colony's Prime Minister, a raiding party under the command of Leander Starr Jameson crossed into the South African Republic with the intention of infiltrating Johannesburg, where they hoped to foment a proxy uprising by the Republic's *uitlanders*, the British expatriate foreign workers who had remained in South Africa after the 1886 gold rush. Had it been successful, the British authorities could have simply remained aloof while the *uitlanders* and the Boers fought it out, with the British military using the conflict as a pretext to move in later as a peacekeeping force that would save the territory from self-destruction by annexing it to the British Cape Colony.

The whole operation was apparently a fiasco from the very beginning. Educated initially as a physician, and ultimately engaged by Cecil Rhodes to help administer his various enterprises in southern Africa, Jameson had no real military experience to guide him. And the Boer intelligence apparatus proved just as effective as Mr Casement's, giving them sufficient advance knowledge of the plan to prepare for a defence. A company of Boer militia surrounded the unsuspecting Jameson party near Krugersdorp, just outside Johannesburg, and after a brief skirmish, the blundering group of British irregulars was forced into an ignominious surrender. As a gesture of good will, President Kruger returned Jameson to the British for trial, and while he was indeed sentenced to fifteen months of imprisonment, he was quickly pardoned and celebrated in the press as a hero. My FO contacts who were in Lourenço Marques at the time certainly did not consider Mr Jameson a hero; they were well aware of the anti-British sentiments that the raid generated among those residing in the territories under their jurisdiction, of the precautions that the Boers were now intent upon taking, and of the international backlash, especially on the part of the German government. All this made further action against the Boers, whether overt or covert, an exceedingly delicate venture, although my contacts all seemed convinced that this was the precursor of an inevitable military confrontation.

As for Mr Casement, he seemed to take inspiration from Jameson's quixotic foray into paramilitary intrigue. My informants were both shocked and amused when they learned about his eventual involvement in what turned out to be an aborted plan to prevent the delivery of German arms to the Boers by blowing up the rail line between Lourenço Marques and Pretoria. Before that incident, however, he had spent a year as Her Majesty's Consul at St Paul de Loanda in Portuguese West Africa, where he was once again called upon to exercise his intelligence-gathering skills, to provide the government with information about the smuggling of arms through the Congo to reinforce those supporting the Mahdist resistance to British expansion in the Bahr el Ghazal region of central Africa. While in St Paul de Loanda, he also received the first of many reports that had begun to surface about the atrocities being committed within the Congo Free State. Before he could follow up on those reports, however, the tensions between Britain and the Boers had finally erupted into full-scale warfare, and he was sent back to Lourenço Marques to once again collect intelligence about outside support for the rebels in the Transvaal.

All this intelligence-gathering activity on behalf of the Crown to undermine insurrection has not been lost on Mr Casement's Irish compatriots. My sources within the Irish Republican Brotherhood acknowledge that they knew about Mr Casement's earlier success in gathering intelligence for the British government about the Boer rebellion and the Mahdist resistance. During their preparations for the recent Easter Rising, they were therefore naturally reluctant to give any credence whatsoever to his overtures of support. Only after his sincerity became apparent from his personal sacrifices on behalf of the cause did they feel at all comfortable taking him into their confidence, and even then with a great deal of hesitation and trepidation.

According to those consular colleagues whom I have been able to interview, his intelligence-gathering efforts upon returning to Lourenço Marques for the final time produced no solid evidence of outside intervention, but in what they insist was a typical act of self-aggrandisement, he cast himself in the role of a Jameson-type para-military leader, proposing that he lead a raiding party to destroy the rail link into the Transvaal and thus cut off any possibility of transporting arms from Delagoa Bay to the Boer fighters. As had been the case with Leander Jameson, Casement had no military experience to qualify him for such a venture and his associates in the Foreign Office dismissed him as a quixotic fraud with delusions of grandeur. To their utter amazement, however, Lord Roberts, the military Commander-in-Chief of British forces, actually approved Mr Casement's proposal in March of 1900 and was about to dispatch the expeditionary force in May. By that time, however, the course of events had rapidly made the mission irrelevant to the prevailing military strategy and Lord Roberts cancelled the raid at the last minute, redirecting the members of the raiding party to other theatres of action where they were more urgently needed. Having declared war against the British on 11

October, just a few months before the planned raid, the Boer forces under Paul Kruger, President of the Transvaal, and Martinus Theunis Steyn, President of the Orange Free State, were proving to be formidable foes with their commando-type tactics. The British military needed every man it could muster to respond to the unexpected initiatives that had been launched by the Boer forces.

While Mr Casement's involvement with the war against the Boer republics was brief, my contacts who served with him in Lourenço Marques suggest that his loyalty to the Crown was beyond reproach. His anger toward the Boers over their mistreatment of the natives complemented British anger toward the Boers over their mistreatment of the *uitlanders*, the British expatriates living in the South African Republic and the Orange Free State. It is therefore an ionic twist of historic fate that the Boer rebellion was supported by an Irish Brigade recruited from British prisoners of war that the Boers had captured on the battlefield. The same John MacBride who was executed just three weeks ago for his involvement with the Easter uprising in Dublin was responsible for organising the Irish Transvaal Brigade that fought alongside the Boers. And as noted in my dispatch of 25 May, a legal precedent for filing charges under the fourteenth-century treason statute was established just fourteen years ago with the trial of Arthur Lynch (for helping to organise that same Irish Transvaal Brigade). And, of course, the Roger Casement who condemned that brigade for supporting the Boer rebellion against the Crown is the same Roger Casement who is now going to trial for attempting to organise a similar brigade in Germany to join the Irish rebellion against the Crown. The ironies indeed abound.

Based on my interviews with some of Mr Casement's Irish compatriots, there is also reason to believe that in spite of his enthusiastic support of the government's efforts, the Boer War might have actually sewn the initial seeds of his disillusionment with the Crown's methods in subduing resistance by dissident groups. With the frustrating successes of the Boers in waging guerrilla warfare against a military still wedded to conventional tactics, Lord Kitchener, the successor to Lord Roberts as the overall military commander of British forces in South Africa, adopted a 'scorched earth' policy of destroying all bases of subsistence for the Boer's agrarian society and a 'relocation' policy of interning Boer families *en masse* in concentration camps. It was the latter especially that led to accusations of atrocities by the outside world. While Mr Casement never became personally involved in actual hostilities, and was therefore not in a position to observe what was happening on site, he had to have been aware of the reports coming back from the field, especially after the Fawcett Commission's documentation of the thousands of deaths brought on by mass starvation, disease, and physical exposure in the camps. With the Boer War having only concluded a year before with the Treaty of Vereeniging in May of 1902, the reports of British atrocities in South Africa had to be fresh in Casement's mind as he set off in the fall of 1903 to investigate reports of state-sanctioned atrocities in the Congo Free State.

My interviews with business and government associates who knew Mr Casement during his seventeen years in Africa before joining the Congo investigative commission suggest that those earlier African experiences left him temperamentally vulnerable to profound disillusionment when he embarked upriver on the *Henry Reed*. He was obviously an idealist who firmly believed in the civilizing benefits that colonial and commercial outreach could bring to the less-developed areas of the world. He was an outspoken and fervid advocate for the oppressed and disadvantaged populations for whom those civilizing benefits were intended. He had an inherent empathy for the downtrodden and exploited communities who survived at the margins of society. And while he may still have been a loyal supporter of the Crown in extending its colonial domain and in confronting those foreign elements that would interfere with the Crown's imperial mission, his faith in the government's methods had probably been shaken by the reports from South Africa. By the time he joined the Congo investigative commission, he was also a skilled bureaucrat and an accomplished intelligence agent, and in what may have been his greatest vulnerability, he was an ardent believer in his own capacity to make a difference in dealing with the loftiest of moral and diplomatic issues.

All these attributes made him eminently qualified to head the commission of enquiry that brought international attention to the atrocities of the Congo Free State. Unfortunately for Mr Casement, they also laid the foundation for the disillusionment brought on by his 1903 mission into the Congo and his 1910 mission into the Amazon, the latter of which will be the subject of my next dispatch, which I hope to file within the week. The idealism that led him to believe in the benefits of colonialism and commercialisation may not have been able to survive what he found in the Congo and the Amazon. And his empathy for the oppressed and downtrodden of the earth may have inevitably led him to question the benefits of British imperialism. Those are matters that I hope to address in subsequent dispatches, as I learn more about Mr Casement and as I follow the events that unfold in the weeks ahead.

THURSDAY 1 JUNE 1916

From the data collected for my previous dispatch, it is clear that Casement's twenty years of intermittent exposure to Africa from 1881 to 1901 were formative years, during which he learned a great deal about African societies, acquired the diplomatic and commercial experience that enabled him to deal effectively with those societies, and seized upon numerous opportunities to apply what he had learned in an idealistic commitment to elevating those societies to a higher level of political, material, and spiritual well-being. It is against this backdrop that his 1903 investigative expedition in the Congo Free State can be seen as a traumatic turning point in his worldview. His belief in the magnanimity of European civilization, and its potential for positively assimilating indigenous peoples into the world of the twentieth century, had to have been seriously challenged, if not destroyed, by what he saw during those few brief weeks in the summer of 1903.

Perhaps the atrocities committed by Leopold's Congo Free State were an aberration in Europe's march to civilizing the African continent. That is surely one consideration to which Casement must have clung when he saw the horrendous impact that commercialisation had wrought along the once pristine banks of the Congo River. With that as a guiding premise, his scathing investigative report could be seen as a corrective measure that might resurrect the original goals of the African enterprise, to bring the benefits of advanced civilisation to the deprived peoples of this primitive continent. By casting the report in that perspective, he could retain some semblance of his original idealism, and indeed my interviews with his colleagues from the Foreign Office suggest that he may very well have taken that tack as one way of preserving his faith in a beneficent and meaningful role for the advanced societies of the world. Reflective of the resentment that has surfaced on more than one occasion during my interviews, however, those same colleagues could not resist the cynical suggestion that while his need to preserve a sense of idealism may have had something to do with it, he really had to see the report in such a light as a way of reinforcing an inflated sense of his own importance: by bringing the atrocities to the attention of the world, Casement was personally setting things right and resurrecting the ideals that had been articulated in the Berlin Agreement of 1885.

Whatever the case, when asked by the Foreign Office to return to its employ and assume responsibility for the Brazilian consulates in Sao Paulo and Paraná, in 1906, after two years of respite from the strain of consular service, he must surely have struggled to recover that earlier sense of idealism in approaching another continent that was outside the mainstream of twentieth-century civilization. How could he have otherwise found the emotional and spiritual strength to take on such a task? While his need for gainful employment may have contributed to his accepting the position, his colleagues have pointed out repeatedly that he was not one to see himself as a mere functionary; in accepting the appointment he undoubtedly assumed that he would be in a powerful and influential position – another opportunity to promote himself, by promoting the humanitarian cause, with which he had become identified, regardless of whether association with that cause was the accidental offshoot of circumstance or the product of philosophical commitment. How disheartening it must therefore have been to find himself almost immediately at the forefront of another investigation into atrocities, that further undermined the idea that outside intervention and commercialisation were a boon to the development of primitive societies.

The Putumayo is a tributary of the upper Amazon River basin, feeding into the main river from a jungle region over which Peru and Colombia are still feuding for political jurisdiction. Inhabited by indigenous peoples who have only recently suffered contact with the outside world (the Witoto, Bora, Ocaína, and Miranya tribes), the area encompasses some of the most inhospitable geography on the face of the earth. Were it not for the discovery that latex from the native *Castilla elastica* and *Hevea guianensis* trees could be processed into the rubber that has become such a highly sought-after commodity on the world market, it is unlikely that the 'white' man would ever have ventured into those forbidding tropical rainforests.

While ignorance can occasionally be bliss, it does not necessarily protect one from the exigencies of fate. In their private world beyond the precincts of modern civilization, the Witoto were obviously unaware of advances that were overtaking the rest of the world; of Charles Goodyear's 1839 discovery of vulcanisation, for example, to process raw latex into rubber with the elasticity and strength needed for adaptation to the needs of modern technology; or of John Dunlop's development of the pneumatic tire in 1888, an invention that would capitalise upon the availability of rubber and the vulcanisation process to revolutionise the transportation industry; or of Henry Ford's assembly-line approach to mass production of the new motor car, generating an insatiable demand for tires and the rubber to produce them. Such developments were totally outside the Witoto universe but ultimately led to their demise.

Just as King Leopold of Belgium capitalised upon the world's insatiable demand for rubber by exploiting the indigenous populations of the Congo, Julio César Arana del Águila, a Peruvian entrepreneur, seized the same opportunity among the Witoto of the Putumayo. Born in the same year as Sir Roger Casement, Arana started his entrepreneurial career by selling the straw hats that his father wove, peddling them on the streets of Rioja, the Andean village where he was born. In the age-old spirit of entrepreneurship, guided by a single-minded and ruthless commitment to making money, he gradually climbed the ladder of commercial success, opening a trading post on the Huallaga River at the early age of twenty-four, buying into a rubber-tapping enterprise just two years later, and finally finding his way into the disputed territory of the Putumayo at the age of thirty-five. The absence of governmental control in a politically contested area, rich in marketable latex, made the region ripe for Arana's unscrupulous approach to personal enrichment. By 1905, through the exercise of shrewd business acumen in conjunction with his no-holds-barred approach to exploitation, swindling, and outright violence, this erstwhile peddler of straw hats reportedly controlled more than 30,000 square kilometres of the finest rubber-producing trees in the Amazon rainforest.

Just as Leopold found in dealing with the indigenous peoples of the Congo, the peaceful and unsuspecting Witoto of the Putumayo were easily reduced to slavery, eliminating the labour costs that constitute one of the most significant constraints on commercial profits. Enforcing slavery, however, inevitably leads to the kinds of atrocities that Casement uncovered in the Congo, and just as Edmund Morel's revelations brought attention to Leopold's atrocities, so the revelations of a young American named Walt Hardenburg brought Arana's reign of terror into public view.

According to the reports to which I have gained access in preparing this background piece, Hardenburg was a young engineering student from Illinois who, along with an American friend named Perkins, set out in December of 1907 to seek adventure in the exotic rainforest of central Brazil. While passing through one of Arana's outposts in a place called El Encanto, they apparently had a run-in with some of Arana's 'enforcers', were viciously beaten, and then thrown into the local jail among native prisoners who were being held for various violations of their labour 'contracts'. While incarcerated, they were shocked by the blatant evidence of physical abuse among those jailed natives. Upon being released, Hardenburg and his friend vowed to go public with what they had witnessed and approached the newspaper in Iquitos with their story, only to find that it, too, was being controlled by the intimidation of Arana and his henchmen. This simply fuelled the fires of outrage harboured by the young American idealist, and at the risk of his own life, he took it upon himself to launch a one-man crusade, collecting as much evidence as he could before fleeing the region in the summer of 1908.

In the process of collecting that evidence, Hardenburg apparently learned that Arana was attempting to capitalise further upon his 'business' venture by listing his Peruvian Amazon Rubber Company on the

London stock exchange. This offered Hardenburg the opening he needed to strike back at the heinous practices that he had observed while in the Putumayo region. Leaving the jungles behind in July of 1908, he headed off to London where he hoped to find a newspaper editor who would take an interest in his story. After several frustrating overtures, he finally found two sources of support: the Revd John Harris of the Anti-Slavery and Aborigines Protection Society, and the editors of a little-known magazine called *Truth*, that was attempting to build a reputation in the field of investigative journalism by revealing potential scandals. Entitled 'The Devil's Paradise: A British Owned Congo', the series of articles it published about Hardenburg's revelations was intentionally inflammatory, suggesting that the company's appearance on the London stock exchange proved that British commercial interests were complicit in an exploitative enterprise that was strikingly similar to the one that Parliament and the Foreign Office had so recently condemned in the Congo.

The report attracted attention in the House of Commons, which discovered to its dismay that a knighted Member of Parliament was actually on the Board of Directors of Arana's company. Like Leopold before him, Arana tried to deflect attention from the atrocities and to discredit the source of the revelations, but memories of the Congo affair were still fresh in the minds of Parliamentarians, and the fact that the company was registered in London, with British businessmen on the Board of Director,s raised a level of concern that could not be ignored. The Board of Directors itself apparently decided that it was in their best interest to support an investigation, but according to my sources in the Foreign Office, it was immediately apparent that the Board's commission of enquiry would be comprised of insiders and sympathisers, very much like the commission of enquiry that Leopold had dispatched to the Congo in response to public pressure.

Recalling how Leopold had tried to predetermine the findings of the Congo commission, Sir Edward Grey and the Foreign Office were determined this time to be a part of the investigation from the very beginning. And who better to lead such an investigation on their behalf than the diplomat who had earned such praise and recognition for what he had accomplished in similar circumstances just five years earlier. The fact that Casement was already in place as the British Consul-General in Rio de Janeiro was a fortuitous turn of events for the Foreign Office, which took little time in ordering him to join the team of investigators. By the middle of September, the team had left Manaus and was on its way up the Amazon and the Putumayo.

With the help of the Anti-Slavery and Aborigines Protection Society, I was able to contact a member of the team that accompanied the Commission into this Amazonian heart of darkness. Like the source who provided me with inside information about Mr Casement's mission into the Congo, my informant for this dispatch insisted on complete anonymity and will therefore be referred to by the pseudonym of Mr Winston throughout the remainder of this dispatch. While he was not an official part of the investigation (his duties were simply to provide logistical support for the official members of the investigative party), Winston was nevertheless in a position to follow the investigation from beginning to end. Privacy was non-existent, so he was privy to every interview and observation that Mr Casement and his colleagues conducted.

According to Winston, much of the substantive input the Commission received during the expedition came from Barbadian overseers in Arana's 'employ'. The Witoto were understandably reluctant to provide direct evidence, although scars and mutilation were themselves a transparent form of evidence. The Barbadians, however, proved more forthcoming in response to Casement's engaging and diplomatic manner, especially since they saw his presence as a potential source of release from their own forced servitude. The fact that they were British subjects also helped: as the British Consul-General representing the interests of the Crown's far-flung subjects, Casement was perceived by them as a protector and advocate. Having been tricked into leaving Barbados to join the Arana crews as overseers and then brutally coerced into remaining and taking part in the exploitation of the natives, the Barbadians saw the Commission as a rescue party dispatched by the British Foreign Office under the official direction of its Consul-General. While the Foreign Office had indeed used their status as British subjects as one of the justifications for taking an official interest in the allegations against the

Peruvian Amazon Company, the Barbadians had no way of knowing the limits of the Foreign Office's influence.

The movements of the investigative party were naturally controlled to prevent any direct observation of abuse, but as was the case in the Congo, the evidence of torture and mutilation was apparent among the natives they met, with their missing limbs and scarred bodies. More importantly, however, the Barbadians who had witnessed and in many cases participated in the abuse were both graphic and detailed in their description of the atrocities. As in the Congo, the most pervasive form of abuse was flogging, which was apparent from the scars on the bodies of those with whom the commission members came into contact. According to the Barbadians, the natives were expected to produce a prescribed quota of latex, which was routinely increased as the appetite for profit grew increasingly insatiable, and for which the natives were never compensated. Quite the contrary; rather than rewarding those who met the quotas, they routinely punished those who failed, with vicious floggings and in some cases with execution to intimidate and horrify anyone who lagged behind or considered flight. Floggings themselves could often result in death, for in the unhygienic conditions and hostile climate of the region, infection could easily result from the open wounds.

In one especially gruesome example of the kind of atrocity occasionally inflicted by sadistic station masters to terrorise their subjects and to give vent to their own unbridled furies, Winston related a story told by one of the Barbadians to the absolute horror of the Commissioners. Discovering that a young woman whom he had taken as his personal sex slave had contracted venereal disease, the station master in question flew into a rage, never once considering the possibility that she might have actually contracted the disease from him. To set an example for any other potential sex slaves that he might call to his bed, the monster had her strung up by her wrists to an overhanging tree limb and publicly tortured until she died of shock before the horrified villagers.

On another occasion, an agent by the name of Augusto Jimenez had a tribal member tortured and executed for refusing to disclose the location of family members who had fled into the surrounding forest. Having sprained her ankle in flight, and unable to keep up with the rest of the family, she was captured and returned to Jimenez, who had her hung by her wrists over an open fire. The Barbadian who witnessed this atrocity described in graphic detail how the skin on the woman's thighs erupted into giant blisters as she writhed and screamed for mercy with the flames licking at her blackened legs. In frustration with her continued refusal to betray her family, Jimenez cut her down by decapitating her with a machete, dropping her then lifeless body into the pit of coals.

While cataloguing the atrocities of which he learned, Casement was also intent this time on seeking justice against the perpetrators. Unlike with his Congo report, in which he made a determined effort to suppress the names of those involved, he was just as determined this time to publicize the names of anyone against whom he could amass sufficient evidence to make a case. While his Congo report might have effectively indicted 'the system', as Mr Casement had begun characterising the commercial order supported by colonialism, it had been much less effective in bringing anyone to justice for the atrocities committed on behalf of 'the system'. In the seven years that had elapsed since completing his mission to the Congo, Mr Casement had apparently concluded that while 'the system' breeds criminals, that 'system' is ultimately comprised of concrete individuals who must be held personally accountable if 'the system' is ever to be reformed. In preparing the Putumayo report, he had obviously decided that names are important.

Next to Julio César Arana himself, the most notorious of the perpetrators appears to have been a Brazilian by the name of Armando Normand, who was in charge of the company's station at Matanzas, the most remote of the stations on the Putumayo tributary. The Barbadians who served him were able to provide testimony confirming that he routinely raided native villages in the Colombian jungles and brought back slaves to take the place of local natives who had died while working the rubber trees. Those who tried to flee were tortured to death in front of their fellow tribesmen to discourage them all from attempting to escape. One of the Barbadians whom Mr Casement interviewed at Matanzas described how on one occasion he had seen Normand tie a number of captured escapees together and cast them alive into a raging bonfire, forcing the rest of the tribe to watch in horror until the screaming stopped. And as was the routine among all the rubber stations, those who failed to meet the impossible quotas imposed upon them were ruthlessly flogged and mutilated without remorse.

Among other company agents whom Winston recalled being mentioned by name in conversations between Mr Casement and his fellow investigators were Elias Martinengui of the Atenas station, Innocente Fonseca of the Sabana station, and Alfredo Montt of the Ultimo Retiro station. The Commissioners met few of the station masters personally, but at the company's main base in La Chorrera, they met one named Victor Macedo, toward whom Winston claims Mr Casement took an immediate dislike. The Barbadians in Macedo's 'employ' were unusually reluctant to discuss the conditions of their 'employment' or the treatment of the natives, but after much encouragement from Mr Casement, they provided the kind of testimony that had become all too familiar to the investigating party and which confirmed Mr Casement's impressions of Macedo. In La Chorrera, company officials also made the mistake of allowing Mr Casement to examine the company's accounts, apparently assuming that he lacked the business background to recognise evidence of corruption and fraud; with the experience he had acquired in working for Elder Dempster and in maintaining accounts at the various consulates to which he had been assigned, Mr Casement was anything but inept when it came to poring over business records.

Also among the agents cited by the Barbadians for abuse of the natives was an Irishman named Andreas O'Donnell, who was in charge of the company's station at Entre Rios. Winston informed me that, based on conversations he overheard between Mr Casement and one of his fellow Commissioners, Mr Casement was especially chagrined by this discovery. Drawing upon those overheard conversations, Winston maintains that Mr Casement was becoming more and more indiscreet with his outspoken and pointed critiques of those for whom he worked. While he had once seen British colonialism as a blessing for the deprived of the world, bringing the economic benefits of international trade and the spiritual benefits of Christian dogma to those born outside the reach of western civilization, his experience in the Congo and now in the Amazon had called all that into question.

And he was astounded by the idea that a fellow Irishman could lend his hand to the most heinous of colonialism's abuses. Based, again, on overheard conversations during the quiet nights spent around their campfires, Winston recounted how Mr Casement had begun reminiscing about his homeland, lamenting the amount of time he had spent away from the island of his birth and regretting that he had not devoted more time to the cultural renaissance taking place without him. It was during these reminiscences that Mr Casement had begun referring bitterly to Ireland's status as just another colonial outpost of the British Empire. On more than one occasion, he suggested that his empathy for the oppressed populations in the Congo and the Amazon grew out of his recognition that they shared with the Irish an experience of exploitation that bound them all together in a common worldview. How O'Donnell could participate in the exploitation of another race seemed beyond Mr Casement's comprehension.

Upon submitting his official report to the Foreign Office, Mr Casement apparently withdrew once again from the public eye, at least until he heard from Sir Edward Grey, on 15 June 1911, that he was to be knighted in recognition of his humanitarian contributions. My anonymous contacts in the Foreign Office confirm that he was not nearly as abrasive or confrontational over the handling of the Putumayo report as he had been over the handling of the Congo report – and this in spite of the fact that the Foreign Office once again had to accommodate at least a modicum of diplomatic niceties. Perhaps he had learned the importance and the value of diplomacy, or perhaps it was simply that he found the Foreign Office more aggressive under Sir Edward Grey than it had been under Lord Lansdowne in following up on his input. As a matter of fact, based upon input from my FO sources, it would appear that the follow-up this time was indeed more aggressive, but the international situation was quite different, as well: the government did not have to be as cautious in approaching Peru in 1911 as it had been in its dealings with Belgium in 1904. And after the experience with Leopold and the Congo Free State, Members of Parliament were less inclined to be patient this time in waiting for the cooperation of a foreign government.

In the judgement of several of my sources, the Putumayo report itself was more laden with passion and condemnation than the Congo report had been. As a junior officer in 1904, Mr Casement would have naturally been more careful to couch his official documents in bureaucratic language and obfuscation in an attempt to project objectivity. In his 1911 Putumayo report, Mr Casement apparently dispensed with any pretence of dispassionate objectivity, and levelled his accusations and denunciations in direct terms. Perhaps his experience with the Congo report led him to believe that such an approach would be more effective in stimulating the kind of action that he felt was needed. Perhaps he had simply grown even less patient with official form and protocol – never a personal strength, in any case. Or perhaps, after two traumatic exposures to the dehumanising effects of unbridled greed and commercialism, he had lost all faith in the civilizing influence of colonialism or in the benevolence of human nature. While the Congo atrocities had been horrifying enough, the sheer viciousness and sadism that he uncovered in the jungles of South America had to raise serious questions in his mind about the human capacity for evil.

Whatever the reason, my sources within the Foreign Office confirm that there was much less deference in dealing with President Leguia of Peru than there had been in dealing with King Leopold of Belgium. Initially, of course, the Peruvian government proved to be totally unco-operative, in spite of their assurances that they were taking the case seriously. Sir Edward Grey however, proved less than patient and quickly recognised that he was being stonewalled. While the British government had little diplomatic leverage that it could bring to bear, the Foreign Office threatened to embarrass the Peruvian government by publishing Mr Casement's report and distributing it throughout the diplomatic community. Grey also shared a copy of the report with Philander Knox, the Secretary of State for the Taft administration in Washington, who in turn threatened to intervene under the rubric of the Monroe Doctrine.

The response from Peru undoubtedly surprised the Foreign Office and Mr Casement, as well. To avoid embarrassment and to impress upon the world that they would not tolerate the kind of activity revealed by

Mr Casement's investigation, the Leguia government issued 200 arrest warrants for those identified in the report and in subsequent inquiries that had been conducted by British and American consular officials onsite. The decision, this time, to include names and direct accusations in the report was vindicated, and it appeared that justice might actually be served as a result. Pablo Zumaeta, Sr Arana's brother-in-law was one of those taken into custody, demonstrating that the warrants were presumably more than just window dressing.

But window dressing is, in fact, what the Peruvian response turned out to be. The Foreign Office soon discovered that Zumaeta had been released, and as the months dragged on with no further arrests being made, it became apparent to my contacts in the FO that the authorities in Lima were deluding them, at every turn, with the same kinds of delaying tactics that King Leopold had employed. Grey once again threatened to make Mr Casement's report available to the diplomatic community, but to no avail. It wasn't until Mr Casement made a personal visit to the State Department in Washington while *en route* back to London that an effective plan of action was finally adopted. The Taft administration agreed to exert whatever pressure it could on the Peruvian government and encouraged Grey to proceed with his original threat to publish and distribute Casement's report, as a way of embarrassing that government into action.

While they seemed reluctant to discuss details that might reflect negatively on their Foreign Minister, my contacts acknowledged that Mr Grey continued to procrastinate – until the *New York Sun* somehow managed clandestinely to obtain a copy of the report and ran it in its 13 July edition, during the summer of 1912. As was the case upon the ultimate release of the Congo report, it was once again the House of Commons that finally intervened. Outraged that British members of the company's board of directors would turn a blind eye to the heinous activities of the Peruvian Amazon Company, Members of Parliament appointed a Select Committee to look into the matter and to make formal recommendations for government action. Since there was no legal recourse available to hold the directors liable, the Committee recommended that legislation be introduced to make it possible in future to hold boards of directors accountable for the activities of their companies.

As the diplomatic and legal wrangling unfolded, Mr Casement seems to have gradually faded into the background. My sources in the Foreign Office have indicated that given Mr Casement's impatience with the delays in following up on his Congo report, they all expected him, once again, to take offence with his colleagues and initiate some kind of personal campaign outside official channels, similar to what he had done in co-operation with Edmund Morel and the Congo Reform Association a half dozen years earlier. To their amazement, nothing like that happened. Whether the result of fatigue, illness from his travails in the jungle, or demoralisation, he seemed inclined to withdraw from the scene once Parliament took an interest. As a matter of fact, when the Foreign Office decided to send him back to Rio as its Consul-General, he declined the assignment and took a medical leave of absence, which suggested to his colleagues that he was indeed too ill and worn out to continue his active involvement in the follow-up. They continued to receive correspondence from him in South Africa, where he had gone to visit his brother and to recuperate in a more welcome climate, and even upon his return, he kept his distance while remaining available to the Select Committee for consultation.

While his Foreign Office colleagues attributed his more subdued demeanour to illness and exhaustion, my contacts in the Irish nationalist movement insist that his ardour for humanitarian causes was in no way diminished but was simply shifting its focus. As noted by Mr Winston, my informant from Mr Casement's Putumayo entourage, his campfire conversations with fellow travellers during their voyage up the Amazon had revealed an increasing preoccupation with the plight of his fellow Irish nationals. My Irish sources are convinced that after waging a noble battle on behalf of the oppressed and the exploited in the far-off jungles of Africa and South America, he was beginning to recognise that he had long neglected the cause of those oppressed and exploited denizens of his own native land. And thus began his final mission, which has bought him to the threshold of a trial that could prove to be of historic proportions, scheduled to begin in just three weeks.

WEDNESDAY 14 JUNE 1916

With his trial scheduled to begin in just twelve days, Sir Roger Casement continues to be held incommunicado in the Tower of London. Efforts to gain an audience with the prisoner have been rebuffed at every turn, and the members of his legal team have been too preoccupied with trial preparations to make themselves available to the media. In the absence of direct input from the defendant and his representatives, we in the media have been forced to rely on acquaintances and erstwhile professional colleagues to learn more about what might have brought this decorated and apparently loyal subject of the Crown to the dock for treason.

As noted in my last dispatch, Mr Casement withdrew from government service after the submission of his Putumayo report, citing the effect of service in the inhospitable regions of Africa and South America on his deteriorating health. According to many of his Irish acquaintances, however, he had grown increasingly disillusioned with his work and with the impact of British imperialism and commercialism on the distant populations for whom he had developed a profound empathy. Along with that disillusionment, was what these acquaintances insist was a gnawing sense of guilt and regret that he had not devoted more time and attention to his own Irish roots – a compunction that intensified each time a holiday or a medical leave afforded him the opportunity to interrupt his professional schedule and make a return visit, however brief, to his native land. According to these sources, the sensitisation that he had acquired to the suffering of exploited groups during his assignments abroad made him increasingly aware of the deprivations being suffered by his fellow countrymen. And that, in turn, made him that much more receptive to the argument of Irish nationalists that British economic exploitation, political subjugation, and cultural suppression were at the heart of the suffering at home.

History is always subject to interpretation (or misinterpretation), depending upon the perspective of the individual or the group looking back upon the events, and there is no doubt that those in the Irish nationalist movement have interpreted their history from the perspective of an abused group. As one who steeped himself in his nation's history, Mr Casement was surely well aware of the historical record, and one can certainly assume that the empathy he had acquired for abused groups provided a perspective that would have made him sympathetic to the nationalist cause. An overview of those events and their impact upon the nationalist movement is therefore germane to understanding what motivated Mr Casement in taking the actions that have brought him before the court today.

On the subject of economic exploitation, it was apparent from my interviews that the shock waves from the Great Famine are still reverberating throughout Ireland, where every family is just a single generation removed from one of the greatest national catastrophes of all time. While the current generation may not have had direct personal experience of the starvation and disease that decimated the country from 1845 to 1850, each and every one is the descendant of someone who did. According to the estimates to which I have had access, the population of Ireland was reduced by almost 20 per cent as a result of the combined effects of starvation, disease, and the emigration of thousands who were forced to flee. While precise figures can never be obtained, an 1841 census reflected a population slightly in excess of eight million, while a similar census ten years later, just after the famine, revealed a population of just over six and a half million – a decline of a million and a half people.

As an agrarian society, the national economy has always been directly tied to land tenure, and many of those with whom I spoke are still convinced that the famine was as much the product of the long-standing tenure system as it was the natural by-product of *Phytophthora infestans*, more commonly known as potato blight. While the potato blight was a natural phenomenon, over which no one had any control, and which completely destroyed the nation's subsistence crop, without warning, and for no apparent natural reason, the Irish nationalists still argue vehemently that it was the economic structure imposed upon Ireland by their British oppressors that made mass starvation, not only a possible, but an inevitable result. The malevolent nature of the economic structure was exacerbated by what my Irish informants insist was a calloused British disregard for the plight of the Irish during those horrific five years, to the point where *laissez-faire* economic policies adopted by the government allowed landlords to continue profiting from the exportation of foodstuffs produced in Ireland – even while the Irish starved.

No less a luminary than John Stuart Mill, the pre-eminent political economist of the time and a Member of Parliament at the time of Mr Casement's birth, made the case for Irish land reform, first in his *Principles of Political Economy* and later in a forty-page pamphlet entitled *England and Ireland* that he published in 1868, after he was able to re-assess his position on property rights and land tenure in light of the recent famine. Proponents for land reform had long argued for a revised relationship between proprietor and tenant, based on the philosophical principle that land has no inherent value, acquiring value only through investment in its utilitarian improvement for the common weal of the people. Following this principle, the conacre system, with its endless subdivision of acreage from landowner to tenant farmer to resident labourers known as cottiers (cottage dwellers), along with the competitive and arbitrary rental policies enforced by the estate managers all the way down through the vast hierarchy of leaseholders and lessees, disenfranchised the very tillers who could have contributed the most to improving and utilizing the land for the common weal. Reduced to virtual servitude in the production of cash crops and beef cattle for absentee landlords to export for profit, the cottiers were left with only one motivation – to survive. With no fixed property rights of their own, and ever vulnerable to losing the few rights they had as rents skyrocketed regularly in response to the competitive demand for land, the cottiers had no vested interest in developing or improving the land itself.

The estate managers naturally reserved the best land for the cash crops and pastures that they needed to ensure profitability for their landlords, leasing the poorer parts of the estates to the cottiers who hired on to provide the necessary agricultural labour. With the small plots of infertile land that they occupied, the cottiers ultimately turned to the potato for survival, capitalising upon its nutritional value, along with its hardy adaptability to the poor soil conditions of the plots allocated to them by the estate managers. Limited by the size of their plots to raising just enough for their families to get by from one year to the next, the cottiers were forever on the precarious edge of starvation. With about a third of the population dependent upon the potato for their very survival, the appearance of the potato blight marked the beginning of a catastrophe of biblical proportions.

The land reform issue became the *cause célèbre* of just about every Irish Member of Parliament, most notably Charles Stuart Parnell, until his fall from grace, and even received support from the Liberal Prime Minister William Gladstone, under whose stewardship the government passed the Landlord and Tenant Act, otherwise known as the Irish Land Act of 1870. But it was Michael Davitt, founder of the Irish National Land League, who most of my sources consider the real driving force behind Irish land reform, and whose contributions to that effort had to have had a marked influence on the economic perspectives of one as steeped in history as Mr Casement. Over the course of what is now known in Ireland as the 'Land War', from the mid-1850s to the mid-1880s, by which time Mr Casement was in his late teens, Davitt led the struggle for what land reform advocates touted as the 'three Fs': fair rent, fixity of tenure, and free sale of property, none of which existed for the cottiers upon whom the landowners depended for their labour.

The Irish Nationalists with whom I have spoken argue that expropriation of land has been a key element of British suppression since the end of the sixteenth century, when Irish estates in Ulster were confiscated and distributed among Scottish planters loyal to the Crown. Known as the Plantation of Ulster, an estimated half a million acres of land belonging to the descendants of the O'Neills and the O'Donnells and other indigenous families in the Counties of Donegal, Tyrone,

Fermanagh, Cavan, Armagh, and Londonderry were divided up among Presbyterian immigrants who could be depended upon to support the Crown. Expropriation continued in the middle of the seventeenth century, when Oliver Cromwell compensated his British soldiers with Irish land, which many then promptly converted to cash by selling their modest holdings to wealthy British aristocrats, who were able to amass great estates by buying up and consolidating these parcels of Irish soil that were of no use to soldiers eager to return to their families in England.

Once the centralisation of land ownership had begun with the sixteenth- and seventeenth-century forced expropriations, the continuation of that process was facilitated by the forces of capitalism, which enabled, what was now becoming, a landed aristocracy to take advantage of Irish impoverishment, to augment their holdings with the purchase of more and more of, what was in fact, the basic staple for survival in an agrarian economy – land. By the beginning of the nineteenth century, the ownership of Irish land was concentrated in the hands of absentee landlords who depended upon resident estate managers to generate as much cash profit as possible from the use of that land. Cash crops and beef cattle for export were the most profitable investment for those landowners, and leasing the land to tenant farmers and labourers who would raise those crops to support their own livelihood was the most profitable management system. Paying tenant farmers in land known as conacre, small holdings that the tenant farmers could use in whatever way served their best interest, including further dividing and leasing the land for profit, was the most convenient way for the estate managers to hire the labour force necessary to produce those cash crops. At the bottom of this pyramid, after all the land had been divided and further subdivided, were the cottiers, who used a portion of their income from working on the landed estates to rent a hut and a small plot for raising the potatoes on which their families subsisted. The tenant farmers could maximise their return by forcing cottiers to compete against each other in bidding for the rent of a subsistence plot, and by doing this annually, rather than on a long-term basis. It was the economic exploitation and instability inherent in such practices that Michael Davitt purportedly hoped to eliminate with his program to promote fair rent, fixity of tenure, and free sale of property.

Based on my cursory review of the land reform movement, it would appear that the sentiments behind the movement gradually evolved to a point, where reform of the existing system was no longer enough for the more ardent nationalists, who arrived at the conviction that land nationalisation was the only real answer to Ireland's economic problem. From their perspective, the land reform initiatives of Mill and Gladstone and Parnell had proven inadequate in overcoming either the economic plight of the Irish peasant or in raising the economic standard of Ireland generally. Many of those whom I interviewed are convinced that Mr Casement found these arguments persuasive, and that he linked this economic premise of the need for land nationalisation to what he and most Irish nationalists considered a history of blatant political oppression, in arriving at the conclusion that complete independence from Britain was the only hope for the Irish to survive as a people.

It is probably safe to say that the Irish have seen themselves as unwilling subjects of Britain ever since Henry II responded in 1167 to Dermot MacMurrough's infamous request for outside assistance in what ultimately proved to be his unsuccessful struggle to attain the high-kingship of Ireland. By opening the door to the British forces, my informants argue, MacMurrough unwittingly consigned his native land to foreign occupation for what has now been almost 750 years. The political relationship between Britain and Ireland has vacillated between periods of deceptively apparent harmony to ones of outright hostility, and as an avid student of Irish history, Mr Casement was undoubtedly steeped in the historical details of all those various periods. Like anyone with a grievance, however, Mr Casement's focus would have naturally been on the periods of hostility rather than harmony. And from the Irish perspective, examples of the former abound, beginning with the English violation of the Treaty of Windsor, almost immediately after they first arrived in Ireland to support the inglorious Dermot MacMurrough. Signed in 1175, by Henry II and the reigning High King Rory O'Connor, to accommodate the new British presence, the treaty provided for the partition of Ireland into separate British and Irish domains, ostensibly to allow the Irish to retain a sense of political and cultural independence. Henry promptly disregarded that provision, impinging upon O'Connor's Irish domain to parcel out pieces of property to his knights and barons, thus becoming the first British sovereign to exercise, what the Irish complain, has been the Crown's routine practice of expropriating Irish land to reward its supporters.

A number of my historically minded Irish informants have cited the year 1366 as one of the lesser known, but most significant moments in the history of the Anglo-Irish relationship. Mr Casement's knowledge of history, and his sensitivity to what many of my sources refer to as cultural genocide, would have made that year's Statutes of Kilkenny an especially odious collection of legal proscriptions in Mr Casement's encyclopaedia of abuses. Out of concern that the British settlers were being too fully assimilated into Irish society and that their loyalty to the Crown was thereby being diluted, those thirty-five Acts, authored by the Duke of Clarence, who had been sent as viceroy to Ireland by his father, King Edward III, were a misguided but ominous harbinger of things to come.

Among other things, the Statutes forbade intermarriage and even sexual intercourse between the British and the Irish, prohibited English adoption or fostering of Irish children, encouraged the substitution of British customs and pastimes for the Irish traditions that were becoming popular, subordinated the Brehon Law of ancient Irish custom to British Common Law, and required British settlers to use only the English language. While the Statutes were primarily motivated by the Crown's concern about maintaining the loyalty of its subjects in Ireland, they also reflected an attitude that denigrated all things Irish as the relics of a primitive and inferior race of people. The Statutes ultimately proved to be unworkable and unenforceable, but they marked what my Irish informants consider the first in a centuries-long series of attempts to subjugate and ultimately eliminate the Irish race – a genocidal inclination that they claim was at the root of Mr Casement's antipathy toward the British.

The fifteenth-century implementation of a series of decrees collectively known as Poynings' Law, is another political milestone to which my informants alluded in citing the historical catalogue of grievances that Mr Casement must surely have believed were exemplary of English policy toward Ireland. While the British had asserted their authority over the island for more than three hundred years at that point, the Irish tried to assert their claim to some semblance of self-governance through a Parliament that they had created just thirty years earlier with their 'Declaration of the Independence of the Irish Parliament'. The very idea that they would issue any kind of 'Declaration of Independence' was an affront to the Crown, and under the aggressive leadership of Garret Mór, that new Parliament had become intolerably assertive in the eyes of King Henry VII. Appointed Lord Deputy of Ireland with specific responsibility for bringing its Parliament into line, Sir Edward Poynings issued his decrees in 1494. Poynings made it eminently clear to the Irish Parliamentarians that any legislation they tried to enact on behalf of Ireland had to be endorsed by Westminster before it could take effect, and that any and all legislation enacted by Westminster had the same legal status in Ireland as in England. The Irish Parliament, in other words, was totally subordinated to the Crown, even in matters pertaining uniquely to Ireland, and the Irish were subject to all the laws passed by the British Parliament in Westminster. As noted by many of my Irish informants, Poynings' Law effectively acknowledged what had already become a *fait accompli* – that Ireland was in fact a British colony.

Irish resistance to being treated as a colonial subject became the abiding characteristic of the Anglo-Irish relationship from that point on. The British response to that resistance became increasingly brutal, running through the Elizabethan army's defeat of the Irish at the Battle of Kinsale in 1601 to the reprisals carried out by Oliver Cromwell and his forces at Drogheda in 1649, and culminating in James's defeat by William of Orange at the Battle of the Boyne in 1690. With the flight of the 'Wild Geese', the 14,000 plus members of the Irish army who left Ireland under the terms of the 1691 Treaty of Limerick, Ireland was left virtually defenceless and leaderless as the seventeenth century came to a close – totally subject to British domination.

To add further to the growing sense of injustice, the British conquerors then passed a body of laws that have become known collectively as the Penal Laws, which further disenfranchised and alienated large portions of the Irish population. In its ongoing struggle with the papacy, British Parliament had been gradually instituting measures that would ensure an uninterrupted Protestant line of succession to the monarchy. Given the predominance of Catholicism in Ireland, Westminster determined that the monarchy had to be protected from any threat that the Catholic majority in Ireland might pose to that Protestant line of succession. Beginning with its 1692 edict, that Catholics would henceforth be excluded from holding office in the Irish Parliament in Dublin, the British Parliament, which had been exercising total sovereignty over both England and Ireland for the 200 years since Edward Poynings' decrees, enacted a series of laws over the course of the next seventy-five years to restrict the access of Catholics, and thus the majority of the Irish population, to a multitude of legal, civil, professional, and social prerogatives.

The ban on serving in the Irish Parliament was extended to include the British Parliament, leaving the Catholic majority with no means of influencing legislation to which they would be subject. The Disenfranchising Act of 1728 denied Catholics the right to vote. Catholics were banned from the legal professions and the judiciary as well as from most public offices. Banning Catholics from all teaching positions helped lay the foundation for the gradual eradication of Irish culture, by ensuring that the majority of Irish children would be educated from a purely British perspective. Catholics were banned from intermarrying with Protestants and from being granted custody of orphans. Catholics were banned from the possession of firearms, from serving in the armed forces, from inheriting Protestant land, from leasing land for more than thirty-one years, and from owning a horse with a value greater than £5. Catholics were denied access to a foreign education and from admission to Trinity College, Dublin. To break up any existing estates under Catholic ownership, Catholics who still owned land after the expropriations of the previous couple of centuries were required to bequeath the property equally among all male progeny –

unless one of the male heirs should convert to Protestantism, in which case he would inherit all. A tithing law required all citizens, including Catholics, to pay 10 per cent of their income to the established Church of Ireland. In order to celebrate Mass, priests had to register with their local magistrate's court, for which they had to pay a bond of about £100 as an assurance of 'good behaviour', and they were not allowed to wear clerical garb in public.

While many of the laws ultimately proved to be unworkable and were rescinded, they represented an effort on the part of the British government that has never been forgotten or forgiven by the Irish. Given Mr Casement's extensive knowledge of Irish history, he had to have been deeply affected by the very fact that a 'foreign occupier' would even attempt to effectively eradicate an essential part of the Irish identity and to deny the majority of the population access to the fundamental prerogatives of a civilized society. The Penal Laws had pretty much disappeared by the end of the eighteenth century, but by then the attempt to codify Irish subordination to the Crown received what Mr Casement and his associates had to have considered the final straw – the 1801 Act of Union.

Inspired by the American War for Independence just recently concluded, Irish separatists under the leadership of Theobald Wolfe Tone staged a rebellion in 1798 that shook the authorities in Westminster. Having just lost the American colonies, and still preoccupied with the Napoleonic wars, Britain looked upon this latest Irish rebellion with a degree of trepidation that exceeded any of its earlier confrontations with its contentious Irish subjects. Prime Minister William Pitt came up with a radically simple solution: do away with the half measures of shared sovereignty and simply absorb Ireland into a United Kingdom of Great Britain and Ireland. Under the terms of the Act of Union, the Irish Parliament in Dublin, tolerated for over 300 years in spite of Sir Edward Poynings's attempt to disenfranchise it, was finally dissolved and the newly designated Parliament of the United Kingdom of Great Britain and Ireland at Westminster became the single, abiding legislative body for both Britain and Ireland, now joined together into a single political entity. While Ireland was given representation in an expanded legislative body at Westminster to accommodate its status as a 'coequal' in this new political entity, the fact remained, that the Irish contingent would forever be in the minority when it came to enacting legislation to which Ireland would be subject. And more importantly, according to my sources among the Irish nationalists, was the fact that the Irish as a people were no longer an autonomous race with their own distinctive identity. In spite of any political influence that their new Members of Parliament might wield on their behalf, the Irish were rapidly becoming British.

This concern with identity was apparently as much of a factor in the Irish nationalist movement as were the political and economic grievances. Those acquaintances whom I have been able to interview insist that like many of those involved in the nationalist movement and the Celtic renaissance, Mr Casement was especially disturbed by the extent to which centuries of economic exploitation and political oppression have purportedly contributed to the near annihilation of a once proud and noble race. From their perspective, many of the cultural characteristics that made the Irish distinct are on the verge of extinction. And one of the most distinctive features of any culture is its language.

An admirer of Douglas Hyde, the founder of the Gaelic League, for reviving Irish as a commonly spoken language, Mr Casement apparently made a belated, but vigorous, effort to learn the language of his ancestors – a task made all the more difficult by the exotic nature of the language. Along with Welsh and Breton, Irish is among the oldest languages in Europe. And contrary to what many would assume, given the geographic proximity of the two islands, it is distinctly different from English: while English and Irish are both members of the Indo-European family of languages, they followed different lines of descent from the mother language, with English following the Germanic branch (along with languages like German and Yiddish and the Scandinavian languages) and Irish deriving from the Celtic line of descent (along with languages like Cornish, Breton, and Welsh). The Celtic branch of the Indo-European language family is descended from an indigenous dialect spoken by tribes that occupied central Europe during the Bronze Age, over four thousand years ago. Over the course of several centuries, invading tribes and native tribes in Ireland intermingled, as did their languages, producing a language now known as Gaeilge.

This separate line of descent for the Irish language has made it one of the cultural characteristics that clearly distinguish Irish culture from British, according to those with whom I have spoken in the Irish nationalist movement. British efforts to suppress and denigrate native Irish customs, including its language, brought Gaeilge to the verge of extinction – until Mr Hyde founded *Conradh na Gaeilge* in 1893. With its bilingual journal *Irisleabhar na Gaedhilge* (The Gaelic Journal) and its widely influential newspaper *An Claidheamh Soluis* (The Sword of Light), the League has been the prime mover in the recent Celtic renaissance. Pádraig Pearse, executed in Dublin just two months ago for leading the Easter Rising, was the editor of its newspaper and a leading proponent for reviving Irish culture and language, which apparently became a driving passion for Mr Casement, as well, over the course of his many return visits to his native land.

Whether Mr Casement and Mr Pearse knew each other personally is a question to which I have not yet obtained an answer, but clearly they were kindred spirits in the cultural revival and the consequent upsurge in nationalism that led ultimately to the insurrection that has brought Mr Casement to the dock. Next to the language revival promoted by the *Conradh na Gaeilge*, the revival of ancient mythology and history has been a centrepiece of the Irish cultural renaissance in its effort to restore a sense of pride in the distinctive nature of the national heritage. Alice Stopford Green's *The Making of Ireland and Its Undoing, 1200-1600*, published just eight years ago, and Standish O'Grady's *History of Ireland: Heroic Period*, published thirty-eight years ago, are monuments to the revival of intellectual interest in Irish history from a distinctively Irish perspective.

Contemporary Irish historians like Mrs Green and Mr O'Grady lay claim to the intellectual heritage of the seventeenth-century historians Geoffrey Keating and a group of Franciscan monks known as the 'Four Masters' – Micheál Ó Clérigh and his three associates Lughaidh Ó Clérigh, Fergus O'Mulconry, and Peregrine O'Duigna. Keating and the Four Masters are regarded among scholars of the

Irish nationalist movement as the first historians to attempt a truly objective interpretation of the historical evidence, free of the imperial bias of a foreign conqueror. Keating's *Foras Feasa ar Éirinn* (The Basis of Knowledge Concerning Ireland), completed in 1634, and the Four Masters' *Annála Ríoghachta Éireann* (Annals of the Kingdom of Ireland), produced in 1632, drew upon the written evidence available to them in the monastic archives as well as the oral evidence that they were able to obtain from surviving Brehons. Reflective of the dominant perspective imposed by the occupying forces, however, their contribution to the field of history did not appear in English translation for over two hundred years. It was only in the latter part of the past century that their work has finally received recognition and was consulted by scholars such as Green and O'Grady.

As a part of the turn-of-the-century attempt to revive a sense of unique national and cultural identity, Irish authors like William Butler Yeats, Lady Augusta Gregory, 'Æ' George Russell, Edward Martyn, and John Millington Synge have drawn upon their literary skills to popularise the ancient history and mythology that the intellectual revivalists were uncovering. Lady Gregory's translation of *An Táin Bó Cuailgne* (The Cattle Raid of Cooley), an ancient Irish epic about the heroic exploits of an Ulster teenager named Cúchulainn who single-handedly defeats the invading forces of the Connacht Queen Medb by prevailing in a horrendous three-day battle with her foremost warrior Ferdiad, has become an icon of the literary revivalist movement. Given its accessibility to the average citizen, poetry, fiction, and especially the theatre are effective instruments for promoting cultural awareness among the masses. With the establishment of the Irish Literary Theatre, the Irish National Theatre Society, and the renowned Abbey Theatre, dramatists like Yeats, Synge, and Lady Gregory have been in the forefront of the literary revival of ancient Ireland. Yeats's *Cathleen Ní Houlihan*, the featured presentation for the Abbey Theatre's opening night in December of 1904, has become a classic among Irish nationalists as an allegory of the struggle for independence and the need for a 'blood sacrifice' among young Irish men who will be called upon to sacrifice themselves as martyrs for the cause.

According to my Irish sources, Casement was not only aware of all this activity during his assignments abroad, he was, in fact, an avid promoter, donating much of his meagre financial resources to their support and participating in various ways during those periods of time when he was able to return on holiday or medical leave. Upon his return to Ireland, after the Putumayo investigation, the cultural revival and the nationalistic cause that it spawned apparently became the guiding lights of Casement's redirected mission. He formally resigned from the Foreign Office just three years ago, and devoted his energies to the increasingly virulent separatist movement. And over the course of the past year or so, he appears to have taken it upon himself to assume, what he perceived to be, a leadership role in that movement. In the spirit of mysticism, which is such an essential part of the Irish identity, perhaps he sees himself as the reincarnation of Fionn MacCumhaill, the mythical warrior, who according to legend has been hibernating in a cave beneath the city of Dublin, just waiting for the day when he can awake and summon his band of warriors known as the Fíanna, more recently dubbed Fenians, to come to the salvation of Ireland at the hour of its greatest need. And so, he now rests in the Tower of London, awaiting the trial that could, and most probably will, bring him the martyrdom so eulogised in Yeats's famous play.

Irish nationalists lay claim to the blessing of the venerable St Patrick himself, who is on record for denouncing the oppression of invaders from across the Irish Sea as early as 1,450 years ago in his Epistle to Coroticus. One of only two written documents from the pen of Ireland's patron saint, the other being his autobiography, the epistle was a denunciation of the Welsh chieftain Coroticus for slaughtering a multitude of Irish peasants whom Patrick had recently baptised into the new Christian faith, and whom Coroticus had captured and enslaved. In words that could easily be the rallying cry of Casement and his Irish associates today, Patrick demands to know, 'Is it a disgrace to be Irish? Have we not, as it is written, one and the same God?'[41] Given the sentiments underlying his actions of the past several years, Mr Casement must be contemplating those same questions as he awaits the trial that will commence in less than two weeks.

MONDAY 26 JUNE 1916

The formal trial of Sir Roger Casement began today in the High Court of Justice, presided over by the Lord Chief Justice Rufus Isaacs, the Viscount of Reading, along with Justices Horace Avory and Thomas Horridge. Representatives for the prosecution included the Attorney General, the Honourable Sir Frederick E. Smith, and the Solicitor General, the Honourable Sir George Cave, along with Mr Archibald H. Bodkin, senior counsel for the prosecution, and Messrs Travers Humphreys and G.A.H. Branson, junior counsels for the prosecution. Representatives for the defence included Mr Alexander M. Sullivan, chief defence counsel and Second Sergeant of the Irish Bar, Mr Thomas Artemus Jones, co-counsel for the defence, and Mr John Hartman Morgan, a professor of constitutional law, along with Mr George Gavan Duffy, Mr Casement's solicitor, assisted by Mr Michael Francis Doyle of the American Bar.

The King's Coroner, the court officer who is empowered, not only to hold formal inquests, but also to oversee the administration of indictments and pleas, opened the proceedings with a reading of the indictment. Consisting of six specific counts encompassing the defendant's efforts to recruit an Irish Brigade among the prisoners of war at Limburg an Lahn, and his eventual landing on the coast of Kerry, the complete indictment already appears in my dispatch of 25 May and will not be repeated here.

Before Mr Casement could even enter a plea upon hearing the

indictment, there was a brief moment of judicial drama when Mr Sullivan challenged the legal basis of the charges levelled against his client. Based on a highly technical reading of the 1351 statute, Mr Sullivan argued that since Mr Casement was not, in fact, physically present within the realm at the time of the alleged acts of treason, there was no court that could exercise jurisdiction and therefore, by definition, there was no crime capable of being adjudicated within the terms of the statute. The judges were obviously taken aback by Mr Sullivan's contention and had to interrupt his oration for a conference. Following their deliberation, they ruled that the argument had no proper place at this point of the proceedings and should be held until the prosecution's case had concluded. Mr Sullivan made no attempt to challenge the ruling further, and deferred to his client for a plea of not guilty. Assuming that the objection was not simply a legal ploy to test the waters at this early stage of the proceedings, we can probably expect to hear more from Mr Sullivan on that issue; it will be interesting to hear what kind of legal reasoning he brings to bear on the subject.

One of the first official items of business was the swearing in of twelve jurors to sit in judgement of Mr Casement. For the record, the jurors sworn by the Chief Clerk were: Frederick T. Wheeler, a shipping clerk; Ernest W. West, a schoolmaster; John C. Watts, a warehouseman; Albert J. Abbott, a clerk; Herbert J. Scoble, also a clerk; Richard C. Scantlebury, a shipping agent; Albert G. Scopes, a leather merchant; John Burdon, a mechanical engineer; William B. Card, a baker; William Cole, a coachman; Hyman Saunders, a tailor, and Albert S. Ansley, a bank clerk. Before allowing them to be sworn, the King's Coroner confirmed that the defendant had been given at least ten days to review the list and that he had no objections to their being sworn for his trial. While it is evident from their occupations that Mr Casement will not be tried by a jury of his peers, he nevertheless filed no objection to having them sit in judgement. Objections would have undoubtedly been fruitless, anyway, and I'm sure Mr Casement had other matters on which to focus in preparing for trial. It is somewhat surprising, however, that Mr Sullivan did not raise some concerns; given their backgrounds, it is unlikely that any of the jurors will be able to have any real appreciation for the nature of Mr Casement's professional or educational background, nor for the kinds of experiences to which he was exposed during the course of his career, all of which are essential to understanding what might have motivated the defendant. And while there may be no empirical evidence to support an assumption of conservative bias, I am sure that most pundits would tacitly acknowledge that the political orientation of such a group favours the representatives of the Crown.

Be that as it may, no objection was raised and the jury was seated, allowing the Honourable Attorney General to proceed with his much-anticipated opening statement. In solemn tones befitting the occasion, Mr Smith impressed upon the jury the gravity of the crime of treason, asserting that 'the law knows none graver,'[42] and began his oration with the unequivocal allegation that the defendant standing before them 'has been guilty of this most heinous crime'[43] and that 'he has adhered to the King's enemies and has attempted to seduce His Majesty's soldiers from their allegiance'[44] to the Crown. Following this dramatic introductory condemnation, he proceeded to give a full and thorough synopsis of Mr Casement's illustrious career in the Foreign Office, inferring that Casement's own actions over the course of more than twenty years had clearly established an implicit acknowledgement on his part that he was indeed a loyal subject of the Crown and thus bound by the laws and responsibilities pursuant thereto. By immediately introducing this line of argument, Mr Smith was presumably laying the groundwork to counter what most observers believe will be one of the major defence premises – that Mr Casement, as an Irishman, was engaged in an act of war rather than an act of treason. And by presenting such a stark contrast between Casement's lifetime of service to the Crown and his more recent collaboration with Germany, the Honourable Attorney General was also able to generate a degree of outrage that will surely influence the jury during this time of war.

He then went on to summarise Casement's activities in Germany, specifically those activities related to the recruitment of an Irish Brigade at the Limburg an Lahn prisoner of war camp – the heart of the prosecution's case for treason. With transparent scorn, he portrayed

Casement as a seducer, taking advantage of innocent young men at a time of maximum vulnerability, using charm when possible, and coercion when necessary, to enlist them in the pursuit of a cause they not only did not share, but actually found abhorrent. With ill-concealed contempt, Mr Smith suggested that while pleading for them to sacrifice their honour, integrity, and most probably their lives in taking up arms against England, it was unlikely that Casement 'dwelt upon his own connection with the country which had afforded him a career, which had decorated him with a title, and from which he had accepted a pension'.[45] The implied hypocrisy was surely not lost upon the jury, a further attempt by Mr Smith to stoke the fires of outrage.

Mr Smith then proceeded to describe in great detail how Mr Casement came to be captured on the coast of Kerry and how a German vessel carrying arms for the Irish insurrection was intercepted and scuttled just off the coast of Ireland, and how all this was linked to the failed insurrection of Easter weekend, implying in no uncertain terms that Mr Casement was a key, if not the central, figure in that tragic and misguided escapade. My Irish sources in attendance today visibly struggled to contain themselves when the Honourable Attorney General introduced his summation of these events by saying that, 'We must now pass to that unhappy country which has been the victim in its history of so many cruel and cynical conspiracies, but surely never of a conspiracy more cruel and more cynical than this.'[46] While Mr Smith was using every rhetorical device at his command to convince the jury of Casement's guilt, it seemed fairly obvious that he was also attempting to portray the defendant in a way that would alienate those for whom he claimed to be fighting.

Mr Smith concluded his remarks with a typical prosecutorial flourish, claiming that, 'The prisoner, blinded by a hatred for this country, as malignant in quality as it was sudden in origin, has played a desperate hazard. He has played it and he has lost it. Today the forfeit is claimed.'[47] The prosecution then opened the formal presentation of its case with a series of witnesses, several of whom had already testified at Mr Casement's arraignment in May at the Bow Street Police Court: John Cronin, formerly a private in the 2nd Battalion of the Royal Munster Fusiliers;

Daniel O'Brien, formerly with the Leinster Regiment and the 19th Hussars; William Egan, a member of the Royal Irish Rifles, and Michael O'Connor, a corporal in the Royal Irish Regiment. These four who testified at the arraignment, were joined by three additional witnesses, including John Robinson, who had been a corporal in the Royal Army Medical Corps; Michael Moore, currently a member of the Royal Army Medical Corps serving on the HMS *Cambria* at Dover, and John Neill, a member of the 2nd Battalion of the 18th Royal Irish Regiment. All seven witnesses had been prisoners of war at Limburg an Lahn, before returning to England as part of a prisoner exchange negotiated with Germany. Mr Smith provided no details about how these particular prisoners happened to be included in the exchange; while I am still attempting to determine whether Germany itself had any ulterior motives in identifying them for the exchange, it is becoming increasingly apparent that this will be a matter for historians to address, given the limited access that we in the media have to German authorities during this time of war.

Through direct examination of the witnesses, the prosecution clearly established that from the end of December 1914 until the middle of February 1915, Mr Casement visited the Irish prisoners at Limburg an Lahn and actively, albeit futilely, recruited them for service in an Irish Brigade that would fight with Germany against England to achieve Irish independence. Mr Sullivan made no attempt to counter that specific charge, effectively conceding that his client had in fact collaborated with Germany to intervene militarily in the Irish independence movement. During his cross-examination, however, he did try to raise a question as to whether that in itself constituted treason. He was able, for example, to elicit testimony to the effect that the Brigade was being formed specifically to land in Ireland for the sole purpose of achieving independence from England, hoping that such testimony would dispel the prosecution's insinuations that the Irish Brigade would have participated in the general German war effort against England. Mr Sullivan also made every effort to question the timeframe of the proposed venture, trying on numerous occasions to lead the witnesses into testifying that the insurrection was to take place after Germany had won the war – presuming, of course, that Germany would indeed win the war. The apparent objective was to further undermine the charge of treason by suggesting that the collaboration with England's enemy was not intended to affect the outcome of the war, but only to take advantage of what was presumed would be an eventual German victory as a way of supporting the Irish independence movement.

The prosecution also went to great lengths to establish that coercion had been used as a part of Mr Casement's recruiting efforts. Several of the witnesses testified, for example, that their rations had been reduced when it became clear that very few of the prisoners were going to sign up for the Brigade. Mr Sullivan tried to counter by establishing through his cross-examination that the reduction in rations was applied universally throughout the camp at Limburg and that nationalities other than Irish were among the prisoners being held at that location. This whole line of questioning struck me as beside the point, since the recruiting methods were technically irrelevant to the key issue: Mr Casement's intentions for the Irish Brigade.

Establishing coercion as a recruiting tool seemed again to be a tactical effort on the part of the prosecution to inflame the emotions of the jury against Mr Casement. This, of course, made it necessary for Mr Sullivan to deflate those emotions as best he could during cross-examination. The back and forth manoeuvring between direct and cross-examination was all part of the traditional courtroom jockeying between prosecution and defence in their attempts to gain favour with the jury. Unfortunately for Mr Casement, this is a case where the composition of the jury, unchallenged by Mr Sullivan at the start of the proceedings, is likely to favour the prosecution.

In their responses to the prosecution's direct examination, several of the witnesses also alluded to a number of publications that they had seen in Mr Casement's hands during his visits to the prisoner of war camp – specifically the *Gaelic American*, the *Continental Times*, and a book called *The Crime against Europe* that Mr Casement himself had authored. Sources whom I interviewed for earlier dispatches in this series had already brought the last of these to my attention, I had an opportunity to obtain a copy and read it before the trial convened this morning. As a lifelong diplomat and widely read historian, Mr Casement had much to draw upon in developing his thesis. The book gives a great deal of insight into Mr Casement's political thought and its role in guiding his actions *vis-à-vis* England, Germany, and Ireland over the past couple of years. It will be interesting to see whether the defence (or the prosecution, for that matter) alludes to the book's content in providing an intellectual context within which to view Mr Casement's actions.

Released in December of 1914, when Mr Casement had already arrived in Germany, the book is a collection of essays that purport to examine the circumstances that made war inevitable and to assign culpability for those circumstances. He draws extensively upon the political insights he acquired from his twenty-year career in the Foreign Service and reinforces those insights with a broad range of historical knowledge, giving the book an authoritative aura designed to make a convincing case for his position. A reading of that book supports the hypothesis that Mr Casement's collusion with Germany was not an impulsive act, which some of his apologists have suggested in promoting an insanity defence, nor that it was simply motivated with a view to gaining Irish independence, although that would have been a significant factor, given the political views articulated in the book. The rationale and the supporting analysis make it clear that Mr Casement's attachment to Germany was well thought out and intellectually founded, although, the prosecution would argue, misguided. Some discussion of the book seems warranted at this point as a way of gaining greater insight into the broader range of thinking that motivated and guided Mr Casement in taking the actions that have brought him to the brink of the scaffold.

He begins his analysis by questioning the pretexts offered by those who have allied themselves against Germany – the Triple Entente or Entente Cordiale, both of which are used by Mr Casement at various times in reference to the alliance among Russia, France, and Great Britain. From his historical perspective, Mr Casement argues that there was no reason to fear Germany's militarisation, suggesting that it was a purely defensive response to what it perceived as a threat from those neighbours who have now come together to form the Triple Entente. From his perspective, Germany has never attempted to impose itself militarily upon its neighbours since it became an empire under Kaiser Wilhelm in 1871, and there is therefore no historical justification for believing that it has any expansionist motives behind its military build-up.

In contrast, he suggests that France and Russia have been building up their ground forces far in excess of what would reasonably be required for their self-defence, implying that they are the ones with expansionist ambitions. Based on that premise, Germany can justifiably feel threatened and therefore compelled to respond in kind, with a massive militarisation effort to defend itself against possible aggression. In Casement's words, German militarism 'was born, not of wars of aggression, but of wars of defence and unification'.[48] The wars of unification, of course, were the internal struggles from which the German Empire emerged in 1871. Referring to the use of its military might since that 1871 unification, Mr Casement goes on to claim that, 'Since it was melded by blood and iron into the great human organism of the last forty years, it has not been employed beyond the frontiers of Germany until last year.'[49] And that, of course, was when Germany found itself at war with the Triple Entente.

He further suggests that Russia and France are both self-sufficient, possessing within their own borders the resources for national survival, and that it is Germany that needs to expand, not necessarily in geographic terms but in commercial terms, in order to sustain itself. And this, according to Mr Casement, is where a confrontation between Germany and England became inevitable. Lacking sufficient natural resources within its own borders, Germany began to expand its commercial reach into the global marketplace. Given the vast global network of commercial enterprises already established by England, this led to an encroachment upon British interests which the Crown then perceived as a threat to its Empire. Based on the assumption that world trade is a zero sum game, England saw German gains as British losses and responded accordingly. In Casement's words, 'Let Germany acquire a coaling station, a sanatorium, a health resort, the ground for a hotel even, on some foreign shore, and 'British interests spring to attention.'[50] The competition finally became too much for England to tolerate; according to Mr Casement's data, 'During the first six months of 1914, German export trade almost equalled that of Great Britain. Another year of peace and it would certainly have exceeded it and for the first time in the history of world trade, Great Britain would have been put in second place.'[51]

Casement paraphrases Britain's response with the words, 'German expansion is not to be tolerated. It can only be a threat to or attained at the expense of British interests.'[52] To contain that threat, Britain exploited the internal tensions within Europe to form the Triple Entente, allying the ground forces of Russia and France with its vast naval force to capitalise upon the circumstances precipitated by the assassination of Arch Duke Franz Ferdinand as a pretext for war with Germany. By convincing Russia and France that it was in their mutual best interest to confront Germany together, Britain was able to bring together nations with disparate interests into an alliance with one shared interest, i.e. the containment of Germany. His argument suggests strongly that the Triple Entente is nothing more than the product of another British ruse to delude other European nations into unwittingly fighting for continued British hegemony on the world stage. Referring to the public perception promoted by the Government that England and its allies intervened to deter German aggression and to protect that empire's smaller, more vulnerable neighbours, Casement contends that, 'England fights not to defend the neutrality of Belgium, not to destroy German militarism, but to retain, if need be by involving the whole world in war, her supreme and undisputed ownership of the seas.'[53]

Mr Casement clearly blames England for the conflict that has devastated the continent with unprecedented savagery for the past two years. From his point of view, Germany's commercial expansion was justified as a necessary step in its national development and England's response to that expansion was nothing more than a projection of raw power in its attempt to maintain a worldwide empire under the domination of the Crown. Driven by its greed to maintain a network of subjugated colonies, rather than by any genuine concern about national security, Britain's suggestion that German expansion would inevitably threaten its own survival was a disingenuous justification for Britain to confront this emerging nation before it could become a major power.

Given British commercial interests as the roots of the current war,

Mr Casement then goes on to discuss how those roots have not only affected the relationship between England and Germany specifically, but have also undermined the development of Europe more generally. With its vast naval power, England has been able to control world trade to its own advantage for decades. But naval power alone was not enough to guarantee that dominance; it was British control over Ireland that made it all possible. As the gateway to the Atlantic and the high seas beyond, Ireland has been the lynchpin in England's global hegemony. And maintaining that stranglehold on the world's economy is England's number one priority, according to Mr Casement. As he puts it, 'To subdue that western and ocean-closing island and to exploit its resources, its people, and above all its position, to the sole advantage of the eastern island, has been the set aim of every English government from the days of Henry VIII onward.'[54] And that, according to Mr Casement, is the essence of England's crime against Europe, its use of Ireland's geographic position to deny free access to the riches of the world for the rest of Europe.

In words that clearly reflect Casement's esteem for the German character over his regard for the British, he asserts that:

> It is evident that some 7 million of the best educated race in the world, physically strong, mentally stronger, homogeneous, highly trained, highly skilled, capable and energetic and obedient to a discipline that rests upon and is moulded by a lofty conception of patriotism, cannot permanently be confined to a strictly limited area by a less numerous race, less well educated, less strong mentally and physically, and assuredly less well trained, skilled and disciplined.[55]

Nor is it the 'ethical superiority of the English race that accounts for their lead'.[56] From Mr Casement's perspective, it is clearly 'the favourable geographical situation from which they have been able to develop and direct their policy of expansion'.[57] He even quotes former British Prime Minister William Gladstone as an authoritative voice for the Crown, 'Can anyone say we should have treated Ireland as we have done had she lain not between us and the ocean, but between us and Europe?'[58]

Mr Casement sums up the first two chapters of his book by para-phrasing what he believes to be the essence of British thought:

> German influence cannot but be hostile to British interests. The two peoples are too much alike. The qualities that have made England great they possess in a still greater degree. Given a fair field and no favour, they are bound to beat us. They will beat us out of every market in the world, and we shall be reduced ultimately to a position like that of France today. Better fight while we are still the stronger. Better hinder now ere it be too late ... To tolerate a German rivalry is to found a German empire and to destroy our own.[59]

By allying the European nations against Germany under the guise of an artificial pretext, Britain will also be able to reinforce its control of world commerce by once again diverting European attention from the real threat to continental prosperity, that being England's control of access to the high seas through Ireland.

It is clear, from his own writing, that Mr Casement's collusion with Germany was based, not simply upon an impassioned reaction to the historical animosity between Britain and Ireland, although that passion is surely evident throughout the text, but also upon a well-thought -out political philosophy. It is also clear that he is temperamentally inclined to regard the German 'race' as superior to the British, attribut-ing British dominance to its ability throughout history to distract the rest of Europe from the significance of its control over Ireland. If Mr Casement's analysis has any basis in fact, his trial may have political dimensions that are not readily apparent to my American readers.

That trial resumes tomorrow, at which time the prosecution is expected to focus on Mr Casement's role in the recent insurrection. It will be interesting to see whether the prosecution makes any effort to introduce *The Crime against Europe* into evidence. The German senti-ments and British antipathies expressed in that book certainly provide a credible motivation for participating in what has now become known colloquially as the Easter Rising.

TUESDAY 27 JUNE 1916

The prosecution in the trial of Sir Roger Casement turned its attention today to his capture on the coast of Kerry, calling upon a number of witnesses who participated, either directly or indirectly, in bringing him before the current tribunal. The grizzled and laconic John McCarthy, the early-rising farmer from Curraghane, led off with the account of his discovery of the abandoned boat and his little daughter's excavation of the Mauser pistol that had been partially buried in the sand. Few new details were added to the testimony that he had provided at the arraignment hearing before the Bow Street Police Court (see my dispatch of 16 May), except for a belated explanation for his early-morning jaunt along the Strand.

The defence was apparently as curious as I about what could possibly have drawn him from his bed at that ungodly hour. In response to Mr Sullivan's prodding, he explained that he had gone out to pray beside a well. To pray beside a well? It took a helpful nudge from the Attorney General for Mr McCarthy finally to intimate that it was a holy well, according to local lore, and that being Good Friday morn, he felt compelled to seek it out as an appropriate place to pray. After a bit of playful cross-examination about the location and significance of this 'holy well', all of which Mr McCarthy took very seriously, opposing counsel tacitly accepted that the reason for Mr McCarthy's presence on the beach was really of no direct relevance to the issue before the court.

Testimony from Thomas J. Hearn, the sergeant from the Royal Irish Constabulary who took Mr Casement into custody at McKenna's Fort on 21 April, from Bernard Riley, the RIC constable who assisted sergeant Hearn in Mr Casement's apprehension, and from Frederick A. Britten, the RIC district inspector for that jurisdiction, established the facts of the case relative to the defendant's arrest (the details are simply a repetition of the testimony provided at the arraignment hearing, covered in my dispatch of 16 May). During his cross-examination of Hearn and Britten, however, Mr Sullivan ventured into interesting territory that had not yet been touched upon publicly, apparently to provide a context that would help explain what led to the armed insurrection. Both RIC officials readily admitted that they were aware of the political tensions surrounding the issue of Home Rule, and that those tensions escalated considerably when the Government of Ireland Act came before Parliament in April of 1912 and again in each of the next two years, ultimately achieving passage on 25 May 1914 (see details in my dispatch of 18 May).

As was reported earlier, the Ulster Unionist Party, under the leadership of Sir Edward Carson (a colleague and immediate predecessor of Mr Smith, the Attorney General presiding over Mr Casement's trial) openly and militantly opposed the Home Rule Bill from the time of its introduction in 1912. During their testimony today, Messrs Hearn and Britten acknowledged that press reports in the *Cork Examiner* and the *Independent* and *The Irish Times* had kept them fully aware of the inflammatory rhetoric at the rallies staged by the Unionists. While it is generally known that Messrs Carson and Smith were among those delivering the inflammatory speeches, Mr Sullivan carefully avoided any questions that would have elicited that information in today's public testimony. He was obviously treading a fine line with Mr Smith, sitting just across the room with the full power and authority of the Crown invested in him as the currently presiding Attorney General.

Messrs Hearn and Britten also acknowledged that the gun-running activities by the Ulster Volunteer Force and by the Irish Volunteers was a matter of common knowledge, as both sides armed themselves in anticipation of civil war over the Home Rule issue. They further acknowledged that the arms were being carried openly and that both sides were engaging in drills and mock combat, all in the open and without any official interference from the police. The volatility of the situation naturally made the population uneasy, to say the least. And as Mr Sullivan elicited from Sergeant Hearn under cross-examination, the pervasive fear of incipient violence was exacerbated by the Curragh 'mutiny' of 20 March 1914.

The Curragh Camp in County Kildare was the main British army base in Ireland. Sir Arthur Paget, commander of the base, received orders from the War Office in London to begin assembling his troops for deployment to Ulster, where they were to be prepared to quell any armed effort by the Ulster Volunteers to oppose the Home Rule Bill that was about to be implemented. Led by Brigadier General Hubert Gough, fifty-seven of the unit's seventy officers tendered their resignations rather than be part of any military action against the Unionists. By offering to resign, rather than directly refusing to obey an order, they avoided an official charge of mutiny, although their action was tantamount to the same thing. The Asquith government immediately backed off, rather than risk the embarrassment of a mass resignation, attributing the entire episode to a 'misunderstanding'. As a result of the 'misunderstanding', however, it was clear that in spite of its official support of Home Rule, the Asquith government was not going to use force against the Unionists who were preparing for armed resistance to its implementation. Clearly, the Ulster Volunteer Force took encouragement from the incident and the Irish Volunteers recognised that they could not depend on the government in any struggle that might ensue.

The clear implication from Mr Sullivan's cross-examination of Messrs Hearn and Britten, was that the political situation in Ireland was like a tinder-box just waiting for a spark to ignite it and turn it into an inferno, and that the officials ostensibly responsible for maintaining order were doing nothing to forestall the impending tragedy. Again, Mr Sullivan was treading a fine line, as he avoided the obvious next level of enquiry, i.e. by whose authority the police inaction became official policy. After all, in spite of the Curragh incident, the police were still charged with enforcing the 1914 Arms Proclamation, under which gun smuggling and the arming of private militia were clearly illegal. As noted in my dispatch of 25 May, the testimony of Colonel E. Johnston, Chief Commissioner of the Dublin Metropolitan Police, when he appeared before the Royal Commission investigating the circumstances surrounding the Easter insurrection, would seem to have established that the authority came from Dublin Castle, presumably from Messrs Nathan and Birrell. Since Johnston, Nathan, and Birrell are not on Mr Sullivan's witness list, it would appear that he is not going to pursue the issue further, apparently assuming that the cross-examination of Sergeant Hearn and Inspector Britten has sufficiently established the volatile context within which the defendant's actions must be judged.

The only additional details of the arrest presented today that were not presented at the arraignment hearing, were details about the content of the slip of paper that Mr Casement dropped as he was being led from McKenna's Fort on 21 April. It will be recalled from my dispatch of 16 May, that a young boy named Martin Collins saw the defendant drop the document clandestinely as he was being led from the scene. Entered on the record as prosecution Exhibit 18, the document was described as a guide for coded communications, presumably with the German authorities who were conspiring with Casement. Constable Riley quoted extensively from the document to illustrate its apparent use. The guide consisted of a long list of phrases, with each phrase preceded by a number, presumably so the transmitter of coded messages could substitute numbers for phrases, ensuring that the message could be deciphered only by someone with an identical guide. 'Cease communications' (preceded by the number 00611) and 'await further instructions' (proceeded by the number 00615), for example, could be transmitted as 00611/00615 and deciphered as 'Cease communications and await further instructions.' Many of the phrases could be clearly understood as having to do with a military operation, like 'further ammunition is needed' or 'will send plan about landing' or 'send more explosives'. The document was a pretty solid piece of circumstantial evidence that Mr Casement had landed on the coast of Kerry as part of a military operation.

The Honourable Sir George Cave, the Solicitor General, then concluded the case for the prosecution by reading the entirety of prosecution Exhibit 4 to the jury. This was the written plea that Mr Casement had circulated to the Irish prisoners at Limburg an Lahn (the same document from which Mr Bodkin had quoted at the arraignment hearing on 15 May). Mr Cave naturally wanted to punctuate the prosecution's case by ending with Casement's own words in evidence against him. While it was naturally difficult to transcribe the text of the document verbatim from Mr Cave's reading in court today, I had already obtained a copy following Mr Bodkin's reading at the arraignment and am able to quote it in its entirety, just as Mr Cave did today in court:

> Irishmen! Here is a chance for you to fight for Ireland! You have fought for England, your country's hereditary enemy. You have fought for Belgium in England's interest, though it was no more to you than the Fiji Islands. Are you willing to fight for your own country? With a view to securing the national freedom of Ireland, with the moral and material assistance of the German Government, an Irish Brigade is being formed. The object of the Irish Brigade shall be to fight solely the cause of Ireland, and under no circumstance shall it be directed to any German end. The Irish Brigade shall be formed and shall fight under the Irish flag alone; the men shall wear a special, distinctly Irish uniform, and have Irish officers. The Irish Brigade shall be clothed, fed, and efficiently equipped with arms and ammunition by the German Government. It shall be stationed near Berlin and be treated as guests of the German Government. At the end of the war the German Government undertakes to send each member of the Brigade who may so desire it to the United States of America, with necessary means to land. The Irishmen in America are collecting money for the Brigade. Those men who do not join the Irish Brigade will be removed from Limburg and distributed to other camps. If interested, see you company commanders. Join the Irish Brigade and win Ireland's independence! Remember Bachelor's Walk! God save Ireland![60]

With those words ringing in the jury's ears, the prosecution rested its case. I was somewhat surprised by the fact that they had not called Mr

Bailey to testify. As my readers will no doubt recall, Mr Bailey is the Irish Brigade member who was captured with Mr Casement on the coast of Kerry, who gave lengthy testimony during the arraignment hearing about Mr Casement's activities in Germany and about how they arrived together in Ireland on a German submarine. Obviously, the prosecution believes it has established a case for treason without the benefit of Mr Bailey's testimony, but without it, there is no official record before the court covering Mr Casement's collusion with Germany, beyond what occurred in the Limburg prisoner of war camp. One can only wonder whether there is something that the prosecution wants to avoid confronting in the person of Mr Bailey.

In listening to Mr Cave read the flyer that Casement distributed to the prisoners at the Limburg camp, I was struck by a phrase, the significance of which escaped me when I heard Mr Bodkin read the same document at the arraignment hearing. 'The object of the Irish Brigade shall be to fight solely the cause of Ireland, and under no circumstances shall it be directed to any German end.' This phrase, integral to the very document that the prosecution considers the lynchpin of its case for treason, is remarkably supportive of the case that Mr Sullivan was attempting to make yesterday during his cross-examination of the returned Irish prisoners – that Casement was not conspiring to support Germany in its war with England, and that he is therefore not guilty of treason.

The prosecution would no doubt argue that unless Britain were simply to concede to the demands of the Irish nationalists, a scenario as unlikely as acceding to the demands of the German High Command, diverting the troops and resources that would be required to deal with such an insurrection would effectively serve the military interests of Germany in its war against the Crown. But since the prosecution ended its case with that document, I really expected Mr Sullivan to do or say something that would immediately highlight the exculpatory significance of that phrase, while the document was still fresh in the minds of the jury as a 'prosecution' exhibit. Instead, he immediately took up the motion that the Lord Chief Justice had suggested he defer until this point in the trial, that being the motion to quash the indictment as unsupported by the 1351 statute, 25 Edward III, under which the charge of treason had been filed. The remainder of the day was consumed by a long and tortuous discussion among Mr Sullivan and the presiding justices over case law, legal precedent, and semantics, all revolving around the interpretation and legal application of the 1351 statute's phrase stipulating that a man is guilty of high treason if he 'be adherent to the King's enemies in his realm, giving to them aid and comfort in the realm or elsewhere'.[61]

Given my lack of legal background and limited understanding of British common law, the arguments back and forth were almost impossible to follow, but Mr Sullivan's approach seemed to follow two general tactics: first, to convince the court that learned legal opinion to the contrary, there was no precedent in case law to support the charge of treason against Mr Casement; and second, to convince them that such a precedent being absent, there was no legal basis upon which to support a charge of treason within the strict terms of the statute being cited by the prosecution. Mr Sullivan took issue with a number of legal authorities whose interpretations of the law were apparently well regarded and generally accepted by scholars in the field. These included: Sir Edward Coke, an eminent seventeenth-century jurist and interpreter of common law, who became Attorney General in 1593, Chief Justice of the Court of Common Pleas in 1606, and Chief Justice of the King's Bench in 1613; Sir Matthew Hale, another eminent seventeenth-century jurist who was the Lord Chief Justice from 1671 to 1676 and author of the authoritative *History of the Common Law of England*; and Baron Colin Blackburn, who was regarded as the highest authority on British common law when he joined the Court of Appeal in 1876.

After going to great lengths to argue against the interpretations inherited from these authorities in the field, Mr Sullivan, obviously approaching a state of both physical and mental exhaustion, tried to summarise his position at the end of the day by stipulating that, 'Textbooks are no authority on the construction of a statute unless they are vouched by judicial decisions that that construction is right. The statute is the primary expounder of its own meaning; the textbook is an excellent

exposition of what was the received opinion of lawyers after the statute.'[62] If I understand his position correctly, he was arguing that in every
example of case law that he cited as constituting generally accepted legal
precedent for defining treason, the interpretations provided by the legal
scholars was irrelevant to the case currently before the court, since, in his
judgement, none of the cases truly involved the jurisdictional issue that
he was attempting to address. The Lord Chief Justice agreed that the statute must speak for itself, but pointed out that three or four centuries of
learned interpretation cannot be easily disregarded 'unless you can find
something which shows that those opinions are entirely wrong'.[63]

In attempting to show 'that those opinions are entirely wrong', Mr
Sullivan's position appears to be that Mr Casement was outside the
realm at the time he committed his acts, and therefore beyond the
jurisdiction of the statute, based on the statute's stipulation that a man is
guilty of treason if he be 'adherent to the King's enemies in his realm'.
Mr Sullivan's parsing of the statute's language seems to be a rather desperate attempt to circumvent the charges on the basis of a technicality,
but Mr Casement's situation is indeed desperate and in need of desperate measures. As seems to be the wont of most legal scholars, the
Lord Chief Justice and his associates on the bench have been enjoying
this opportunity to engage in an intellectual wrestling match over the
esoteric meaning of an ancient statute. After what seemed like hours
of arcane debate, the Lord Chief Justice ended the day on a note of
levity, by asking Mr Sullivan, with regard to his assertion that there
are no direct precedents in the existing body of case law, 'May not the
reason be that you do not get cases of treason or adhering to the enemy
without the realm reported in our textbooks, because when a person
commits treason without the realm he takes care to stay there?'[64]

Having reached the end of an exhausting day of legal argument, the
court adjourned until tomorrow morning, at which time Mr Sullivan
will presumably continue his argument that Mr Casement's actions do
not constitute treason within the terms of the statute, under which he
has been charged. In the meantime, let me elucidate further on the
relevance of Mr Casement's book and what that book can tell us about
his motivations.

As noted in my dispatch of yesterday, Casement holds England directly responsible for the war that has ravaged Europe over the course of the past two years. Writing even before the outbreak of the current conflict, Casement states unequivocally that he believes, 'England to be the enemy of European peace, and that until her "mastery of the sea" is overmastered by Europe, there can be no peace on earth or goodwill among men'.[65] Germany, on the other hand, is portrayed as the victim of British political machinations that have produced an unholy alliance of European nations, all of whom have been duped into believing that they share a common interest with Britain when, in fact, their participation in the alliance will, ultimately, redound to the sole benefit of England and their continued exclusion from the full benefits of world trade. With its hold over Ireland giving it control of access to the high seas, England has monopolised world trade for centuries, all the while managing to conceal the true extent of this 'crime against Europe' from those continental neighbours who have consistently failed to recognise the significance of Ireland's position.

Casement is obviously enamoured of Germany and its people. Given their superiority over the British in every way, there is simply no way for England to answer the perceived threat of Germany's emergence as a world power without manipulating others into supporting the British efforts against Germany. The formation of the Triple Entente was a significant first step in that direction; the ongoing courtship of the United States to join in the struggle against the Teutonic tiger is a step that she continues to pursue. In referring to England's plans to retain world dominance, he makes it clear that, 'Those plans can succeed only by active American support, and to secure this is now the supreme task and aim of British stealth and skill.'[66]

By suggesting that Germany could eventually threaten American interests, specifically in the Latin American sphere of influence encompassed by the Monroe Doctrine, England hopes to convince the United States that it, too, should join those nations that have come together in opposition to German ascendancy. Mr Casement is scathing, however, in his characterization of British attitudes toward the United States as totally hypocritical, drawing upon historical examples to illustrate a tradition of hostility toward her former colony – a hostility that has only been tempered by the pragmatic need for additional support against a superior 'race' that it cannot hope to defeat on its own, and perhaps not even with the support of its Triple Entente allies. But pragmatism is ultimately the basis for all political alliances, and Britain is counting on the United States to believe that it is in its national interest to forget the past and ally itself with its former sovereign against a potentially new threat.

Despite British success in mobilising allied support against Germany, Casement remains confident throughout that the superior qualities of the German nation and its people will ultimately prove decisive in gaining a military victory for this upstart nation. But a German military victory will not resolve the issue of British dominance if the Irish question remains unaddressed. As Casement states categorically:

> ...to realise the economic and political fruits of that victory, Ireland must be detached from the British Empire. To leave a defeated England still in full possession of Ireland would be not to settle the question of German rights at sea or in world affairs, but merely to postpone the settlement to a second and possibly far greater encounter.[67]

Indeed, leaving Britain in possession of Ireland, even in spite of a military defeat, would allow her to continue to benefit from the 'crime against Europe' that she has been perpetrating for well over three hundred years.

There is no doubt that Mr Casement is passionately opposed to British control over Ireland and would do whatever he could to relieve Ireland of its historical subordination to the Crown. This is no more clearly stated than in his use of a quote from a Michael Davitt letter to Morrison Davidson in August of 1902:

> The idea of being ruled by Englishmen is to me the chief agony of existence. They are a nation without faith, truth or conscience ... They profess Christianity and believe only in Mammon. They talk of liberty while ruling India and Ireland against the principles of a constitution, professed as a political faith but prostituted to the interests of class and landlord rule.[68]

Achieving Irish independence from Britain is obviously an underlying objective in his entire argument.

But by casting the situation in a much larger European context, Casement makes every intellectual effort to suggest that it is not just Germany and Ireland that will suffer if England is allowed to prevail, but Europe generally. Germany will be denied its rightful place in world affairs and Ireland will continue to be a subjugated and exploited island. But on a much larger scale, the entire continent of Europe will suffer the consequences of a crime that has never been rectified. The cause of Irish independence is directly served by his plea that Ireland be detached from the British Empire, but by placing that cause in the broader context of a European struggle for greater economic prosperity and political influence, Mr Casement gives his argument a more universal and less nationalistic provenance. In that context, Germany emerges as Europe's potential saviour in its struggle with England.

To quote Mr Casement at length:

> The honesty and integrity of the German mind, the strength of the German intellect, the skill of the German hand and brain, the justice and vigour of German law, the intensity of German culture, science, education and social development, these need a great and healthy field for their beneficial display, and the world needs these things more than it needs British mastery of the seas. The world of European life needs today, as it needed in the days of a decadent Roman Empire, the coming of another Goth, the coming of the Teuton. The interposing island in the North Sea alone intervenes. How to surmount that obstacle, how to win the freedom of the 'Seven Seas' for Europe, must be the supreme issue for Germany.[69]

He concludes his paean to Germany as Europe's presumptive saviour with the words, 'The challenge of Europe must be to England, and the champion of Europe must be and can be only Germany. No other European people has the power, the strength of mind, of purpose and of arm to accomplish the great act of deliverance.'[70] Twice before in the past 315 years, a potential European saviour had emerged to intervene in the Irish struggle for independence – first in 1601, when Spain joined the forces of Hugh O'Neill as they went down to ignominious defeat at the Battle of Kinsale, and again in 1798, when France attempted unsuccessfully to intervene on behalf of the insurrection launched by Theobald Wolfe Tone. In both cases, however, the interventions were motivated more by the need to divert English forces from ongoing conflicts between those nations and the Crown, than by genuine interest in Irish independence. In neither case did the intervening power recognise the greater significance of what British control over Ireland meant to the continent as a whole. In any case, both interventions failed for a variety of reasons and as Mr Casement reminds the reader throughout his book, defeating England militarily is never enough anyway: freeing Ireland must be integral to the overall campaign, or all will ultimately be for naught.

Whether Mr Casement truly believes in the underlying argument of this political treatise, or is simply using that argument to leverage his appeal for Irish independence, is a question that can be debated *ad nauseam*. What cannot be debated, however, is the clear appeal for a German victory in the conflict with England, whether in the long run that appeal will truly benefit Europe as a whole or simply benefit Ireland alone. At one point, he very clearly states that, 'I have no fear … of a German triumph: I pray for it.'[71] It seems to this reporter, at least, that such a sentiment can certainly be construed as treasonous.

WEDNESDAY 28 JUNE 1916

The trial of Sir Roger Casement resumed today with an unexpected turn of events. As noted in my dispatch yesterday, Mr Sullivan appeared to be both mentally and physically exhausted after the long, arduous legal argument that he presented over the course of several hours. He did not appear to be capable of continuing this morning and asked the Lord Chief Justice to allow his associate, Mr John Hartman Morgan, to take up the issue on his behalf.

Mr Morgan is widely known and well regarded within governmental and judicial circles alike. He is a professor of constitutional law, who has been consulted extensively by officials in the Home Office about the constitutional issues affecting the status of Ireland during the run-up to the Home Rule vote in Parliament. As a matter of fact, he edited a significant volume on that subject, just four years ago, when he released *The New Irish Constitution*. He is known, most recently, for an investigative report that appeared earlier this year on German atrocities that have been committed during the ongoing conflict on the continent, primarily in Belgium.

Mr Sullivan's request created an immediate dilemma for the Lord Chief Justice. As Lord Reading pointed out, when he approved the appointment of defence counsel on Monday, the defence is limited by law to just two official legal representatives, whom the defence team agreed would be Mr Sullivan and Mr Jones. Lord Reading nevertheless agreed to allow Messrs Morgan, Duffy, and Doyle to join the team as advisers, no doubt to ensure that Mr Casement receives every benefit of the doubt in this highly politicised public trial, but by asking permission for Mr Morgan to officially address the court in oral argument, Mr Sullivan's request today effectively elevated Mr Morgan to a significantly higher status than that of mere 'adviser'. Lord Reading handled the dilemma well, by agreeing to hear Mr Morgan as *amicus curiae* in the matter, rather than as official defence counsel, thus once again allowing the defence some latitude, in order to forestall any future claim that Mr Casement was denied reasonable opportunity to defend himself. I suspect that there was also some intellectual curiosity involved; as noted in my dispatch of yesterday, the justices appeared to enjoy the intellectual jousting match with Mr Sullivan. I'm sure they were eager to hear what a noted academic in the field of constitutional law can contribute to the argument about the statute's applicability.

Unfortunately, I was no better able to follow Mr Morgan than I was Mr Sullivan, although the exchanges between him and the presiding justices were a bit more pointed than the exchanges with Mr Sullivan yesterday, so the justices themselves seemed to be more fully engaged in the substance of Mr Morgan's argument. Once again there were frequent references to the legal texts of Sir Edward Coke and Sir Matthew Hale and to examples in the body of case law. Mr Morgan's initial line of argument again appeared to be an effort to establish that there are, in fact, no real precedents upon which to depend in the current case but that taken as a whole, the combination of available case law, scholarly legal interpretation, and judicial logic all point to the conclusion that 'treason committed abroad could not be ... tried here by common law'.[72] If I understood him correctly, he was effectively arguing that while treason may very well have been committed, there is no legal venue for adjudicating the offence under British common law.

Not to be outdone, the Attorney General naturally weighed in on the issue, providing a lengthy and equally tortuous rebuttal to all that Messrs Sullivan and Morgan had argued over the course of the past two days. At the risk of simplifying an extremely complex legal thesis, his basic position seemed to be that the defence had stretched its interpretation of the law to an absurd extreme by suggesting that Mr Casement was not guilty of treason simply because he was outside the legal jurisdiction of the court at the time he committed the offences, none of which has been denied. In arguing his case, Mr Smith made a very convincing point in his prefatory statement with the observation that, 'The view taken by the law has always been that allegiance, that impalpable and almost indefinable idea which connects the subjects with the Sovereign, is carried by the subject wherever that subject goes and wherever the subject sojourns.'[73]

With respect to legal venue, he seemed to concede that British common law recognised a court's legal authority as applying only to those offences committed within its geographic jurisdiction but that in recognition of this limitation, the statute 35 Henry VIII, passed in 1544, established the King's Bench in the county of London as the statutory venue for treasonous acts committed outside the realm. Quoting from that statute, entitled 'An Acte concerning the triall of Treasons comytted out of the King's Majesties dominions', the Lord Chief Justice supported the Attorney General's interpretation with the passage stating, 'Be it enacted by authority of this present Parliament that all manner of offences being already made or declared or hereafter to be made or declared by any of the laws and statutes of this realm to be treasons shall be tried by the King's Justices.'[74]

So after almost two days of legal wrangling over the interpretation of law, the Lord Chief Justice finally denied the defence motion that the indictment be dismissed. He clearly disagreed with the defence's argument that a strict reading of the statute's language supported the conclusion that no treason had actually been committed. He also disagreed with the argument that there is no legal venue before which the crime can be adjudicated. Justices Avory and Horridge concurred, and the trial finally moved to the formal presentation of a defence. At this point, the proceedings took another unexpected turn when, rather than calling witnesses on his behalf or testifying under oath, Mr Casement asked for permission to read a prepared statement to the court. Again, the Lord Chief Justice seemed prepared to compromise normal procedure in his effort to accommodate Mr Casement, allowing him to proceed without being sworn as a witness and thus avoiding exposure to standard prosecutorial cross-examination.

As it turned out, Mr Casement's statement was relatively brief (certainly in contrast to the legal exchanges that had preceded it) and proved to be a straightforward refutation of four points in the prosecution's case. In a firm voice, that had not been heard since his appearance at the arraignment in May, he asserted that:

(1) There was never any attempt to enlist Irishmen to fight with the Turks against the Russians – an allegation made by John Neill under direct examination by the prosecutor (an allegation that obviously offended Mr Casement and to which he took grave exception).

(2) He never asked any Irishman to fight for Germany in its war against the Crown.

(3) He never condoned the reduction of rations as a form of punishment directed against his own people.

(4) He never accepted payment of any kind for his actions. Otherwise, he did not deny the charges that he attempted to enlist the services of Irish POWs to participate in an armed insurrection directed toward the achievement of Irish independence.

I am sure the Honourable Attorney General would have welcomed the opportunity to cross-examine, but having filed no objection to the Lord Chief Justice's ruling, he had to settle for having the statement incorporated into the record without challenge. And at that point, the defence rested its case and proceeded immediately to its closing argument.

After having deferred to Mr Morgan for the better part of the day, Mr Sullivan seemed to have recovered sufficiently to present the defence's closing argument himself. As I had expected, and noted in my dispatch yesterday when the prosecution closed its case with the document that Mr Casement had circulated among the prisoners at Limburg, Mr Sullivan built the centrepiece of his defence around Mr Casement's written declaration that, 'The object of the Irish Brigade shall be to fight solely the cause of Ireland, and under no circumstances shall it be directed to any German end.' Mr Sullivan drew extensively upon the testimony of the prosecution's own witnesses, citing from his cross-examination the numerous responses, like that of Mr Cronin, to the effect that the members of the Irish Brigade were to fight, 'For nobody else, only for Ireland.'

It was a strong and convincing performance, designed to make the case that Mr Casement never intended to give 'aid and comfort' to the King's enemies and was therefore never guilty of having committed treason. As he noted in summing up the testimony of all the prosecution's witnesses regarding the role of the Irish Brigade:

> Under no circumstances were they to be asked to fight for any country except their own. They were to be landed in Ireland and in Ireland alone was the Irish Brigade to be used, if their use became necessary. All are agreed on that, every witness that I have read.[75]

In anticipation of the prosecution's argument, that the effect of such an action would inevitably benefit Germany in its struggle with Britain, Mr Sullivan insisted that 'intent' was crucial in judging Mr Casement's actions, and while 'intent' of the German government may have been to use him and the Irish Brigade to their advantage, that had nothing to do with Mr Casement's 'intent'.

Most of the courtroom observers with whom I have spoken this afternoon agree that Mr Sullivan did a commendable job of using the testimony of the prosecution's own witnesses to raise serious questions about whether Mr Casement's intentions can be fairly characterised as treasonous. Perhaps the most daring part of Mr Sullivan's argument came with a lengthy attempt at the end, not just to defend Mr Casement against the charge of treason, but to actually justify the actions that he and the Irish nationalists had taken. Drawing upon the testimony elicited from his cross-examination of Sergeant Hearn and Inspector Britten, Mr Sullivan painted a dismal picture of the political situation in Ireland leading up to the vote on the Home Rule Bill, with the pervasive threat of unchecked violence affecting every aspect of life. As an Irishman himself, his feelings obviously ran deep in this regard – a fact that could not be missed when he solemnly declared before the court that:

> It is a dreadful thing, gentlemen, a dreadful thing to contemplate that anyone within the King's peace in any part of his United Kingdom should be subjected to the bullying and intimidation and threat of armed force to be exercised against the liberties secured to him by the constitution and by the Parliament of Great Britain and Ireland; and yet that was the state of affairs in Ireland as you see by the evidence.[76]

While he had to tread carefully, given the Honourable Attorney General's known association with the Ulster Unionists, there was no doubt that Mr Sullivan was referring to the fact that the Ulster Volunteer Force had armed itself in preparation for rebelling against the implementation of the Home Rule Bill and that the official representatives of the Crown had turned a blind eye to their intimidating and illegal activities. Had it not been for the intervention of the war and the subsequent postponement of Home Rule, it is likely that an insurrection would still have occurred in Ireland, except that it would have been the Ulster Volunteer Force, rather than the Irish National Volunteers, rising up against the Crown. It was an impassioned plea for understanding of the desperation and frustration that prompted the actions taken by the Irish National Volunteers.

Again with obvious emotion in his voice, Mr Sullivan lamented:

> What are you to do when, after years of labour, your representatives may have won something that you yearn for, for many a long day, won it under the constitution, had it guaranteed by the King and the Commons, and you are informed that you should not possess it because those that disliked it were arming to resist the King and Commons and to blow the statute off the book with powder?[77]

Mr Sullivan's clear implication was that the Irish nationalist sentiments were, not only understandable, but justifiable, given the fact that those who were arming against them were in fact arming against the will of the Crown and Parliament. Presumably, had the Home Rule Bill been implemented as scheduled, it would have been the Ulster Unionists fighting against the Crown and the Irish Volunteers on the side of the

King's men – a historical irony that Mr Sullivan was trying as tactfully as possible to impress upon the court.

It was an eloquent and commanding performance, approaching the defence of Mr Casement from a variety of angles. In concluding his remarks, Mr Sullivan came back once again to the key element of his argument against the charge of treason, that Mr Casement's actions provided 'no military aid to Germany; none whatever', either by intent or by outcome.

It was also an understandably exhausting performance. At the conclusion of a rather innocuous statement about Mr Casement having left the consular service prior to the events in question, Mr Sullivan paused noticeably, leaving everyone in the courtroom suspended in anticipation of one final, dramatic statement. To everyone's astonishment, however, he addressed the Chief Justice with the comment that, 'I regret, my Lord, to say that I have completely broken down,'[78] and with that he literally collapsed upon his chair. Lord Reading immediately adjourned for the day and Mr Sullivan's colleagues helped him from the room.

Mr Casement's association with Germany is obviously a critical element in the trial, which is, of course, why I devoted a significant portion of my last two dispatches to his publication about what he characterises as *The Crime against Europe*. In an effort to learn more about that association, I have also consulted with my anonymous sources within the Irish Republican Brotherhood, and most of what follows is a reconstruction of events in Germany, based on the input that I received from those sources.

Apparently, Mr Casement's mission to Germany was somewhat serendipitous. Upon retiring from the Foreign Office in 1913, he fully intended to continue his involvement with those organisations that were promoting a revival of Irish culture and nationalistic causes. By that time, however, political tensions had escalated, especially in view of the militant activities of the Ulster Unionists and their Ulster Volunteer Force, which led Mr Casement to become actively involved with the Irish Volunteers and their struggle for total independence rather than the limited devolution of political power promised by the Home Rule Bill.

The Irish Volunteers had already been receiving extensive support, both moral and financial, from Irish expatriates in the United States, specifically from the Clan na Gael under the leadership of John Devoy. Given Mr Casement's name recognition among Irish expatriates, the Irish Volunteers became convinced that he would be a public-relations asset in the fund raising efforts being spearheaded in the United States by the Clan na Gael. Mr Casement was apparently flattered by the idea that his name might be effectively put to use on behalf of the national-ist cause and was more than happy to accept the assignment, leaving for the United States in July of 1914. As best I can determine, there was no plan at that time for Mr Casement to represent Irish interests anywhere other than in the United States. As a matter of fact, in spite of the political sentiments articulated in the essays that he was already writing and which ultimately appeared in *The Crime against Europe*, Mr Casement had never actually been to Germany and did not speak the language.

Apparently his name recognition was not as great as anticipated; while a significant amount of money poured into the Clan na Gael coffers as a result of Mr Casement's speaking engagements, it was nowhere near what Mr Devoy or the Volunteers had expected. And what they apparently did not expect was the increasingly militaristic nature of Mr Casement's pronouncements, along with the correspond-ing impact of those pronouncements upon both sides of the campaign in Ireland. Mr Casement made no attempt to conceal his pro-German sentiments, and when war broke out in August, he paid a visit to the German Embassy in Washington, where he met with the Ambassador, Count Johann Heinrich von Bernstorff, and his military attaché, Franz von Papen.

His outspoken defence of Germany and his meeting with officials of the German government began to attract the attention of the British Foreign Office, from which Mr Casement had just recently retired. But the real *coup de grâce* was a letter he sent to the *Irish Independent* just a month after the outbreak of war, proclaiming that the first priority for all Irish men and women was to fight on behalf of Ireland; he urged all young Irishmen to defy conscription into the British army and refuse to take up arms on behalf of England against a nation with whom they had no quarrel. Such public defiance of the British call to arms could not go unnoticed by the Crown. And since Mr Casement was still subject to recall by the government should he ever return to the UK, a recourse that the Foreign Office could use to either silence him or make him subject to disciplinary action, it became quite obvious that returning to Ireland was out of the question.

So, given the contacts that he had already made with officials at the German Embassy, Clan na Gael and the Irish Volunteers decided that rather than send Mr Casement home after doing as much as he could in support of their fund raising efforts, it would now be in the best interest of the nationalist cause to dispatch him to Germany. After just three months in the United States and no initial expectation of remaining abroad when all the real action was at home, Mr Casement found himself in the friendly arms of the enemy. Given their many years of dealing with British intelligence, my sources within the IRB are convinced that spies from the Foreign Office had targeted Mr Casement for close observation after his meeting with the German diplomats in Washington. It is therefore almost certain that the authorities in London were well aware of his departure from the United States and of his likely destination.

While his mission to Germany effectively cut him off from direct lines of communication with the IRB and his nationalist compatriots, the sources with whom I have conferred were nevertheless able to follow his activities through correspondence between Mr Casement and officials within the movement, and by reference to reports sent back from Joseph Plunkett and Robert Monteith, both of whom joined Mr Casement at one time or another as a part of the ongoing effort to enlist German support for the cause. Knowledge about his efforts to recruit Irish prisoners of war for service in an Irish Brigade is now widely held, as a result of the trial testimony; his other activities during the year and a half that he spent in Germany are less widely known, but also bear a direct relationship to the charges levelled against him. Based on the limited input available to my IRB sources, I have attempted to piece together some of the details and to consider what that reflects about his attitudes and inclinations at the time.

I am just now learning some of the details about an intrigue involving Mr Casement and the British Ambassador in Christiania, Norway, while he was *en route* from the US to Germany. I hope to be able to report more about that in a later dispatch; for the time being, suffice it to say that the very existence of the intrigue clearly proves that the British were fully aware of Mr Casement's movements. And if Mr Casement ever had any hope of entering into a clandestine relationship with the German government, that hope was dashed shortly after his arrival in Germany, when on 20 November, the Foreign Ministry in Berlin released an official acknowledgement that it had formally received him and entered into diplomatic discussions about the status of Ireland. The announcement included a stipulation, that based on negotiations with him, the government could assure the people of Ireland, that should German troops eventually land on the shores of the Emerald Isle, they would represent a government 'that is inspired by good will towards a country and a people for whom Germany desires only national prosperity and national freedom.'[79] The allusion to German troops invading Ireland and assurances of amity toward the people of Ireland had to raise eyebrows in the British Foreign Office, and surely led to an even more vigorous intelligence-gathering effort.

Based on feedback from Plunkett and Monteith, as well as the occasional correspondence between Casement and officials within the IRB and the Clan na Gael, my sources report that Mr Casement's initial impressions of Germany and of the prospects for a German–Irish alliance quickly faded. His disillusionment with the prospect for support from the Irish prisoners of war has already been well documented by the trial testimony; his disillusionment with Germany was no less profound and morally devastating, especially in light of how deeply enamoured he had been with the German character. From paragons of virtue who would emerge as the saviours of Europe, Germany and its people were transformed into self-serving aggressors who were not above committing the kinds of atrocities that Mr Casement had devoted his life to combating.

The disillusionment apparently began rather abruptly, when Mr Casement was escorted by his German hosts through some of the war-torn areas on the borders of France and Belgium, presumably to impress him with the nation's military prowess and to convince him of the ultimate justice of the war effort. While evidence of the former may have been apparent from the devastation he observed, my sources are convinced that any illusions he might have had with respect to the latter were forever extinguished. The sheer scale of destruction and human misery was unprecedented, and whatever the political justification for the war, the human cost was simply beyond the pale.

He apparently reached the nadir of disillusionment when he and his military escorts visited the Ardennes, scene of the most vicious fighting of the war to date. Led by Duke Albrecht of Württemberg and Crown Prince Wilhelm, the German Fourth and Fifth Armies had totally routed the French forces commanded by Generals Pierre Ruffey and Fernand de Langle de Cary during the three-day battle, from 21 to 23 August. With barely three months having elapsed between that battle and Mr Casement's visit, the destruction and carnage were still overwhelming. And while the left-over evidence of unbridled savagery may have shaken Mr Casement's faith in human nature generally and in the efficacy of warfare as a solution to national differences, it was the coincidental visit to a mass grave that totally undermined his once-glowing image of the German character. How his German military escorts could have been so foolish as to let him have access to the site is beyond explanation; it was apparently the scene of a mass execution where more than 300 Belgian partisans had been lined up and shot, in retaliation for an ambush by unknown assailants. One can only imagine how devastated he must have been, after extolling the German character in his own mind and in his writing, and after leaving the familiar world of his upbringing to ally himself with this Teutonic saviour of the western world.

But Mr Casement had made a commitment that could not be rescinded. While he now recognised that he was making a Faustian bargain with the devil, he felt compelled to continue his efforts to gain German support of the Irish independence movement. The future of his beloved homeland was in the balance and too many people were depending upon him to gain that support. And therein lay the roots for his final disillusionment. While the authorities with whom he had met in the Foreign Ministry had been cordial and encouraging, it soon became apparent that their sincerity about coming to the aid of Ireland was not much more than rhetorical. Had Mr Casement been more realistic in his assessment of the international situation, he would surely have realised that Germany had much more pressing concerns to address. While his case for supporting Ireland certainly had merit, it necessarily had a lesser priority among the German High Command than the deteriorating conditions brought on by the military stalemate on the continent. And so, as the months slipped by and the war continued to take its ghastly toll, with no apparent prospect of a civilised resolution for any of the combatants, let alone Ireland, Mr Casement began to wither away physically, emotionally, and spiritually. By the beginning of the year, just six months ago, he had apparently reached the point of total collapse.

And collapse he apparently did. What few details my sources could provide were apparently gleaned from reports that Robert Monteith sent back to the IRB. Having served with the British forces during the Boer War before becoming an avid nationalist and member of the Irish Volunteers, Monteith had the kind of military experience that the Brotherhood felt would be useful in training the Irish Brigade that Casement was supposedly recruiting. They therefore dispatched him to Germany in December of 1915 to join Casement and to help prepare the Irish Brigade for its role in the rapidly approaching insurrection. His reports about the status of the recruitment efforts naturally disappointed the IRB, apparently raising concerns on the home front about Mr Casement's suitability for the job. Monteith's feedback in January did little to assuage those concerns, as he was present to observe the total physical and nervous collapse of the man upon whom Ireland was depending for the enlistment of outside support.

It was from Monteith's reports that the IRB became aware of Mr Casement's confinement to a Munich sanatorium, at which point, with only two months left before the projected rising, they began to depend more and more on John Devoy and the Clan na Gael for co-ordination with the German authorities through their contacts at the

German Embassy in Washington. Those preparing for the rising had pretty much given up on the idea of receiving support from either an Irish Brigade or from a contingent of German soldiers; according to my sources, however, they were still expecting a major infusion of arms and ammunition. It was through those rather circuitous lines of communication that they arranged for what they assumed would be a shipload of arms to arrive a day or two before the rising, just in time for distribution to the IRB and its supporters.

My sources indicate that after the arrangements had been made, they communicated with Monteith through the Foreign Ministry in Berlin, expecting him now to assume responsibility for any on-site logistical arrangements. To their dismay, they heard back from Monteith that while all this was going on, Mr Casement had been released from hospital and was now reviling the German authorities with whom he had been working for months, raising a major concern about the sincerity of the German commitment and the level of support that might be forthcoming. The news was unsettling to those in Ireland who had been assuming and depending upon the goodwill and support of the German Empire. While it may have been the product of wishful thinking, they were inclined to attribute Mr Casement's total change of attitude toward Germany as the product of his unstable mental condition. They were therefore reluctant to make decisions based on his latest judgements. After all, it was he who had led them to assume all along that Germany would be a staunch and dependable ally. The intensity of the vilifications reported by Monteith, in contrast to Mr Casement's earlier sentiments toward Germany, suggested to them that their envoy had probably suffered a complete mental breakdown. Besides, preparations had reached a point of no return, so they decided that they had to proceed with whatever level of support they might receive.

At this point, my sources insist they lost contact with both Mr Casement and Mr Monteith. Using the Clan na Gael connections, they proceeded with preparations for the rising, including arrangements to receive the arms shipment that would be arriving on a German vessel disguised as a Norwegian fishing trawler – which we now know was the *Aud*. As far as Messrs Casement and Monteith are concerned, the

IRB and their colleagues were as surprised as the British authorities when they showed up on Banna Strand. Since Mr Casement was taken into immediate custody (and Mr Monteith has disappeared), there has been no opportunity for anyone in the nationalist movement to discuss his intentions with Mr Casement directly. They can only speculate as to what really brought him to Banna Strand on Easter weekend, just days before the planned insurrection.

Rumours, of course, are rampant. Many are inclined to believe that Mr Casement recognised the futility of the planned rising and wanted to arrive in time to be included among those who would be forever enshrined as martyrs to the Irish cause – the 'blood sacrifice' that has become an essential ingredient of the revolutionary mystique. Others believe that the same recognition of futility had inspired him to make a desperate effort at intervening before calamity could strike, intending to arrive just in time to forestall the imminent rising. A few believe that he was mentally deranged, as evidenced by his confinement just prior to the Banna Strand incident, and assume that he was in pursuit of a quixotic fantasy, believing that he was indeed the reincarnation of Fionn MacCumhaill, rising from centuries of hibernation to lead a modern army of Fianna in liberating the motherland. With his trial rapidly approaching, its conclusion and the possibility of execution increasingly probable, time is running out for those of us who would like to know.

With the trial scheduled to resume in the morning, there has been much speculation about whether Mr Sullivan will be able to continue with his closing argument and if not, how that will impact the defence. Mr Sullivan was obviously in no condition to argue anything when his colleagues helped him from the courtroom this afternoon. He will need to make a hasty recovery if he is to give Mr Casement any chance at avoiding the gallows.

THURSDAY 29 JUNE 1916

As noted at the conclusion of yesterday's court session, the physical and mental stresses have together taken a serious toll on Mr Sullivan. When court convened today, he was not even in attendance. Mr Jones pointed out to the court that Mr Sullivan's medical adviser had urged him not to continue, and Mr Jones asked and received permission to conclude the closing argument for the defence.

Among the various reasons offered by speculators about what brought Mr Casement to the coast of Ireland on Good Friday, one particular rumour had emerged, which some courtroom observers believed would become a basic tenet of the defence's final argument; that Mr Casement arrived in Ireland over Easter weekend not to participate in the imminent insurrection but to stop it. Given his state of mind after returning from the German asylum, to which he had been briefly committed last spring, that proposition may not be totally implausible. As noted in the reports from my interviews with his IRB associates, Mr Casement had become totally disillusioned with the sincerity of Germany's commitment to the cause of the Irish Brigade. Without the level of material support that he had anticipated and that he had promised his Irish colleagues, Mr Casement no doubt felt that the insurrection was bound to fail and that he would bear a heavy burden of responsibility for that failure. It is therefore not beyond the realm of possibility that he did indeed embark for Ireland, in the hope of forestalling a tragedy. His arrival on Good Friday, two days before the scheduled rising, lends itself to either scenario – arriving just in time either to head off the rebellion or to participate in it. While the defence may indeed offer the former as a plausible alternative explanation, the prosecution has amassed a solid base of circumstantial evidence to support the latter explanation.

In any case, Mr Jones did not make that argument a centrepiece of his closing today, as many had anticipated. He focused the initial remarks of his closing statement on the testimony of Sergeant Hearn and Inspector Britten concerning the political situation in Ireland. His major point seemed to be that Mr Casement was primarily concerned, not so much with fomenting insurrection against England, as with providing Ireland with the military wherewithal to defend itself against the pending violence that was being fomented by Unionist resistance to the Home Rule Bill. During its opening argument, the prosecution had used Mr Casement's stellar record of service with the Foreign Office as a counterpoint against which to contrast his more recent actions. Mr Jones seemed to be making an effort to turn that around by suggesting that opposition to the Ulster Unionists was, in fact, a patriotic act directed against those who were preparing for armed opposition to the Crown's implementation of a Bill that had been duly and legitimately passed by Parliament.

Given the fact that Home Rule had been postponed until the cessation of hostilities with Germany, thus temporarily eliminating the reason for any Unionist revolt against the will of the Crown, Mr Jones's argument is plausible only if one assumes that Mr Casement was preparing in advance for a Unionist uprising at the end of the war. The events in Dublin, just three months ago, clearly negate that assumption. Arming the Irish Volunteers may have made sense in the climate that Mr Jones describes as existing prior to the war, but with the postponement rather than cancellation of the Bill's implementation, the threat of civil war was also postponed. The insurrection of the Irish Volunteers and their supporters nevertheless proceeded, two years into the conflict with Germany, and well after the threat of civil war had become at least temporarily irrelevant. And as Mr Smith reminded the jury later in the day, during his own closing address, the testimony in evidence clearly indicates that the landing of the Brigade in Ireland was to occur not at the end of the war, but after Germany had established sufficient control of the seas to make such a landing possible.

Mr Jones's hypothesis would also appear to be at odds with the clearly stated purpose of the Irish Brigade, as articulated in the written document that had been circulated among the prisoners and entered in evidence on Tuesday, i.e. that the Brigade was being formed 'With a view to securing the national freedom of Ireland' and that members were being recruited to 'Join the Irish Brigade and win Ireland's independence!' Several of the witnesses had also testified that in his speeches to the prisoners at Limburg, Mr Casement had clearly stated that the Brigade was being organised to fight against England. In other words, the most logical explanation for Mr Casement's continued involvement with the Irish Volunteers after the outbreak of war, would appear not to be in preparation for a potential revolt by the Ulster Volunteer Force, but in fact to be in preparation for armed revolt against the Crown. Given the prevalence of the evidence before the court, it was difficult to see how Mr Jones could reasonably expect the jury to accept his argument, and in fact, the Honourable Attorney General was quick to scoff at the suggestion and effectively demolish its credibility during his closing argument later in the day.

More to the point of the charge, however, Mr Jones did try to expand upon Mr Sullivan's argument that Mr Casement had no intention of aiding Germany in its war with England – only of aiding Ireland in its struggle to become a free-standing nation. To enhance his position, he tried to introduce a favourable interpretation of the 'aid and comfort' clause of the statute, by suggesting rhetorically to the jury that, 'Aiding and comforting the enemy means supplying them with information or with forces or with material for the purpose of levying war against the King.'[80]

Unfortunately, this drew an interjection from the Lord Chief Justice that totally undermined the point Mr Jones was trying to make. Assuring Mr Jones that he was only trying to prepare him in advance, so he could craft his argument accordingly, Lord Reading told him that his closing instructions to the jury would contradict what he had just said by defining 'aid and comfort' as 'any act which strengthens or tends to strengthen the enemy in the conduct of the war against us'[81] as well as 'any act that weakens or tends to weaken the power of this country to resist or to attack the enemy'. Clearly, this broadened interpretation favours the prosecution, which Mr Smith naturally capitalised upon in his closing argument this afternoon. Mr Jones nevertheless made every effort to convince the jury that there was a major distinction between supporting Ireland and supporting Germany and that Mr Casement's intent was specifically to support Ireland. There was no mention in his closing argument about any alternative scenario for Mr Casement's arrival in Ireland.

In his summation for the Crown, Mr Smith was quick to discredit the idea that the defendant was simply trying to prepare a defence against a Unionist uprising, and used the testimony in evidence to support his inferences about Mr Casement's true motives. While he conceded Mr Sullivan's point that no one can ever truly get into the mind of another when it comes to determining intent, one can certainly infer intent from an individual's actions and their consequences, which is one of the responsibilities of those assessing legal culpability.

Given that as a premise, he repeatedly raised the rhetorical question of why Mr Casement ever went to Germany in the first place. It was obvious from the evidence that Mr Casement had been graciously received by a nation with which his country was at war, allowed unfettered access to the prisoners at Limburg an Lahn, and promised material support for his venture in Ireland, all of which pointed to a relationship that was suspect, at best. One could certainly infer that Germany expected something in return, something from which it could benefit in its war with England. While Mr Casement may have had a political agenda of his own, he could not disclaim responsibility for the consequences of his negotiations, that as a *quid pro quo*, Germany expected to gain a military advantage over England by entering into collusion with Mr Casement. And under the 'aid and comfort' definition that the Lord Chief Justice had already announced would be included in his instructions to the jury, this clearly constituted treason.

To complement the testimony of the witnesses, Mr Smith also cited the coding document that had been entered into evidence as another example of circumstantial evidence from which one could infer a treasonous relationship with a foreign power. He also reviewed the testimony about the sinking of the *Aud* as further support for his theory of the crime: given the expectation of material support for the Irish uprising, it could not have been sheer coincidence that a German vessel laden with arms and ammunition would have appeared just off the coast of Ireland at precisely the time that Mr Casement himself was landing on Banna Strand. As Mr Smith argued, all of these circumstantial threads could be woven into a tapestry that clearly illustrated treasonous intent. If Mr Bailey had been available to testify, as he did at the arraignment hearing, about their arrival in Ireland on a German submarine, Mr Smith would have had just one more circumstantial thread for his tapestry. And then, of course, there is the fact of the insurrection itself, launched in Dublin just three days after Mr Casement's arrest on the Irish coast – another circumstance that the prosecution insisted could not have been mere coincidence.

After the tedium of dealing for two days with the defence motion for dismissing the indictment, the closing arguments for both sides brought the trial to a dramatic conclusion. The Lord Chief Justice then addressed the jury at length with his legal instructions, impressing upon them the enormous burden of their responsibility in determining whether the most grievous of crimes had been committed. As promised, at the beginning of Mr Jones's argument earlier in the day, he defined 'aid and comfort' in the broadest terms, giving the jury a great deal of latitude in assessing whether Mr Casement's activities were encompassed by that definition. Not content to define the clause in the broadest of terms, he even offered illustrations, pointing out, for example, that:

> It does not need a very vivid imagination to see that if Germany could introduce arms and ammunition into Ireland for the purpose of helping to create a rebellion there, or strife of a serious character, so as to occupy the attention of the British Executive, and also to necessitate the maintaining of a considerable number of His Majesty's soldiers in Ireland, that that would be assisting Germany.[82]

While Lord Reading had prefaced his remarks to the jury by stating that trial procedure required him to interpret and define the law for them in his final instructions, this sort of illustration seemed to stray well beyond that of simply 'interpreting the law'. It remains to be seen whether the defence can make this an issue before the Court of Criminal Appeals.

Given the nature of the instructions, it was difficult to see how the jury could reach any verdict other than guilty. After all, Mr Casement had never denied the actions summarised in the indictment: his only defence was to argue that the actions did not constitute treason. Lord Reading's definition and illustrations of the statute's 'aid and comfort' clause seemed to effectively undermine the plausibility of that argument. In any case, the Lord Chief Justice closed his address to the jury with the admonition that:

> … if you have a reasonable doubt in the matter after considering the evidence, it is your duty to acquit the prisoner. But if, after viewing all the facts and circumstances, the conviction is borne in upon you that the prisoner has committed the offence with which he is charged, then, gentlemen, it is your duty to return a verdict to that effect, and to take no regard of the consequences which must follow.[83]

The consequences to which he was alluding, of course, was death, such being the prescribed sentence for treason. With that he released the jury for their deliberations at 2.53p.m.

Then came the next startling turn of events. At 3.48p.m, just fifty-five minutes later, the jury returned with its verdict. The Lord Chief Justice's instructions about the gravity of their responsibility took longer than their deliberations! One can only wonder just how heavy that burden of responsibility had really proven to be – or how seriously they had taken it. Even with the latitude allowed by Lord Reading's liberal interpretation of the 'aid and comfort' clause, there must surely have been some discussion about whether Mr Casement's actions were truly intended to provide aid and comfort to Germany – intent being the operative factor, since no real aid or comfort actually materialised.

The brevity of the deliberations eliminated any element of suspense regarding the outcome. With the word 'guilty' hanging in the air, the Lord Chief Justice asked the defendant if he had anything to say before sentencing. Having obviously anticipated just such a verdict, Mr Casement responded with complete equanimity that he would like to read from a statement that he had prepared twenty days ago. While granting such a request was another deviation from established protocol, Lord Reading again made it quite evident that he wanted to give every appearance of having accommodated the defendant and gave him permission to proceed. Had he know in advance how long and politically oriented the address would prove to be, he might have ruled differently. It was ultimately apparent that Mr Casement intended for the oration to become a part of the historical record, and copies were made available after the trial had concluded today. At over 4,500 words, the document is not one that can easily be included in a dispatch of this nature, but an abridged version has been appended for the benefit of those readers who are interested in learning more about Mr Casement's political and philosophical convictions.

Mr Casement began the reading of his statement in a trembling voice, the first time he had revealed any sign of nervousness during the entire length of the trial. He soon overcame his trepidation, however, and read forcefully and with conviction straight through to the end of the document. After pausing for just a moment, as he folded the sheaf of papers before him, he looked the jury squarely in the eye and added an impromptu addendum to his statement. 'Gentlemen of the Jury,' he said:

I wish to thank you for your verdict. I hope you will not think that I made any imputation upon your truthfulness or your integrity when I said that this was not a trial by my peers. I maintain that I have a natural right to be tried in that natural jurisdiction, Ireland, my own country, and I would put it to you, how would you feel in the converse case, or rather how would all men here feel in the converse case, if an Englishman had landed here in England and the Crown or the Government, for its own purposes, had conveyed him secretly from

England to Ireland under a false name, committed him to prison under a false name, and brought him before a tribunal in Ireland under a statute which they knew involved a trial before an Irish jury? How would you feel yourselves as Englishmen if that man was to be submitted to trial by jury in a land inflamed against him and believing him to be a criminal, when his only crime was that he had cared for England more than for Ireland?[84]

With the statement officially entered into the record, Lord Reading then brought the trial to an end, with the most sombre words that can ever be delivered at a capital trial:

Sir Roger David Casement, you have been found guilty of treason, the gravest crime known to the law, and upon evidence which in our opinion is conclusive of guilt. Your crime was that of assisting the King's enemies, that is the Empire of Germany, during the terrible war in which we are engaged. The duty now devolves upon me of passing sentence upon you, and it is that you be taken hence to a lawful prison, and thence to a place of execution, and that you be there hanged by the neck until you are dead … May the Lord have mercy on your soul.[85]

To my astonishment, Mr Bailey was brought before the court immediately upon the removal of Mr Casement. As noted earlier, he had not been called upon to testify during the trial, so I was both surprised and curious when he took his place in the dock. I was even more surprised to hear the Honourable Attorney General then proceed to excuse Mr Bailey's actions in joining the Irish Brigade and accompanying Mr Casement to Ireland as those of an innocent and misguided man. Apparently, after consulting with Mr Bailey's defence counsel, Mr Smith had agreed to seek a directed verdict of acquittal. The rationale presented to the court by the Attorney General himself was that Mr Bailey had joined the Irish Brigade not to become a traitor to his country but to use that as a subterfuge in gaining release from the German prisoner of war camp so he could return to his army unit and continue serving his country in the struggle with Germany.

Mr Holman Gregory, lead counsel for the defence, stood briefly to confirm that Mr Smith had correctly characterised the defence's position. In a matter of moments, the jury concurred with Mr Smith's recommendation and Mr Bailey walked out of the court a free man – no doubt to return to his unit and continue his glorious service to the Crown.

Final Statement of Sir Roger Casement

My Lord Chief Justice, as I wish my words to reach a much wider audience than I see before me here, I intend to read all that I propose to say. What I shall read now is something I wrote more than twenty days ago. I may say, my lord, at once, that I protest against the jurisdiction of this court in my case on this charge, and the argument, that I am now going to read, is addressed not to this court, but to my own countrymen.

There is an objection, possibly not good in law, but surely good on moral grounds, against the application to me here of this old English statute, 565 years old, that seeks to deprive an Irishman today of life and honour, not for 'adhering to the King's enemies', but for adhering to his own people. When this statute was passed, in 1351, what was the state of men's minds on the question of a far higher allegiance – that of a man to God and His kingdom? The law of that day did not permit a man to forsake his Church or deny his God save with his life. The 'heretic', then, had the same doom as the 'traitor'.

Today a man may forswear God and His heavenly realm without fear or penalty, all earlier statutes having gone the way of Nero's edicts against the Christians, but that constitutional phantom 'the King' can still dig up from the dungeons and torture-chambers of the Dark Ages a law that takes a man's life and limb for an exercise of conscience.

If true religion rests on love, it is equally true that loyalty rests on love. The law that I am charged under has no parentage in love, and claims the allegiance of today on the ignorance and blindness of the past. I am being tried, in truth, not by my peers of the live present, but by the fears of the dead past; not by the civilization of the twentieth century, but by the brutality of the fourteenth; not even by a statute framed in the language of the land that tries me, but emitted in the language of an enemy land – so antiquated is the law that must be sought today to slay an Irishman, whose offence is that he puts Ireland first. Loyalty is a sentiment, not a law. It rests on love, not on restraint. The government of Ireland by England rests on restraint, and not on law; and since it demands no love, it can evoke no loyalty.

But this statute is more absurd even than it is antiquated; and if it be potent to hang one Irishman, it is still more potent to gibbet all Englishmen. Edward III was King not only of the Realm of England, but also of the Realm of France, and he was not King of Ireland. Yet his dead hand today may pull the noose around the Irishman's neck, whose Sovereign he was not, but it can strain no strand around the Frenchman's throat, whose Sovereign he was. For centuries the successors of Edward III claimed to be Kings of France and quartered the arms of France on their Royal shield down to the Union with Ireland on January 1, 1801. Throughout these hundreds of years these 'Kings of France' were constantly at war with their Realm of France and their French subjects, who should have gone from birth to death with an obvious fear of treason before their eyes. But did they? Did the 'Kings of France,' resident here at Windsor, or in the Tower of London, hang, draw, and quarter as a traitor every Frenchman for 400 years who fell into their hands with arms in his hands? On the contrary, they received Embassies of these traitors, presents from these traitors, even knighthood itself at the hands of these traitors, feasted with them, tilted with them, fought with them – but did not assassinate them by law.

Judicial assassination today is reserved only for one race of the King's subjects – for Irishmen, for those who cannot forget their allegiance to the realm of Ireland. The Kings of England, as such, had no rights in Ireland up to the time of Henry VIII, save such as rested on compact and mutual obligation entered into between them and certain princes, chiefs, and lords of Ireland. This form of legal right, such as it was, gave no King of England lawful power to impeach an Irishman for high treason under this statute of King Edward III of England until an Irish Act, known as Poynings' Law, the tenth of Henry VII, was passed in 1494 at Drogheda, by the Parliament of the Pale in Ireland and enacted as law in that part of Ireland. But if by Poynings' Law an Irishman of the Pale could be indicted for high treason under this Act, he could be indicted in only one way and before one tribunal – by the laws of the Realm of Ireland and in Ireland. The very law of Poyning, which, I believe, applies this statute of Edward III to Ireland, enacted also for the Irishman's defence 'all these laws by which England claims her liberty'.

And what is the fundamental charter of an Englishman's Liberty? That he shall be tried by his peers. With all respect, I assert this court is to me, an Irishman, charged with this offence, a foreign court – this jury is for me, an Irishman, not a jury of my peers to try me on this vital issue, for it is patent to every man of conscience that I have a right, an indefeasible right, if tried at all under this statute of high treason, to be tried in Ireland, before an Irish court and by an Irish jury. This court, this jury, the public opinion of this country, England, cannot but be prejudiced in varying degrees against me, most of all in time of war. I did not land in England. I landed in Ireland. It was to Ireland I came; to Ireland I wanted to come; and the last place I desired to land was in England.

But for the Attorney-General of England there is only 'England' – there is no Ireland, there is only the law of England – no right of Ireland; the liberty of Ireland and of Irishmen is to be judged by the power of England. Yet for me, the Irish outlaw, there is a land of Ireland, a right of Ireland, and a charter for all Irishmen to appeal to, in the last resort, a charter that even the very statutes of England itself cannot deprive us of – nay more, a charter that Englishmen themselves assert as the fundamental bond of law that connects the two kingdoms. This charge of high treason involves a moral responsibility, as the very terms of the indictment against myself recite, inasmuch as I committed the acts I am charged with to the 'evil example of others in like case'. What was the 'evil example' I set to others in 'the like case,' and who were these others? The 'evil example' charge is that I asserted the rights of my own country and the 'others' I appealed to, to aid my endeavour, were my own countrymen. The example was given, not to Englishmen, but to Irishmen, and the 'like case' can never arise in England, but only in Ireland. To Englishmen I set no evil example, for I made no appeal to them. I asked no Englishman to help me. I asked Irishmen to fight for their rights. The 'evil example' was only to other Irishmen who might come after me and in 'like case' seek to do as I did. How, then, since neither my example nor my appeal was addressed to Englishmen, can I be rightfully tried by them?

If I did wrong in making that appeal to Irishmen to join with me in an effort to fight for Ireland, it is by Irishmen, and by them alone, I can be rightfully judged. From this court and its jurisdiction I appeal to those I am alleged to have wronged and to those I am alleged to have injured by my 'evil example' and claim that they alone are competent to decide my guilt or innocence. If they find me guilty, the statute may affix the penalty, but the statute does not override or annul my right to seek judgement at their hands.

This is so fundamental a right, so natural a right, so obvious a right, that it is clear that the Crown were aware of it when they brought me by force and by stealth from Ireland to this country. It was not I who landed in England, but the Crown who dragged me here, away from my own country to which I had returned with a price upon my head, away from my own countrymen whose loyalty is not in doubt, and safe from the judgement of my peers whose judgement I do not shrink from. I admit no other judgement but theirs. I accept no verdict save at their hands.

I assert from this dock that I am being tried here, not because it is just, but because it is unjust. Place me before a jury of my own countrymen, be it Protestant or Catholic, Unionist or Nationalist, Sinn Féineach or Orangemen, and I shall accept the verdict and bow to the statute and all its penalties. But I shall accept no meaner finding against me, than that of those whose loyalty I have endangered by my example and to whom alone I made appeal. If they adjudge me guilty, then guilty I am. It is not I who am afraid of their verdict – it is the Crown. If this is not so, why fear the test? I fear it not. I demand it as my right.

That, my Lord, is the condemnation of English rule, of English-made law, of English government in Ireland, that it dare not rest on the will of the Irish people, but exists in defiance of their will – that it is a rule derived not from right, but from conquest. Conquest, my Lord, gives no title; and if it exists over the body, it fails over the mind. It can exert no empire over men's reason and judgement and affections; and it is from this law of conquest without title to the reason, judgement, and affection of my own countrymen that I appeal.

My Lord, I beg to say a few more words. As I say, that was my opinion arrived at many days ago while I was a prisoner. I have no hesitation in reaffirming it here, and I hope that the gentlemen of the press who did not hear me yesterday may have heard me distinctly today. I wish my words to go much beyond this Court.

I would add that the generous expressions of sympathy extended me from many quarters, particularly from America, have touched me very much. In that country, as in my own, I am sure my motives are understood and not misjudged – for the achievement of their liberties has been an abiding inspiration to Irishmen and to all men elsewhere rightly struggling to be free in like cause.

My Lord Chief Justice, if I may continue, I am not called upon, I conceive, to say anything in answer to the inquiry your lordship has addressed to me why sentence should not be imposed upon me. Since I do not admit any verdict in this Court, I cannot, my Lord, admit the fitness of the sentence that must of necessity follow it from this Court. I hope I shall be acquitted of presumption if I say that the Court I see before me now is not this High Court of Justice of England, but a far greater, a far higher, a far older assemblage of justices – that of the people of Ireland. Since in the acts which have led to this trial it was the people of Ireland I sought to serve – and them alone – I leave my judgement and my sentence in their hands.

Let me pass from myself and my own fate to a far more pressing, as it is a far more urgent theme – not the fate of the individual Irishman who may have tried and failed, but the claims and the fate of the country that has not failed. Ireland has outlived the failure of all her hopes – and yet she still hopes. Ireland has seen her sons – aye, and her daughters, too – suffer from generation to generation always for the same cause, meeting always the same fate, and always at the hands of the same power; and always a fresh generation has passed on to withstand the same oppression. For if English authority be omnipotent – a power, as Mr Gladstone phrased it, that reaches the very ends of the earth – Irish hope exceeds the dimensions of that power, excels its authority, and renews with each generation the claims of the last. The cause that begets this indomitable persistency, the faculty of preserving through centuries of misery the remembrance of lost liberty, this surely is the noblest cause men ever strove for, ever lived for, ever died for. If this be the case I stand here today indicted for, and convicted of sustaining, then I stand in a goodly company and a right noble succession.

My counsel has referred to the Ulster Volunteer movement, and I will not touch at length upon that ground save only to say this, that neither I nor any of the leaders of the Irish Volunteers who were founded in Dublin in November, 1913, had quarrel with the Ulster Volunteers as such, who were born a year earlier. Our movement was not directed against them, but against the men who misused and misdirected the courage, the sincerity, and the local patriotism of the men of the north of Ireland. On the contrary, we welcomed the coming of the Ulster Volunteers, even while we deprecated the aims and intentions of those Englishmen who sought to pervert to an English party use – to the mean purposes of their own bid for place and power in England – the armed activities of simple Irishmen. We aimed at winning the Ulster Volunteers to the cause of a united Ireland. We aimed at uniting all Irishmen in a natural and national bond of cohesion based on mutual self-respect. Our hope was a natural one, and if left to ourselves, not hard to accomplish. If external influences of disintegration would but leave us alone, we were sure that Nature itself must bring us together.

It was not we, the Irish Volunteers, who broke the law, but a British party. The Government had permitted the Ulster Volunteers to be armed by Englishmen, to threaten not merely the English party in its hold on office, but to threaten that party through the lives and blood of Irishmen. The battle was to be fought in Ireland in order that the political 'outs' of today should be the 'ins' of tomorrow in Great Britain. A law designed for the benefit of Ireland was to be met, not on the floor of Parliament, where the fight had indeed been won, but on the field of battle much nearer home, where the armies would be composed of Irishmen slaying each other for some English party again; and the British Navy would be the chartered 'transports' that were to bring to our shores a numerous assemblage of military and ex-military experts in the congenial and profitable business of holding down subject populations abroad. Our choice lay in submitting to foreign lawlessness or resisting it, and we did not hesitate to choose.

But while the lawbreakers had armed their would-be agents openly, and had been permitted to arm them openly, we were met within a few days of the founding of our movement, that aimed at uniting Ireland from within, by Government action from without directed against our obtaining any arms at all. The manifesto of the Irish Volunteers, promulgated at a public meeting in Dublin on 25th November, 1913, stated with sincerity the aims of the organisation as I have outlined them. If the aims contained in that manifesto were a threat to the unity of the British Empire, then so much the worse for the Empire. An Empire that can only be held together by one section of its governing population perpetually holding down and sowing dissension among a smaller but none the less governing section, must have some canker at its heart, some ruin at its root. The Government that permitted the arming of those whose leaders declared that Irish national unity was a thing that should be opposed by force of arms, within nine days of the issue of our manifesto of goodwill to Irishmen of every creed and class, took steps to nullify our efforts by prohibiting the import of all arms into Ireland as if it had been a hostile and blockaded coast. And this proclamation of the 4th December, 1913, known as the Arms Proclamation, was itself based on an illegal interpretation of the law, as the Chief Secretary has now confessed. The proclamation was met by the loyalists of Great Britain with an act of still more lawless defiance – an act of widespread gun-running into Ulster that was denounced by the Lord Chancellor of England as 'grossly illegal and utterly unconstitutional.' How did the Irish Volunteers meet the incitements of civil war that were uttered by the party of law and order in England when they saw the prospect of deriving political profit to themselves from bloodshed among Irishmen?

I can answer for my own acts and speeches. While one English party was responsible for preaching a doctrine of hatred, designed to bring about civil war in Ireland, the other, and that the party in power, took no active steps to restrain a propaganda that found its advocates in the Army, Navy, and Privy Council – in the House of Parliament, and in the State Church – a propaganda the methods of whose expression were so 'grossly illegal and utterly unconstitutional' that even the Lord Chancellor of England could find only words and no repressive action to apply to them. Since lawlessness sat in high places in England and laughed at the law as at the custodians of the law, what wonder was it that Irishmen should refuse to accept the verbal protestations of an English Lord Chancellor as a sufficient safeguard for their lives and liberties? I know not how all my colleagues on the Volunteer Committee in Dublin reviewed the growing menace, but those with whom I was in closest co-operation redoubled, in face of these threats from without, our efforts to unite all Irishmen from within. Our appeals were made to Protestant and Unionist as much almost as to Catholic and Nationalist Irishmen.

We hoped that by the exhibition of affection and goodwill on our part toward our political opponents in Ireland, we should yet succeed in winning them from the side of an English party whose sole interest in our country lay in its oppression in the past, and in the present in its degradation to the mean and narrow needs of their political animosities. It is true that they based their actions, so they averred, on 'fears for the Empire,' and on a very diffuse loyalty that took in all the peoples of the Empire, save only the Irish.

That blessed word 'Empire' that bears so paradoxical a resemblance to charity! For if charity begins at home, 'Empire' begins in other men's homes – and both may cover a multitude of sins. I, for one, was determined that Ireland was much more to me than 'Empire' and that if charity begins at home, so must loyalty. Since arms were so necessary to make our organisation a reality, and to give to the minds of Irishmen menaced with the most outrageous threats a sense of security, it was our bounden duty to get arms before all else. I decided, with this end in view, to go to America, with surely a better right to appeal to Irishmen there for help in an hour of great national trial, than those envoys of 'Empire' could assert for their weekend descents upon Ireland, or their appeals to Germany.

If, as the right honourable gentleman, the present Attorney General, asserted in a speech at Manchester, Nationalists would neither fight for Home Rule nor pay for it, it was our duty to show him that we knew how to do both. Within a few weeks of my arrival in the United States, the fund that had been opened to secure arms for the Volunteers of Ireland amounted to many thousands of pounds. In every case the money subscribed, whether it came from the purse of the wealthy man or from the still readier pocket of the poor man, was Irish gold.

Then came the war. As Mr Birrell said in his evidence recently laid before the Commission of Inquiry into the causes of the late rebellion in Ireland, 'the war upset all our calculations'. It upset mine no less than Mr Birrell's, and put an end to my mission of peaceful effort in America. War between Great Britain and Germany meant, as I believed, ruin for all the hopes we had founded on the enrolment of the Irish Volunteers. A constitutional movement in Ireland is never very far from a breach of the constitution, as the Loyalists in Ulster had been so eager to show us. The cause is not far to seek. A constitution to be maintained intact must be the achievement and the pride of the people themselves; must rest on their own free will and on their own determination to sustain it, instead of being something resident in another land whose chief representative is an armed force – armed not to protect the population, but to hold it down. We had seen the working of the Irish constitution in the refusal of the army of occupation at the Curragh to obey the orders of the Crown.

And now that we were told the first duty of an Irishman was to enter the army, in return for a promissory note, payable after death – a scrap of paper that might or might not be redeemed, I felt over there in America that my first duty was to keep Irishmen at home in the only army that could safe-guard our national existence. If small nationalities were to be the pawns in this game of embattled giants, I saw no reason why Ireland should shed her blood in any cause but her own, and if that be treason beyond the seas I am not ashamed to avow it or to answer for it here with my life. And when we had the doctrine of Unionist loyalty at last – 'Mausers and Kaisers and any King you like,' and I have heard that at Hamburg, not far from Limburg on the Lahn – I felt I needed no other warrant than these words conveyed – to go forth and do likewise. The difference between us was that the Unionist champions chose a path they felt would lead to the woolsack; while I went a road I knew must lead to the dock. And the event proves we were both right. The difference between us was that my 'treason' was based on a ruth-less sincerity that forced me to attempt in time and season to carry out in action what I said in word – whereas their treason lay in verbal incitements that they knew need never be made good in their bodies. And so, I am prouder to stand here today in the traitor's dock to answer this impeachment than to fill the place of right honourable accusers.

We have been told, we have been asked to hope, that after this war Ireland will get Home Rule, as a reward for the lifeblood shed in a cause which, whomever else its success may benefit, can surely not benefit Ireland. And what will Home Rule be in return for what its vague promise has taken and still hopes to take away from Ireland? It is not necessary to climb the painful stairs of Irish history – that treadmill of a nation whose labours are as vain for her own uplifting as the convict's exertions are for his redemption – to review the long list of British promises made only to be broken, of Irish hopes raised only to be dashed to the ground. Home Rule when it comes, if come it does, will find an Ireland drained of all that is vital to its very existence – unless it be that unquenchable hope we build on the graves of the dead.

We are told that if Irishmen go by the thousand to die, not for Ireland, but for Flanders, for Belgium, for a patch of sand in the deserts of Mesopotamia, or a rocky trench on the heights of Gallipoli, they are winning self-government for Ireland. But if they dare to lay down their lives on their native soil, if they dare to dream even that freedom can be won only at home by men resolved to fight for it there, then they are traitors to their country, and their dream and their deaths alike are phases of a dishonourable fantasy.

But history is not so recorded in other lands. In Ireland alone in this twentieth century is loyalty held to be a crime. If loyalty be something less than love and more than law, then we have had enough of such loyalty for Ireland and Irishmen. If we are to be indicted as criminals, to be shot as murderers, to be imprisoned as convicts because our offence is that we love Ireland more than we value our lives, then I know not what virtue resides in any offer of self-government held out to brave men on such terms. Self-government is our right, a thing born in us at birth, a thing no more to be doled out to us, or withheld from us, by another people than the right to life itself – the right to feel the sun, or smell the flowers, or to love our kind. It is only from the convict these things are withheld, for crime committed and proven – and Ireland, that has wronged no man, has injured no land, that has sought no dominion over others – Ireland is being treated today among the nations of the world as if she were a convicted criminal.

If it be treason to fight against such an unnatural fate as this, then I am proud to be a rebel, and shall cling to my 'rebellion' with the last drop of my blood. If there be no right of rebellion against the state of things that no savage tribe would endure without resistance, then I am sure that it is better for men to fight and die without right than to live in such a state of right as this. Where all your rights have become only an accumulated wrong, where men must beg with bated breath for leave to subsist in their own land, to think their own thoughts, to sing their own songs, to gather the fruits of their own labours – and even while they beg, to see things inexorably withdrawn from them – then surely it is a braver, a saner and a truer thing to be a rebel, in act and deed, against such circumstances as these, than to tamely accept it as the natural lot of men.[86]

TUESDAY 4 JULY 1916

Last Friday, just one day after Roger Casement's conviction of high treason, King George moved quickly to strip the erstwhile knight and distinguished diplomat of all his official honours. By the issue of letters patent, under the seal of the United Kingdom, the King directed that he be degraded from the rank of Knight Bachelor. He also ordered that he be removed from membership in the Distinguished Order of Saint Michael and Saint George, to which he had been appointed a Companion in 1905, and that his name be stricken from the Register of that Order.

Sergeant Sullivan and his defence team have filed an appeal that was immediately placed on the docket for the Court of Criminal Appeals, to be heard already next Monday as the Crown moves quickly to dispose of the case. In anticipation of a denial and in response to the death sentence, a number of appeals for clemency have reportedly begun to filter in to the Home Office and the Prime Minister's Office. In the meantime, Mr Casement has been placed on what is commonly referred to as 'death row' in Pentonville Prison, his fate now rapidly approaching a resolution.

In a related development, the Royal Commission charged with looking into the matter of the Irish Easter Rising, which Mr Casement is accused of masterminding, has now filed its report. Chaired by Lord Hardinge of Penshurst, with Mr Justice Shearman and Sir Mackenzie Chalmers serving as associates, the Commission concluded that the rebellion was the direct result of the unchecked lawlessness that has prevailed throughout the island over the past several years, maintaining that those responsible for maintaining law and order had preferred to turn a blind eye to the rapidly deteriorating security situation rather than take action that would have required a confrontation with the opposing factions. The Commission specifically cited the importation of arms and the military-style manoeuvres that the authorities had chosen either to ignore or to tolerate, producing a volatile situation that was bound to result in violence.

While it has become a matter of common knowledge that the Ulster Unionists began the practice of importing arms, the Commission was more distressed by the arming of those factions that may have initially been concerned about defending themselves against the Unionists, but which ultimately used those arms to rebel against the Crown while the nation was at war. The report made specific reference to the founding of the Citizen Army during the 1913 industrial strikes in Dublin, citing that as the point at which the responsible authorities should have taken action to suppress the arming of civilian paramilitary organisations. The Commission also noted that upon the outbreak of war in August 1914, the passage of the Defence of the Realm Act gave those responsible for law and order in Ireland the additional authority to suppress arms shipments as inimical to national security. Unfortunately, in the judgement of the Commission, the Defence of the Realm Amendment Act of 1915 weakened that authority by giving those charged with sedition the option of a jury trial as opposed to a more expeditious military court martial.

In addition to the arming and drilling of civilian paramilitary groups, the Commission cited the inflammatory public rhetoric of those who opposed military recruitment of Irish soldiers for the war against Germany, condemning the authorities' failure to suppress that rhetoric as a seditious violation of the Defence of the Realm Act, thus allowing the various factions to believe that they could pursue their objectives with impunity, and paving the way for an inevitable descent into civil conflict. The report was especially critical of the failure to suppress the anti-recruitment rhetoric that permeated the nationalist press after the outbreak of hostilities with Germany, a campaign in which we now know Mr Casement participated with his submissions to tabloids like *The Nation*, *The Irish Volunteer*, *The Irish Review*, and *The*

Fortnightly Review. The report creates the distinct impression that while the Unionist rhetoric against Home Rule may have generated internal conflict within Ireland, it was the nationalist rhetoric against military recruitment that crossed the line to sedition and treason.

If action had been taken from the outset to suppress the hostile rhetoric, interrupt the flow of arms from abroad, and outlaw military-style training by the paramilitary units on both sides, the conditions that made the rebellion possible would never have materialised, according to the report. Unfortunately, the deteriorating situation led one side (those represented by the Irish Volunteers and the Irish Citizen Army) to ally itself with a foreign power at war with the Crown. Once that occurred, regardless of what prior negligence and provocation might have led to such a juncture, immediate action should have been taken against the seditious factions under the Defence of the Realm Act, including the identification and arrest of anyone connected with the Irish Volunteers, the Irish Citizen Army, and anyone else involved in forging the foreign alliance.

While generally condemning the inaction of those charged with maintaining peace and order in Ireland, the Commission specifically excused the Lord Lieutenant, Sir Ivor Guest of Wimborne, pointing out that his position is purely ceremonial and that in any case, he had been in the position only since February of 1915 and could therefore not be held answerable for established government policy toward Ireland. It was the Chief Secretary, Mr Augustine Birrell, upon whom they placed primary responsibility for the situation, pointing out that it is the Chief Secretary who acts as the administrative head of His Majesty's government in Ireland. Mr Birrell's culpability was mitigated, however, by the fact that Parliament has been in almost continuous session for the last two and a half years of Mr Birrell's nine-year tenure in the position, and since one of his paramount responsibilities is to sit in on Parliamentary sessions and be available for consultation on matters related to Ireland, he had been away from the island during most of the critical lead-up to the insurrection, making it difficult for him to be as responsive as he should have been to the deteriorating state of affairs. However, the Commission was not as kind in its assessment of the role played by Sir Matthew Nathan, the permanent Under Secretary who served as the on-site extension of the Chief Secretary in representing His Majesty's government in Ireland and in enforcing the government's Irish policies. Having held that office since September of 1914, Mr Nathan, in the Commission's judgement, should have been well aware of the deteriorating security situation and should have been more assertive in making that known to the Chief Secretary.

The Commission did take pains to compliment Sir Neville Chamberlain, the Inspector-General of the Royal Irish Constabulary, and Colonel Edgeworth-Johnstone, the Chief Commissioner of the Dublin Metropolitan Police, for their efforts to keep Dublin Castle informed about what was happening under their very noses. The Commission is clearly of the opinion that the reports compiled by the RIC and the DMP provided all the evidence that was necessary to prompt the kind of action that it feels should have been taken at a much earlier date, well before anyone on the nationalist side might have even contemplated the need for an armed insurrection. This opinion naturally reinforces the Commission's main conclusion, that primary responsibility for the failures that led to the insurrection must be laid at the feet of Sir Matthew Nathan, the permanent Under Secretary who would have been the recipient of the RIC and DMP reports and who was responsible for the day-to-day management of government affairs in Dublin Castle.

The only criticism of the RIC and the DMP was not directed at them, *per se*, but at the organisational structure that impeded their response when violence erupted in Dublin. The two organisations function under separate commands, and unlike the RIC, the DMP is not armed. Whereas cities like Cork and Belfast are policed by the RIC, Dublin's law enforcement responsibilities fall under the purview of the independent DMP. And while an unarmed DMP is fully capable of fulfilling its law enforcement responsibilities under normal circumstances, it is obviously not in a position to deal with armed conflict. Had the RIC been directly responsible for law and order in Dublin, the report contends, the rebellious factions would have been less inclined to resort to violence in the first place. And if the two forces had at least been under a unified command, their joint response to the civil disorder would have been more immediately effective.

In further supporting its case against Mr Nathan, the Commission pointed out that the British military could not be held responsible for failing to take action in settling a domestic matter until called upon by the civil authorities, which never occurred until the violence of Easter week actually erupted. To make matters worse, according to the report, the military had clearly informed Dublin Castle (i.e. Mr Nathan) that it was severely undermanned, and that its efforts to recruit soldiers in Ireland were being undermined by opposition from Sinn Féin, making it difficult either to maintain adequate strength at its home bases, or to raise the forces needed by the Crown in its war with Germany. In spite of its warnings, Sinn Féin was allowed to continue with its seditious activities, laying the foundation for what finally occurred this past April. All in all, this was not a good day for Mr Nathan.

The report also maintains that it has long been a matter of common knowledge that the Irish Volunteers, one of the nationalist factions involved in the rising, had been receiving financial support from foreign sources for quite some time, primarily from Irish expatriate organisations in the United States. Furthermore, according to the report, Germany has also been suspected of providing support for the nationalist cause, and while Roger Casement is not named in this section of the report, the prominent media coverage of his trial and conviction of collusion with Germany will undoubtedly lead the public to infer that he was personally involved in masterminding the German support to which the report alludes. The only direct mention of Mr Casement comes near the end of the report, with the suggestion that advance intelligence about an arms shipment from Germany, supported by Mr Casement's capture on the coast of Kerry, should have alerted Dublin Castle to the impending insurrection, which in fact did follow Mr Casement's capture by just three days. The Commission's report, coming as it does only days after Mr Casement's conviction, will certainly not enhance his chances of success before the Court of Criminal Appeals.

The prosecution in last week's trial went to great lengths to suggest that Mr Casement's landing on the coast of Kerry was a clear indication that he had masterminded the entire affair and was returning to take charge of the uprising. His impeccable credentials as a diplomat and his proven qualities of leadership were invaluable assets that would have served him well in that role, had he succeeded in joining the forces that were indeed mobilising as he made his way from Germany. The prosecution would have us believe that no one else involved in the rising had comparable leadership qualities and that it was therefore self-evident that Mr Casement had to be the moving force behind the rebellion. By implication, the failure of the rising, which was almost farcical in its execution, could be directly attributed to the capture of Mr Casement before he could take effective command.

My contacts within the Irish Republican Brotherhood scoff at that entire idea. They point out, for example, that Mr Casement had been away from Ireland for two years – the very period of time during which the plans for the rising were being made. Given his clandestine activities in Germany and the difficulties of communication, he had only limited contact during that time with those who were actually dealing with the situation on the home front. And for a couple of months just prior to the rising, he had been confined to a sanatorium for a complete nervous breakdown – not exactly something that would inspire great confidence in his leadership. Furthermore, as my informants pointedly reminded me, Mr Casement was still regarded with some suspicion by members of the IRB, all of whom were well aware of Mr Casement's loyal service to the Crown throughout his illustrious career.

According to those sources, it was Pádraig Pearse who was the inspirational leader of the rising. An academic and a poet, founder of St Enda's school for boys, Pearse may have been more at home in the classroom than on the battlements, but according to my sources, he was almost obsessive in his nationalism and in his commitment to the revival of the Irish language and culture. His emulation of Robert Emmett, the Irish poet and revolutionary who was executed by the British just over a century ago, apparently led him to fancy himself another in the long line of romantic martyrs to the Irish cause, and his belief in the efficacy of 'blood sacrifice' in both the Celtic and the Christian traditions left him willing, if not eager, to surrender his life as an inspiration to others.

Typical of his romantic notion that a small band of guerrillas could arouse an entire population to rebel against what he considered an oppressive and exploitative government, Mr Pearse's first act of defiance was his posting of a proclamation at the entrance of the General Post Office, the adopted headquarters for his ragtag army, announcing the formation of a provisional government for the new Irish Republic. That proclamation is appended in full at the end of this dispatch. Signed by Pearse along with Thomas Clarke, Sean MacDiarmada, Thomas MacDonagh, Eamonn Ceannt, James Connolly, and Joseph Plunkett, the proclamation reflects, what my IRB informants insist, is the idealistic vision of a poet, not the bureaucratic formula of a diplomat.

According to these IRB sources, the 'blood sacrifice' of those who participated with Pearse in the Easter Rising, may very well have been the inspiration needed to arouse the otherwise complacent Irish populace. As those informants were happy to point out with obvious irony, the British authorities under General Sir John Maxwell could not have been more obliging in their facilitation of the 'blood sacrifice'. Ireland, Britain, and indeed the world are still reeling from the news about the series of executions over which General Maxwell presided this past May. Fifteen of the key participants in the rebellion, including Mr Pearse and his brother Willie, were tried in secret and summarily shot behind the walls of Kilmainham Gaol over the course of ten days in early May. Recognising that the secrecy and haste of the proceedings, along with the denial of counsel and a jury could be in violation of the Defence of the Realm Act, and seeing the potential for a public relations debacle, Prime Minister Asquith intervened in the middle of May to terminate the executions. By that time, however, the 'blood sacrifice' that Mr Pearse considered necessary to the Irish cause had become a matter of record. And with Mr Casement now convicted and condemned, he could very well become the sixteenth person executed for planning and promoting the recent insurrection.

While public outrage initially swept across Ireland in response to the army's ruthless suppression of the rebellion, it is still too early to tell whether the 'blood sacrifice' and the highly publicised Casement trial, just concluded, will have any lasting impact upon relations between

Britain and Ireland. With the war against Germany still preoccupying the majority of those in Britain and Ireland both, the Easter rising, its bloody aftermath, and the spectacle of a knight on trial for treason may all be just part of a passing episode in the public consciousness. The trial of Roger Casement, obviously intended to be in sharp contrast with the hastily contrived, secret courts martial and executions in May, has kept the issue alive for the time being, but the prosecution has gone to great lengths to ensure that the trial does not occupy the headlines any longer than is absolutely necessary.

The trial testimony of the soldiers whom Mr Casement tried to recruit into his Irish Brigade reflects a patriotic sentiment that may be difficult for militant separatists to overcome, as long as the war rages on the continent: a sense of common purpose with their British brethren in the face of German aggression may subdue the fires of nationalism that Mr Pearse and Mr Casement tried to stoke. Parliament is on record as supporting the Home Rule that Ireland has been seeking. Given the government's assurance that the Home Rule Bill, which has in fact been passed, is simply on hold until the cessation of hostilities with Germany, the people of Ireland may dismiss the recent uprising as a tragic but unnecessary engagement precipitated by a small group of romantic idealists who were too impatient to await the promised devolution of power. At least that is the hope of the British government, which is eager to turn media attention to other matters.

The Proclamation of The Provisional Government
Of the Irish Republic
To the People of Ireland

Irishmen and Irishwomen: In the name of God and of the dead generations from which she receives her old tradition of nationhood, Ireland, through us, summons her children to her flag and strikes for her freedom.

Having organised and trained her manhood through her secret revolutionary organisation, the Irish Republican Brotherhood, and through her open military organisations, the Irish Volunteers and the Irish Citizen Army, having patiently perfected her discipline, having resolutely waited for the right moment to reveal itself, she now seizes that moment, and, supported by her exiled children in America and by gallant allies in Europe, but relying in the first on her own strength, she strikes in full confidence of victory.

We declare the right of the people of Ireland to the ownership of Ireland, and to the unfettered control of Irish destinies, to be sovereign and indefeasible. The long usurpation of that right by a foreign people and government has not extinguished the right, nor can it ever be extinguished except by the destruction of the Irish people. In every generation the Irish people have asserted their right to national freedom and sovereignty; six times during the last three hundred years they have asserted it to arms. Standing on that fundamental right and again asserting it in arms in the face of the world, we hereby proclaim the Irish Republic as a Sovereign Independent State, and we pledge our lives and the lives of our comrades-in-arms to the cause of its freedom, of its welfare, and of its exaltation among the nations.

The Irish Republic is entitled to, and hereby claims, the allegiance of every Irishman and Irishwoman. The Republic guarantees religious and civil liberty, equal rights and equal opportunities to all its citizens, and declares its resolve to pursue the happiness and prosperity of the whole nation and of all its parts, cherishing all of the children of the nation equally and oblivious of the differences carefully fostered by an alien government, which have divided a minority from the majority in the past.

Until our arms have brought the opportune moment for the establishment of a permanent National Government, representative of the whole people of Ireland and elected by the suffrages of all her men and women, the Provisional Government, hereby constituted, will administer the civil and military affairs of the Republic in trust for the people. We place the cause of the Irish Republic under the protection of the Most High God, Whose blessing we invoke upon our arms, and we pray that no one who serves that cause will dishonour it by cowardice, inhumanity, or rapine. In this supreme hour the Irish nation must, by its valour and discipline and by the readiness of its children to sacrifice themselves for the common good, prove itself worthy of the august destiny to which it is called.

TUESDAY 18 JULY 1916

The Court of Criminal Appeals today completed its review of the legal briefs filed by Mr Alexander Sullivan on behalf of Sir Roger Casement. Presiding over the Court were Justices Darling, Bray, Lawrence, Scrutton, and Atkin. Representatives for both the prosecution and the defence were the same as at trial.

After covering the appeal for the last two days, it has become apparent to me that it requires a special kind of intellect to deal with arcane legal issues like those that Mr Sullivan insisted on presenting to the court and with which the appeal's court justices appeared to enjoy grappling as much as the trial justices. Mr Sullivan's appeal was based on two counts: the applicability of the statute under which Mr Casement has been convicted; and the appropriateness of the legal instructions that Lord Reading gave the jury at trial. The first basis of his appeal was a rehash of the argument that he made to the trial court over the course of two days – and which left him so exhausted that he had to ask Mr Jones to replace him during a portion of that trial. The mind-numbing review of ancient statutes and case law and scholarly legal interpretation would leave any normal human being in a state approaching the comatose. It only seemed to invigorate Justice Darling and his colleagues on the bench.

Again, the basis of his argument seemed to be that the statute under which Mr Casement has been convicted does not technically apply, since Mr Casement was outside the judicial jurisdiction of any legal authority under British common law. According to Mr Sullivan, the Treason Act of 1351 (25 Edward III, statute 5, chapter 2), which is the statute under which Mr Casement had been charged, did not provide judicial jurisdiction for crimes committed outside the realm. In other words, there is no legally prescribed court that can appropriately adjudicate a charge of treason when the 'treasonous' acts are committed outside the realm. And as Mr Sullivan succinctly pointed out, nothing is treason unless it can be adjudicated treason'.[87] Referring to the lack of a proper judicial venue for adjudicating the crime, Mr Sullivan went on to state that:

> You must not be presumed to have committed a crime until you have been lawfully condemned, and if there exists no machinery, not only for condemnation but for inquiry, I submit that is overwhelming proof that the act cannot be a crime when its legal quality cannot be inquired into.[88]

Based on what appeared to be a much more thorough and coherent review of ancient statutes than he had been able to present to the trial court, Mr Sullivan argued that proper legal venue for adjudicating an act of treason committed outside the realm did not exist until the passage of 26 Henry VIII, almost 200 years after the enactment of 25 Edward III. As a matter of fact, according to Mr Sullivan's scholarly analysis, 26 Henry VIII was enacted precisely because of the limitations inherent in the earlier statutes, governing the crime of treason, i.e. to statutorily establish the judicial venue that was lacking in common law. But Mr Casement was not charged under 26 Henry VIII; he was charged specifically and exclusively under 25 Edward III. Alluding once again to the standard legal interpretations upon which the courts have relied in their interpretation of case law, Mr Sullivan took the position that 26 Henry VIII, not the earlier 25 Edward III, is, 'the foundation of all that has been said in Hale and Coke with regard both to procedure and to treason out of the realm'.[89] In other words, all the scholarly legal interpretations upon which the courts have relied in trying charges of treason, according to Mr Sullivan, are irrelevant to the case currently before the court, since those interpretations are based on assumptions inherent in a statute that did not even exist until 200 years after the statute under which Mr Casement was tried. And furthermore, according to Mr Sullivan, this is the first true case on record in which treason has been charged for actions committed outside the realm.

As he had attempt at trial, Mr Sullivan was once again trying to persuade the justices not to consider the scholarly interpretations that would normally play such a significant role in their deliberations, since those interpretations were based on a later statute (and would obviously favour the prosecution rather than the defence). In order to open the way for a fresh consideration of the language in the statute, Mr Sullivan had to first convince the court that the interpretations upon which they would normally rely are irrelevant. He tried to illustrate his point by quoting from a Lord Esher, drawing a parallel between a case upon which Lord Esher was working and the case now before the court, 'This case would be a perfectly plain case to any man who did not commence by confusing his mind with reading a large number of other cases.'[90] To which Lord Darling quipped from the bench that, 'That is a dangerous doctrine when you have been addressing the court for two hours.'[91]

Two hours quickly turned into two days, with an often spirited but esoteric exchange between Mr Sullivan and the five justices before him. One could not help but wonder, on occasion, whether they had all lost sight of the actual case before them and become intellectually sidetracked into a maze of legal precedent that challenged their judicial acumen. To the credit of the presiding justices, I must say that they seemed genuinely interested in Mr Sullivan's argument and asked questions that appeared to my untutored perspective as attempts to clarify the law rather than to poke holes in Mr Sullivan's defence. In spite of it all, the outcome was never really in doubt. No one was at all surprised when Justice Darling finally brought the debate to an end with his declaration that 'the appeal is dismissed'.

In retrospect, it is difficult for the average courtroom observer to understand just what any of it had to do with the real issue before the court: the question of whether Mr Casement's conviction of treason was justified, even if it met the strict legal interpretation of 25 Edward III. After all, even if Mr Sullivan had persuaded the presiding justices to ignore legal and scholarly precedent, they would still have had to interpret the law in the context of current legal and political realities. Regardless of what Messrs Hale and Coke may have had to say about the statute, it is unlikely that the trial justices or the appeal's court justices or even the trial jury, for that matter, would have seen Mr Casement's acts as anything other than treason, when seen from the perspective of a nation at war. One cannot help but wonder, however, whether Mr Sullivan's entire defence strategy might have been misguided from the beginning: Mr Casement may have been better served if the focus had indeed been on current political realities, as George Bernard Shaw and others have vehemently suggested since the trial verdict was announced.

One example of such a political reality, of course, is the conflict between the unionists and the nationalists in Ireland over the passage of the Home Rule Bill and the fact that Mr Casement's initial involvement in that conflict was actually on the side represented by Parliament. A more thorough argument along those lines, as Mr Jones started to pursue when he replaced Mr Sullivan briefly after Mr Sullivan's collapse, might not have been persuasive, but it would have at least been an argument that a reasonable jury might have been able to grasp.

In any case, dismissing the appeal on the basis of a legal interpretation of 25 Edward III was not at all surprising – indeed expected. But Justice Darling's next comment from the bench this afternoon was definitely a surprise, at least to this observer, 'The other points taken in the notice of appeal questioning the summing up of the Lord Chief Justice are entirely withdrawn by the appellant's counsel and it is needless to say more about them.'[92] At what point this occurred and for what reason are a total mystery. Perhaps Mr Sullivan had simply run out of energy and could proceed no further. Perhaps he had given up and assumed that any further appeal was futile. Perhaps he had second thoughts about the legal basis for that point of his appeal. Whatever the reason, I will be making every attempt to sort it out over the next several days, especially since that appeared to be the strongest element of his appeal: the esoteric argument about legal precedent and interpretation of the statutes had already been played out unsuccessfully at trial, whereas the appropriateness of Lord Reading's closing address to the jury had not yet been contested.

Since Mr Sullivan never presented the argument he had intended to deliver with regard to the jury instructions from the Lord Chief Justice, we can only speculate as to the probable content of that argument. In my dispatch of last Thursday, the final day of the trial, I alluded to Lord Reading's broad definition of 'aid and comfort' as an indirect suggestion to the jury that Mr Casement's actions, while not providing direct material support to the cause of Germany, would have indeed provided 'aid and comfort' to the enemy, if his venture had succeeded.

The key issue according to Lord Reading's instructions was whether Mr Casement intended for the Brigade to land in Ireland after the war was over or at the first opportunity afforded by a German sea victory. If the landing was planned for after the war, then Mr Jones's argument, that the Brigade was being assembled to oppose any action on the part of the Ulster Volunteer Force to resist implementation of the Home Rule Bill that was scheduled to take effect upon the cessation of hostilities with Germany, might be plausible. If, on the other hand, the landing was to take place at the first practical opportunity for such an operation (after Germany had established sufficient control of the seas to enhance the probability of success), then according to Lord Reading, there could be no doubt that the operation would provide 'aid and comfort' to the enemy, given the broad definition already put forward by the Lord Chief Justice. This, according to the Lord Chief Justice, was the key issue for the jury to address in determining whether Mr Casement's collusion with Germany constituted treason.

Lord Reading then quoted extensively from the trial transcript, citing specific examples of witness testimony that the Lord Chief Justice considered germane for the jury to take into account in forming its judgement on this key issue. I'm sure that Mr Sullivan could have easily argued that each example cited was in direct support of the prosecution's interpretation of events; every witness from whose testimony Lord Reading quoted stated categorically that the landing in Ireland was to take place, not when the war was over, but when

Germany had won a sea battle that would pave the way for an amphibious landing on the Irish coast. One could also argue, of course, that Mr Sullivan himself had to bear some responsibility for that, since he had never called any witnesses who could have provided contrary evidence for Lord Reading to cite. In any case, given the witness testimony from which the Lord Chief Justice quoted concerning the projected landing of the Brigade and his insistence that the timing was the crucial factor in determining whether the insurrection would provide 'aid and comfort' to the enemy, it would have been difficult for any jury to arrive at a judgement other than the one put forward by the trial jury in this case. Mr Sullivan's decision to drop the jury instructions from his appeal will forever leave open the question of whether the appeal's court justices might have found those instructions prejudicial in determining the ultimate outcome of the trial.

Whatever the reason for Mr Sullivan's decision, the trial and appeal processes have now run their course, leaving Mr Casement condemned to die by hanging in less than three weeks. I understand that Mr Sullivan has filed a petition for the House of Lords to intervene and overturn the sentence. My legal sources have explained to me that in a capital case, this is a recourse that is available to the defence, but the petition must go through the Attorney General, who must in turn certify that the petition raises a legal issue of such paramount importance that an additional review is either necessary or desirable. It isn't difficult to predict the fate of Mr Sullivan's petition when it reaches Mr Smith's desk.

In probing for more background information about Mr Casement's collusion with Germany, my sources have only now revealed an interesting but tangential subplot that casts a somewhat different light on what and when the Crown knew about his activities, and how government authorities used that knowledge in dealing with Mr Casement. It is a tale of intrigue that could have almost come from the pages of a spy thriller. My sources insist that Mr Sullivan had to have been aware of the incidents, if from no other source then certainly from Mr Casement himself, in which case one must wonder why Mr Sullivan didn't avail himself of the information to introduce another set of mitigating circumstances for the trial court to consider.

According to my sources in the Irish Republican Brotherhood, who in turn had access to information from associates in the Clan na Gael in the United States, when Mr Casement left the US for Germany in October 1914, he was accompanied by a Norwegian travelling companion and personal assistant by the name of Adler Christensen. In spite of every effort to conceal his identity and his travel plans, those sources are convinced that British intelligence was able to track him almost from the beginning of his journey. Government apprehension about his outspoken advocacy for Germany and what that might portend in terms of Irish–German relations had already drawn their attention. They would naturally have given high priority to following his activities and movements. Among Irish nationalists, who see informers and intelligence agents around every corner, there was concern from the very beginning about allowing Mr Casement to travel in the company of an unknown Scandinavian, but Mr Casement insisted that his new-found companion could be fully trusted.

Whatever the source of their intelligence, British authorities were apparently able to follow Mr Casement while *en route* to Germany, in spite of his effort to throw off any surveillance by taking a circuitous route through Christiania, Norway. It was in Norway that things seem to have gotten especially interesting from the perspective of those who relish tales of international intrigue. My IRB sources were astonished and unsettled to hear from Mr Casement, when he finally arrived in Germany, that he had narrowly avoided being kidnapped and perhaps assassinated while in Norway.

According to the reports that my IRB sources received from Mr Casement, Mr Christensen had informed him that he (Mr Christensen) had been approached by a representative of the British embassy in Christiania and told that the government was intent upon waylaying Mr Casement before he could proceed any further in his contacts with Germany. Mr Christensen apparently claimed to have met with Mansfeldt Findlay, the British foreign minister to Norway, and that Mr Findlay had tried to coerce him into cooperating with the British plot, by making some veiled threats about having Norwegian authorities take formal action against him, for associating with a known subversive.

Using a 'carrot and stick' approach, that threat was then followed by the offer of a bribe to help British agents arrange for Mr Casement's disappearance: Mr Christensen's story, as related by Mr Casement in his reports, was that the Foreign Office knew Mr Casement was travelling on a false passport to conceal his identity and that it would therefore be a simple matter for him to disappear without a trace. Upon hearing all this from his trusted companion, Mr Casement proceeded post haste to Germany before anything might happen to him.

I naturally attempted to verify the story with my contacts in the Foreign Office, expecting them to deny any knowledge of such an affair. To the contrary, they acknowledged that Mr Christensen and Mr Findlay had indeed met in Christiania, but their version of the meeting was quite different. According to them, it was Mr Christensen who initiated the meeting, informing Mr Findlay of Mr Casement's presence in Norway and offering to set him up if the price were right. According to my FO sources, the embassy in Christiania had no prior knowledge of Mr Casement's movements (IRB suspicions to the contrary), and the contact from Mr Christensen was met with great scepticism. In response to Mr Findlay's request for some kind of proof to support his claims, Mr Christensen provided the embassy with copies of a pro-Germany article as well as a pamphlet called 'The Elsewhere Empire', both of which Mr Casement had allegedly written, and claimed that he had purloined the documents from his travelling companion's bag. Still sceptical and uncertain about how to proceed, Mr Findlay passed the documents along to the Foreign Office in London, which is how my contacts supposedly learned about them.

Whichever version is true, a cat-and-mouse game apparently ensued between Mr Casement and Mr Findlay, with Mr Casement attempting to mislead British authorities about his activities through false leads to the embassy in Christiania, and Mr Findlay attempting to spearhead British efforts to capture and detain Mr Casement. As a bizarre example of the fallout from this back and forth intrigue, I've learned that Captain Reginald Hall, Chief of Naval Intelligence, and Inspector Basil Thompson, Head of Scotland Yard's Criminal Investigation Division, chartered a yacht called the *Sayonara* to intercept Mr Casement when he returned to Ireland, assuming that he was about to make his way back in accordance with a false and misleading plan that he had fed them through the Christiania embassy. Ironically, Mr Casement ultimately did return to Ireland – aboard the German submarine that dropped him off on the coast of Kerry just three months ago. And the collaboration that began almost two years ago between Captain Hall and Inspector Thompson, based initially on a fake plan that had been fed back to them through the embassy in Christiania, finally bore fruit with the bizarre plan that ultimately did materialise for Mr Casement's return.

The intrigue between Mr Findlay and Mr Casement reached its height when Mr Findlay actually signed a note promising Mr Christensen a handsome reward for helping to arrange for Mr Casement's capture. I have still not been able to get a grasp on how Mr Christensen was manipulating the intrigue to his advantage, but for whatever reason, he apparently made Mr Casement aware of the note and the offered reward. Outraged by Mr Findlay's official imprimatur on the plan to 'kidnap' him, Mr Casement responded with a furious letter to Sir Edward Grey, the Foreign Secretary. My contacts in the Foreign Office were dismayed, not only by the content of the letter, but also by that fact that Mr Casement had the audacity to distribute copies to a number of embassies and news outlets. Mr Casement used the letter to publicly reveal the facts of the Findlay affair, as he knew them, and to use that affair as an example of how nefarious the British government could be. Expressing outrage over the treatment to which he had been subjected, he renounced all his past honours, including his knighthood, and relinquished any claim to a government pension, which the government had terminated anyway. If there had been any hope of reconciliation before, it is clear that with this latest escalation, the ties between Mr Casement and the Crown were now permanently severed.

While all the facts of the affair may never be fully known, it is nevertheless evident that the British government had attempted clandestine action of some sort against Mr Casement, well before he had entered into any treasonous collusion with Germany. Whatever the motive for that action, the fact remains that while Mr Casement may have been a noisome tormentor and an exponent of subversive opinions, he was not at that point a traitor; the charges of treason upon which he was convicted all relate to activities in which he engaged several months later. It seems reasonable to wonder why Mr Sullivan did not see fit to introduce this affair as a possible mitigating circumstance in the ensuing developments, which culminated in Mr Casement's treasonous relationship with the German government. If nothing else, he could have perhaps cast the Crown in a less positive light; it may not have helped Mr Casement avoid execution, but it might have given the jury some reason to pause before condemning him outright.

All in all, there is reason to question why Mr Sullivan chose to pursue the issue he did (the technical interpretation of an archaic statute) and to rule out the use of other issues, one of which seemed to this observer, at least, to have judicial merit (the prejudicial jury instructions from the Lord Chief Justice) and some of which might have offered room for a plea of mitigating circumstances (the conflict over the status of Home Rule, the Irish nationalist claim of colonial exploitation, the Findlay affair just cited, etc.). For Mr Casement, unfortunately, the question is moot: his fate now rests solely in the hands of the Attorney General, who must decide whether to certify that a sufficiently paramount question of law merits consideration by the House of Lords. Given Mr Smith's stated position during the trial and appeal process, along with the history of his relationship with Mr Casement, that is not a good place for Mr Casement's fate to rest. Any hope of avoiding execution more likely rests with public appeals for clemency, which have apparently begun to pour into the Prime Minister's office.

TUESDAY 25 JULY 1916

As expected, the Honourable Attorney General was quick to deny Mr Sullivan's petition for a House of Lords review of the Casement appeal. With less than two weeks left before the scheduled execution, it appears that Mr Casement's only hope now is for clemency from the Prime Minister. Reports coming into the media room suggest that His Majesty's government has been inundated by clemency petitions. One such petition, according to reports from my colleagues in the British media, was forwarded to Mr Asquith by Colonel Maurice Moore, Inspector General for the Irish National Volunteers, and bore the signatures of six bishops, twenty-six members of parliament, and fifty-one affiliates with various universities. According to those same media colleagues, the Prime Minister also received a personal appeal from Mrs F. Sheehy Skeffington, widow of the *Irish Citizen* editor who was shot and killed under mysterious circumstances after being taken hostage by British militia during the recent Easter uprising.

We in the media have also been made aware of a petition for clemency from a number of influential British dignitaries, among them Sir Arthur Conan Doyle, G.K. Chesterton, Sir Francis Darwin, Sir James G. Frazer, and John Galsworthy. While they readily acknowledged his guilt, they asked that some consideration be given to the possibility that his recent actions, so at variance with his long record of loyalty to the Crown, might be the combined product of 'severe strain during his honourable career of public service', the lifelong affliction of 'tropical fevers' that he had contracted while on official business in the Congo and the Amazon, and the stress of the two high-profile international investigations that he had conducted on behalf of the Foreign Office. In effect, they are supporting what has become a widely shared perception that Mr Casement's judgement was adversely affected by the combination of physical and mental afflictions that have beleaguered him – a suggestion that I'm not sure would be a welcome argument for clemency from Mr Casement's point of view.

They also suggested that his execution would be used, 'however unjustly', as a propaganda weapon against England in the United States and 'other neutral countries', whereas 'magnanimity upon the part of the British Government would soothe the bitter feelings in Ireland and make a most favourable impression throughout the Empire and abroad'. In an interesting allusion to the American Civil War, they concluded their appeal by pointing out that none of the Confederate officers in that war had been executed after their surrender, in spite of the fact that they had participated in armed conflict against the Republic to which they had sworn allegiance, and that 'this policy of mercy was attended by such happy results that a breach which seemed to be irreparable has now been happily healed over'. It will be interesting to see whether the analogy resonates at all in government circles, where passions are still running high, given the fact that Mr Casement, not only supported insurrection against the government to which he had sworn allegiance, but also colluded with a foreign power that was waging war against that government.

According to inside sources in the Prime Minister's office, a number of similar appeals have been placed before Mr Asquith. And in a very public appeal this past Saturday, George Bernard Shaw, the noted Irish dramatist and social critic, published a letter of protest in the *Manchester Guardian*. Responding to media coverage in England, which has roundly denounced Mr Casement as a traitor and hailed the justice that will be meted out by his execution, Mr Shaw introduced his letter by asking rhetorically that he 'be allowed to balance their judgement by a reminder of certain considerations, easily overlooked in England, which seem glaringly obvious in Ireland'.[93] The Irish point of view that

Mr Shaw claims to represent in his letter is one that makes a review of his letter especially germane in attempting to tap the prevailing mood in the aftermath of this highly politicised and public trial.

Appealing as an Irishman, he suggests strongly that political bias was behind the sentence, contrasting Mr Casement's death sentence with the leniency of the sentence imposed upon one Christian De Wet, from which one could only conclude that 'there is no other apparent ground for this discrimination than the fact that Casement is an Irishman and De Wet a Boer'.[94] Mr De Wet was a former Boer guerrilla leader who had, like so many of his fellow Boers, signed an oath of allegiance to the government of the Crown's Commonwealth dominion in South Africa at the end of the Boer War in 1902, but who had, upon the outbreak of the war with Germany two years ago, taken advantage of Britain's preoccupation with that conflict by staging another Boer revolt in an attempt to restore the former Boer republics. To Irishmen like Mr Shaw, that revolt was not unlike the recent Irish insurrection, but the leniency shown to the leaders of that revolt has been in stark contrast to that of the Irish rebels. To an Irishman, of course, the bias is obvious and incendiary.

Mr Shaw goes on to fault Mr Casement's counsel for failing to mount a proper defence – a sentiment that seems to be gaining wider credence among Irish sympathisers since the trial and subsequent appeal. It is clear from Mr Shaw's letter that he would have preferred to see Mr Casement mount his own defence, based, not on the legal technicalities put forward by Mr Sullivan, but on the political convictions articulated in Mr Casement's own writings – presumably the essays that were collectively published in his *The Crime Against Europe*, which I discussed at length in my dispatches during the trial. Alluding to a parallel that Casement draws with Serbia in his writings, he paraphrased Mr Casement as saying that:

> ... five centuries of Turkish rule in the Balkans had not, in the opinion of the British nation, abrogated the right of every Serbian to strike for independence, and he concluded quite logically that the same period of British rule could not abrogate the right of every Irishman to do the same.[95]

With that principle in mind, Shaw asserts that from the point of view of an Irishman, Mr Casement must be seen as a rebel rather than a traitor and therefore treated as a prisoner of war – again, a sentiment that has gained wide currency among Irish nationalists since the trial. Clearly, Mr Shaw, and perhaps many of Mr Casement's compatriots, would have preferred to see the trial unfold as a piece of political theatre, rather than a legal contest. Given the bellicose nature for which he has become famous (or notorious, depending on one's point of view), Mr Shaw would have no doubt been happy to write the script. One can only wonder whether he would have been equally happy to play the lead role.

In his final paragraph, Mr Shaw captures another significantly widespread point of view that has emerged among Irish followers of the trial and appeal. In closing an otherwise loosely organised argument against execution, he succinctly points out that, 'In Ireland he will be regarded as a national hero if he is executed, and quite possibly a spy if he is not.'[96] The British authorities should have already learned from the reprisals ordered by General Maxwell in May that executions merely create martyrs for the pantheon of Irish nationalists. What they may not fully appreciate, however, is the significance of the latter assertion from Mr Shaw. Given Mr Casement's lifetime of loyal service to the Crown and the honours he derived, Irish nationalists have viewed his recent association with their cause as suspect. My sources inside the nationalist movement have acknowledged his contributions to the cause, but they have also made it clear that those contributions were always seen through a veil of suspicion, precisely because of his history of distinguished service in the British Foreign Office. My sources point out quite passionately that Ireland's long struggle with England has been so beset by treachery and infiltration that they tend not to trust even the most ardent of nationalists, let alone someone with Mr Casement's record. So as Mr Shaw astutely suggested in his letter, it would be in Britain's best interest to spare Mr Casement's life, not only to avoid the creation of another martyr to the Irish cause, but also to fuel the kind of suspicion that a formal government reprieve would help generate throughout Ireland.

The letters from Mr Shaw and from Messrs Doyle, Chesterton, Frazer, and Galsworthy reflect the overall tenor of the various appeals being made to the British government; that sparing Mr Casement would be in the best interest of the Crown. Authorities outside the British Commonwealth, including the Vatican and American government officials, have also lodged appeals on Mr Casement's behalf. Authorities have confirmed, for example, that US Ambassador Page met with the Foreign Minister earlier this month to share with him the outpouring of concern from the US While there is nothing official that the US an do to overturn the death sentence, the sentiments expressed by Mr Page could have a significant influence on His Majesty's government as it continues to seek US support in the war against Germany.

My colleagues in the United States have reported on efforts within the U.S. Senate to adopt a formal congressional resolution seeking a stay of execution. Senator Martine of New Jersey, with the support of Senators Phelan of California and Vardaman of Mississippi, has led the movement within the Senate Foreign Relations Committee. During debate generated by the resolution's introduction, Senator O'Gorman of New York made an especially impassioned appeal for passage, expressing a 'hope for clemency in behalf of one whose only offence is love for his native land'.[97] Senator O'Gorman went on to suggest that, 'If Sir Roger is a criminal, then George Washington and John Hancock and John Adams were criminals. They were all rebels protesting against wrong and tyranny.'[98] Senator O'Gorman even cited precedents for such interventions by the US government – Thomas Jefferson's appeal in 1793 for Congress to seek the release of General Lafayette in France; Secretary Seward's 1867 attempt to save the life of Maximilian in Mexico; and President Grant's 1869 appeal to the British government on behalf of Irish political prisoners.

Senator Stone of Missouri, the Chairman of that Committee, has apparently stalled the effort, arguing that Ambassador Page's submission to the Foreign Minister should be an adequate representation of the government's position and that a formal congressional resolution would be inappropriate and perhaps counterproductive. Senator Martine even went so far as to try to attach the resolution to the Naval Appropriations

Bill currently before Congress, a procedural tactic that is often employed by members of Congress when a motion lacks sufficient support to stand on its own. While the resolution's fate is still uncertain, the sentiments that gave rise to the resolution will certainly not go unnoticed by His Majesty's government, even if the resolution itself fails to gain passage.

The Roman Catholic Church has also gone on record as opposing the execution, with Michael Cardinal Logue, the Archbishop of Armagh and Primate of All Ireland, submitting a plea for the government to demonstrate its capacity for Christian mercy, in spite of the gravity of the crime. As with the other petitions, Archbishop Logue supplements his appeal for mercy with the more pragmatic argument that a commutation of the death sentence would be in the government's best interest, obviously hoping that if the Prime Minister cannot be swayed by an appeal to the heart, he might be receptive to more concrete practical concerns about the political ramifications.

According to anonymous but reliable sources within the Prime Minister's office, Mr Asquith has received a rather stunning letter from the Cardinal Secretary of State at the Vatican, claiming that the Holy See has evidence to support the claim that Mr Casement arrived in Ireland this past April, not to participate in the insurrection, but in fact to stop it. According to these sources, the Vatican claims to have received a letter from Dr Charles Curry, an Irish-American who apparently befriended Mr Casement when they were in Munich at the same time last year – a letter in which Dr Curry insists that Mr Casement informed him, before leaving Germany, that he needed to stop the rebellion before needless blood was shed. The Cardinal Secretary of State has purportedly urged the Prime Minister to commute the death sentence in recognition of this attempted humanitarian intervention on the part of the condemned man. My media colleagues' government sources have indicated, however, that the Prime Minister is sceptical to say the least about the credibility of any such input on behalf of Mr Casement from an Irish-American friend.

While these and other clemency appeals seemed to be pouring in from all directions at first, my sources within the government have indicated that the influx has fallen off significantly in recent days, presumably in response to shocking rumours that have been circulating about a secret diary that Mr Casement maintained during his investigation of the Putumayo atrocities. The rumours began shortly after Mr Casement's arraignment in May, gained momentum in early June when American journalists were summoned to Whitehall and shown select excerpts from the alleged diary, and have reached a crescendo over the course of the past couple of weeks, not coincidentally as appeals for clemency began arriving in the Prime Minister's office. The diary reportedly contains a graphic record of homosexual liaisons that Mr Casement pursued among young native boys while travelling upriver on the Amazon and its tributaries. Generally regarded as the most perverse of deviant human behaviour and strictly forbidden by law, no activity is more widely loathed than homosexuality, especially when it occurs between a man and a young boy.

The uproar surrounding the trial for 'gross indecency' of another noted Irishman, Mr Oscar Wilde, is still fresh in the minds of the public after more than twenty years. Ironically, Mr Travers Humphreys, who helped prosecute the case against Mr Casement, was a junior counsel for the prosecution in that trial as well. Many readers of this column may be familiar with Mr Wilde's *Ballad of Reading Gaol*, written shortly after his incarceration in that institution after being convicted of paederasty. There is no doubt that the stigma attached to Mr Casement's character by rumours of similar behaviour cannot help but blunt the sentiments behind appeals for clemency.

No one outside the government has actually seen the diary, but reports have surfaced from anonymous sources inside the Attorney General's office that Sir Basil Thompson of Scotland Yard came across it during his criminal investigation into Mr Casement's activities. Casement sympathisers and Irish Nationalists share the general sense of shock precipitated by what the allegations say about Mr Casement as a human being. They have also expressed outrage that such a story would be released by the prosecutor's office, at precisely the time when it will do the most damage to their clemency efforts. Demands for access to the diary have been brushed off, with what many consider a disingenuous claim by the prosecution, that it would be unseemly and insensitive to place such a document before the public at a time when Mr Casement is awaiting execution. The lack of access has also generated widespread suspicion about the diary's authenticity, especially among those in Ireland who are always prepared to believe the worst about the British authorities and their methods.

My sources within the Irish community claim that such a suspicion is especially credible among the Irish who remember a similar tactic that was directed at Charles Stewart Parnell. In 1887 *The Times* of London accused Mr Parnell of complicity in the 1882 Phoenix Park murders of Lord Frederick Cavendish, the newly appointed Chief Secretary for Ireland, and the Permanent Undersecretary Mr Thomas Henry Burke. *The Times* based its accusation on incriminating letters that had come into its possession, purportedly from Mr Parnell to personal associates. An official parliamentary inquiry ultimately determined that the letters were forgeries, created by a disgruntled journalist named Richard Piggott. While there has never been any suggestion that the British government was behind the forgeries, the very fact that the letters were given such credence by the leading British newspaper and directed against the most famous Irish politician of his generation at a time when he was leading the cause for Irish Home Rule, left a lingering sense of outrage about the use of duplicity in discrediting advocates for Irish autonomy. None of my Irish sources doubt the capacity of the Crown to engage in such duplicity.

Those who refuse to believe in the authenticity of the diary support their position with a number of arguments. As an example, they argue that until now, no one, not even Mr Casement's closest associates, has ever had any reason to suspect him of deviant behaviour. Surely, they insist, there would have been some hint of perversity that would not have gone unnoticed over the course of an entire lifetime. Nor is it plausible that, as busy as he was in conducting an intensive investigation in a hostile environment while beset by a variety of physical maladies (including an eye infection that would have made it difficult for him even to make such a record), he would still have had the time and the energy to maintain a second diary, separate from his official one, let alone engage in the multitude of sexual exploits that the diary purportedly catalogues. Nor is it credible that he would have been so indiscrete as to maintain such a damning piece of evidence, even if he had had the time and the stamina to create such a record.

The advocates of the forgery theory claim that whoever produced the false diary probably altered or embellished the journal entries that Mr Casement had made, in his own handwriting, about the promiscuous behaviour of the young natives whom he encountered during his investigation of the Putumayo atrocities. Defenders of his character suggest that Mr Casement was probably as appalled by the behaviour he observed in the jungle as the public is now by the behaviour alleged against him, and that he therefore felt compelled to record it for future reference. And while Mr Casement was apparently obsessive about maintaining a diary throughout his career, it isn't clear at this point whether the authorities are claiming the existence of similar entries in diaries before his excursion into the Amazon rainforest. As his apologists contend in arguing that hints of deviant behaviour would have surfaced at some point during the course of his lifetime, they also argue that if Mr Casement felt inclined to make diary entries about personal sexual proclivities, such entries would have appeared in his earlier diaries, as well.

Those who claim to have seen the excerpts provided by the prosecutor's office insist that no one can reasonably doubt their authenticity. The sources with whom I have spoken suggest that there may indeed be earlier diaries that document the same kinds of behaviour that have surfaced from the Amazon diaries; there just hasn't been time yet to archive all the documents that were collected during the criminal investigation. Those sources have also indicated that Adler Christensen, the Norwegian companion who accompanied Mr Casement to Germany (see my dispatch of last Tuesday), actually offered to testify in support of the allegations that Mr Casement was indeed a homosexual. What bearing such testimony might have had on the charge of treason is, of course, questionable, but reference to Mr Christensen and his alleged offer helps lend credence to the attacks against Mr Casement's character. Whatever the case may be with regard to his sexual orientation, there is no doubt that the rumours have had a significantly negative impact on public perceptions and appeals for clemency.

The dissemination of those rumours does seem to have been well orchestrated, suggesting that whether the evidence is authentic or fabricated, someone is intent upon using that evidence to discredit Mr Casement, just as the appeals for clemency appeared to be gaining currency within government circles. In a column published earlier this week in the *Manchester Guardian*, the noted British journalist Henry Nevinson has been one of the few to take umbrage with the spreading of 'insinuations against Casement's private character',[99] comparing it to tactics employed by the Inquisition and by some of the seamier nations on the continent where 'one could imagine the police or even the government spreading such rumours with the object of poisoning the public mind against a man whom they wished to destroy'[100]. As he points out in his column, 'These insinuations have no bearing on the charge of which he was convicted nor have they been established or mentioned in court.'[101] He concludes by insisting that:

> … anyone who may have attempted by any such means to blacken the character and prejudice our feelings toward a man who stands in acute danger of a degrading and hideous death is, in my opinion, guilty of a far meaner and more loathsome crime than the worst which could possibly be unearthed in the career of the criminal himself.[102]

There is certainly no doubt that the 'revelations' about Mr Casement's questionable morality have had a chilling effect on the clemency campaign. As just one example, it is rumoured that Archbishop Davidson of Canterbury was prepared to join those campaigning on Mr Casement's behalf, until he learned about the content of what are now being characterised as the 'black diaries'. His signature is conspicuously absent from those appeals bearing the names of other noted clerics. While those who initially appealed the sentence have not retracted their pleas, there have been no notable follow-up submissions since the diary excerpts began circulating. And whether or not the government authorities were complicit in either generating or circulating the diary excerpts, they are undoubtedly exploiting them to the fullest, in dampening any efforts to spare Mr Casement from execution. Sources who have been privy to the internal deliberations have informed us in the media that Sir Ernley Blackwell, for example, the legal adviser to the Home Office, has unabashedly alluded to sexual degeneracy and perversion in his written opinions opposing any stay of execution.

Mr Nevinson's outrage may well be justified and to the point, but the campaign of innuendo and character assassination has obviously had a marked effect on the level of public support for any clemency consideration that might have emerged from the recent petitions. With only a week left before the scheduled execution, the effect need only be temporary and short-lived; by the time anyone can get around to initiating a formal enquiry into the authenticity of the diary and the ethics of leaking select excerpts to the public, Mr Casement will have long since been dispatched to the next world.

THURSDAY 3 AUGUST 1916

Roger Casement was executed behind the walls of Pentonville Prison, this morning at nine o'clock, in accordance with the order issued by the Lord Chief Justice, presiding judge of the trial court. In what was obviously a surprise to everyone following the appeal process, the Crown rejected all petitions for clemency and allowed the execution to proceed as scheduled. It had been generally believed that the Prime Minister would relent under the pressure of international opinion, if for no other reason than for political expediency. One can only speculate as to the rationale for its decision. Most of those to whom I have spoken over the course of the past week, shared the opinion that the government had much to lose in terms of international regard by proceeding with the execution, and much to gain if it had chosen to show mercy in dealing with a convicted traitor. Obviously, there had to be some compelling rationale for the Crown to go against what most perceived to be its best interest.

The adverse impact of the 'black diaries' on Casement's character certainly made it easier to reach that decision. Home Office informants who understandably insist upon anonymity maintain that those 'black diaries' were used to wage an intense internal campaign against the politically expedient course that was apparently being considered. Those informants claim that Sir Ernley Blackwell, the legal adviser to the Home Office, was especially vociferous in his opposition to a reprieve, his conduct bordering on reprehensible in the judgement of some of those with inside knowledge. His legal memoranda were apparently laced with allusions to Mr Casement's 'lewd' and 'degenerate' character, suggesting, in one instance, that Mr Casement 'seems to have completed the full cycle of sexual degeneracy and from a pervert has become an invert – a woman, or pathic, who derives his satisfaction from attracting men and inducing them to use him'.[103] While the graphic discussion of alleged paederasty was surely intended to offend the sensibilities of those considering a reprieve, and thus prejudice them against Mr Casement, Mr Blackwell purportedly justified the use of such allusions in his legal advice by insisting that the intent was to address the issue of insanity, which several of the clemency petitions had raised as a mitigating factor. According to those who were privy to Mr Blackwell's arguments, he was determined to convince his Home Office clients that Mr Casement was indeed a pervert and was so by nature, not by reason of mental imbalance.

Mr Blackwell's rationale appears to be disingenuous at best. As far as any of us in the media can determine, no one has used the allegations of homosexuality to support a plea of insanity, so alluding to the insanity defence was beside the point in justifying the references to the diaries. As a matter of fact, Mr Sullivan reportedly declined to accept the 'black diary' excerpts when Mr Smith offered them to the defence, as possible evidence of a mental disorder. According to sources close to the defence, Mr Sullivan recognised the offer as a trap, knowing full well that Mr Casement was in full command of his faculties and that Mr Smith was simply hoping he could trick the defence into introducing the documents to the court, since Mr Smith himself had no legal basis to do so. Having failed in his ploy, my defence sources contend, the Honourable Attorney General had to depend on Mr Blackwell to use the issue of insanity as a justification for parading the documents before those Home Office authorities responsible for considering the clemency appeals.

The Home Office informants who shared this information with us in the media seemed convinced that Mr Blackwell had developed an almost pathological hatred for Mr Casement and was determined to use his official capacity in the Home Office to ensure that appeals for clemency would fail. What is interesting, is the impression from those informants that Mr Blackwell's campaign of character assassination was not used as a direct justification for executing the man, rather as a way of enabling the execution to proceed in accordance with a decision that had already been made by Mr Samuel, the Home Secretary, and by Mr Asquith, the Prime Minister. In light of the clemency efforts, the government's primary reservations about proceeding with the execution were political – the apprehension about creating a martyr to the Irish cause and the concern about world opinion. Mr Blackwell's exploitation of the 'black diaries' in his legal opinions mitigated both those concerns by projecting the image of a man with whom few would be able to sympathise, no matter their political sentiments. In effect, the government decided to execute Mr Casement's reputation as a necessary prelude to executing his body.

Why Mr Samuel and Mr Asquith were so determined to proceed with the execution that they would sanction that kind of character assassination is open to conjecture. The Home Office and the Prime Minister's Office will undoubtedly insist that they were simply complying with the law, that Mr Casement had been fairly tried and convicted of the most heinous crime that one cannot commit during a time of war, and that to spare his life would be a violation of legal and political principle. While clemency is always an option for the highest authorities within the government, they will also argue, I am sure, that given Mr Casement's service to the Crown and the honours bestowed upon him, a reprieve would have been perceived as an unfair act of favouritism for one of their own: they had to hold him to a higher standard than they might have otherwise enforced.

Critics will certainly argue that personal vendettas and long-suffering vindictiveness among those who knew and interacted with Mr Casement in various capacities over the past twenty years, must surely have affected the judgement of those who ultimately bore responsibility for the decision. Otherwise, they will argue, how could they have run the risk of alienating those in the world whose opinion they needed to court, even with the protection that the 'black diaries' campaign afforded them. Some of my media colleagues are suggesting that political intrigue of some sort must have also played a part in the decision and that future historians will have to ferret out the details.

Whatever the reason, the clemency appeals failed. As the hour of execution approached this morning, a small crowd, probably no more than 200 to 250 and made up primarily of women and children from the neighbourhood, along with a handful of local munitions workers on their way to work, had gathered along several blocks of Caledonian Road in front of the prison. A smaller group of supplicants knelt separately at the back door of the prison to offer prayers for the salvation of Mr Casement's soul. There was nothing otherwise unusual about the day, except for the sombre tolling of the prison bell as it counted down the last twenty minutes of Mr Casement's life. At precisely nine o'clock, the bell ceased to toll, and nine minutes later, a single haunting strike of the bell signified that the end had come. A few derisive cheers from the assembled labourers erupted when the bell struck, after which the crowd quickly dispersed and the street returned to its normal daily routine. Mr Casement's departure from this world was as quiet and unnoticed as his arrest and trial were raucous and sensational.

About half an hour after the tolling of the bell, a routine notice was posted, outside the main prison doors, to announce that the execution had officially taken place. Signed by R. Kynaston Metcalfe, the acting Under-Sheriff of London, O.E.M. Davies, the governor of the prison, and Fr James McCarroll, the Roman Catholic pastor of Eden Grove church, who had been ministering to Mr Casement's spiritual needs as he awaited execution. A formal death certificate signed by P. R. Mander, the senior medical officer of the prison, was posted alongside the notice of execution to confirm that Mr Casement was indeed dead. Sources from within the prison confirm that Mr Gavan Duffy was in attendance at the post-execution inquest, to confirm the identity of the body. Mr Duffy reportedly asked that the body be released into the custody of his family, but it is my understanding that Mr Casement's remains will, in fact, be buried in quicklime within the confines of the prison.

In a brief interview with the press, Fr McCarroll announced that Mr Casement had converted to Catholicism in the waning hours of his life and had made his final confession and received Holy Communion. Fr McCarroll did not entertain many questions and naturally refused to discuss the nature of Mr Casement's 'confession'. It has been widely known among Mr Casement's associates, however, that his mother had him quietly baptised a Catholic at an early age, so it is not clear what Fr McCarroll meant when he spoke of Mr Casement's conversion during the death-watch of these past several days. Some of my press colleagues have also learned that Fr Crotty, the chaplain of the Limburg prisoner of war camp at the time Mr Casement was attempting to recruit an Irish Brigade, had praised Mr Casement for his spirituality during their interaction in Germany, claiming that he even carried a prayer book with him at all times and spoke reverently of his regard for the Church Fathers, reflecting a Catholic sensibility that Mr Casement may have harboured for some time.

I have otherwise been able to learn very little about Mr Casement's religion over the course of his career, but since he was raised a Protestant following his mother's death, the 'conversion' of which Fr McCarroll speaks may simply have been a formal acknowledgement of the faith into which he was baptised. Or it may have signified a more profound recognition of a spiritual affinity for the faith of his mother, as opposed to the faith that had been an established part of his adulthood. Or, if he had been an undeclared Catholic all along, as we might deduce from Father Crotty's observations, then Fr McCarroll may have simply misread the significance of Mr Casement's final confession and 'first' Communion. In any case, one can only hope that Fr McCarroll will eventually see fit to expound further on the conversations he had with Mr Casement during the final days of his life. Insight into Mr Casement's religious convictions may shed some light on the motivations that guided him, from the moment he descended into the African heart of darkness, until he ascended the scaffold this morning.

Eager to bask for a few moments in the reflected limelight of a media event, a couple of the guards who were present at the execution were more than happy to pass along some of the details about Mr Casement's final hours. Apparently he was allowed to wear his civilian clothes rather than prison garb for the occasion, and in spite of any hostility the prison officials may have felt toward a convicted traitor, everyone involved was respectful toward the condemned man, right up until he met his fate on the scaffold. The guards were especially impressed by

Mr Casement's own demeanour, which they characterised as calm and unruffled, almost to the point of indifference toward the fact of imminent death. They were obviously impressed by the courage he displayed as he mounted the scaffold and stood calmly in place as Mr Ellis, the executioner, placed the noose around his neck. Upon being asked if he had any final words, Mr Casement simply stated that, 'I die for my country' and quietly stepped onto the trap. The guards claim that even Mr Ellis remarked upon Mr Casement's courage, commenting that he was probably the bravest man he had ever had to execute.

Immediately following the execution, the government released a rather startling and pointed statement that left no doubt about its official position with respect to the clemency appeals submitted on behalf of its former knight and honoured consul. Given the significance of the statement, it is worth quoting in full:

All the circumstances in the case of Roger Casement were carefully and repeatedly considered by the Government before the decision was reached not to interfere with the sentence of the law. He was convicted and punished for treachery of the worst kind to the Empire he had served and as a willing agent of Germany.

The Irish rebellion resulted in much loss of life, both among soldiers and civilians. Casement invoked and organised German assistance to that insurrection. In addition, though himself for many years a British official, he undertook the task of trying to induce soldiers of the British army, prisoners in the hands of Germany, to forswear their oath of allegiance and join their country's enemies. Conclusive evidence has come into the hands of the government since the trial that he had entered into an agreement with the German Government which explicitly provided that the brigade which he was trying to raise from among the Irish soldier prisoners might be employed in Egypt against the British Crown. Those among the Irish soldiers, prisoners in Germany, who resisted Casement's solicitations of disloyalty were subjected to treatment of exceptional cruelty by the Germans; some of them have since been exchanged as invalids and have died in this country, regarding Casement as their murderer.

The suggestion that Casement left Germany for the purpose of trying to stop the Irish rising was not raised at the trial and is conclusively disproved not only by the facts there disclosed, but by further evidence which has since become available.

Another suggestion, that Casement was out of his mind, is equally without foundation. Materials bearing on his mental condition were placed at the disposal of his counsel, who did not raise the plea of insanity. Casement's demeanour since his arrest and throughout and since the trial gave no ground for any such defence and indeed was sufficient to disprove it.[104]

As was to be expected, my Irish sources have reported outrage and horror throughout the Irish community, where the statement has been characterised as an appalling example of the Crown's high-handed approach to justice, when it comes to its Irish 'citizens'. Their outrage was fuelled first by the news that Mr Casement's remains would be interred within the prison walls – an act normally reserved for common criminals. It was well known among his compatriots that Mr Casement's solemn wish was to be buried at Murlough Bay in Co. Antrim. While it is understandable that the government would not want him to receive a funeral suggestive of state honours, which would surely have been the case if his remains were returned to Ireland, burying him in quicklime in an unmarked grave among common criminals seems, from the point of view expressed by my Irish associates, designed to heap further disgrace upon a man whom the government has already fully dishonoured.

The statement from the government stoked the fires of outrage even further, with its allusions to evidence never presented in open court, especially the claim that Mr Casement had entered into a secret agreement with the government of Germany to use the Irish Brigade as reinforcement for German troops fighting against English forces in Egypt. Without ever having been called upon to present such evidence for cross-examination by defence counsel, the government is obviously assuming that it will be taken at its word – an assumption that is totally unfounded when it comes to the Irish. The average British citizen will undoubtedly accept that claim as fact, especially since it further supports their firm belief that Mr Casement was a vile traitor who deserved to be hanged, but among the Irish, that claim is seen as just another underhanded attempt by the British government to cast further aspersions upon the already besmirched reputation of its former consul. Until they can examine the evidence that the government claims to have in its possession, the Irish can only believe that the claim is an outright falsehood.

The penultimate paragraph struck me and all my media colleagues as somewhat odd. As noted at the beginning of that paragraph, 'the suggestion that Casement left Germany for the purpose of trying to stop the Irish rising was not raised at the trial', and as best we can determine, that suggestion was not widely credited, even among the rumour mongers who were eager to generate as much controversy as possible. As noted in my last dispatch, inside sources in Mr Asquith's office have revealed that a communication from the Cardinal Secretary of State at the Vatican claimed that the Hole See had evidence to that effect; otherwise, there has been virtually no official discussion of such a notion. Certainly Mr Casement, who was eager to be seen, in his final performance, as an ardent supporter of the uprising and a martyr to the cause, would not have wanted such a defence made on his behalf, even if it were true. Why the government felt compelled to respond to, what most consider, a non-issue is a mystery – unless they were trying indirectly to plant seeds of doubt among Mr Casement's Irish sympathisers as to his true intentions, and thus further undermine any tendency to see him as a martyr. Or perhaps they found it necessary, for whatever reason, to provide additional written reinforcement of their own conviction that his return was indeed with treasonous intent.

We also found the statement that 'materials bearing on his mental condition were placed at the disposal of his counsel' to be suspiciously revealing. Most of us agree that the statement is a veiled reference to the 'black diaries', that had allegedly been discovered during the investigation. This is the first intimation that defence counsel was given access to the documents, which naturally raises a number of questions about why the prosecutor did that and why Mr Sullivan chose not to introduce them. The prosecution has certainly made effective use of them in the court of public opinion, but since they did not have any direct bearing on the formal charges against Mr Casement, the Honourable Attorney General would have been precluded from introducing them in the court of legal opinion. Rumours are already circulating that Mr Smith wanted to be able to blandish the diary contents openly, and since he could not do that legally in the courtroom, he was hoping that Mr Sullivan would do it for him, introducing them in support of an insanity plea. According to these rumours, either Mr Sullivan saw the trap and refused to bite, or he felt that Mr Smith would be able to effectively counter an insanity defence anyway, leaving the diary contents in evidence without having served any useful purpose. Assuming that such rumours have merit, it would make sense for the government to include this paragraph in its final proclamation, allowing the prosecution its only remaining opportunity to make some official reference to the 'black diaries' and their relevance to an insanity plea.

The Irish reaction to the posting was entirely predictable, which begs the question of why the Government would issue an inflammatory statement that was sure to exacerbate an already tense situation. The Prime Minister's Office clearly felt that some explanation of its refusal to grant clemency had to be put forward, but that could have easily been done on the basis of the trial evidence alone. There was no need to suggest that new evidence had come into its possession in support of a trial verdict that no one was contesting anyway. The content of the statement certainly seems consistent with the Irish contention that the government was not satisfied with simply putting Mr Casement to death, but felt that it had to sufficiently tarnish his reputation, to preclude any further expressions of sympathy. Its undisclosed 'proof', that he had conspired with Germany to use the Irish Brigade against British troops in Egypt, not only contradicts Mr Casement's defence that the Brigade was being formed specifically and solely to fight for Irish independence, but also taints his image as an Irish freedom fighter. In one unsubstantiated allegation, the government has apparently hoped to solidify British public opinion and at the same time raise doubts about Mr Casement's true intentions among Irish nationalists, who may still harbour some ambivalence about the sincerity of his commitment to Ireland.

The tenor of world opinion outside Ireland and Britain may not be fully known or appreciated for quite some time, although it has become known in just the past few days that the resolution put before the US Senate and which had been stalled for some time in the Foreign Relations Committee did eventually receive majority support and was transmitted to the Foreign Office this past weekend – obviously to no effect. Media coverage had already begun to decline once the appeals court had rendered its ruling, and with international tensions continuing to dominate the headlines, interest in the case may wane rapidly now that it has reached a final resolution. Which may well explain the government's aggressive pursuit of the matter: from arrest to trial to appeal to execution – the entire case occupied the world's attention for little more than three months. By dispatching the matter so quickly, the Crown has perhaps disposed of what might otherwise have been a public-relations debacle, weathering an intense but brief firestorm on the assumption that it would flame out quickly, leaving Mr Casement and his reputation to disintegrate anonymously in the quicklime of Pentonville Prison.

FRIDAY 1 SEPTEMBER 1916

Today would have been Roger Casement's fifty-second birthday. While only a month has elapsed since his execution, this may nevertheless be an appropriate time to reflect upon the significance of his life and death. Already his name has disappeared from the major media: he is rapidly becoming of more interest to historians than to his contemporaries.

With the excitement of the trial having subsided, the two-year-old war on the continent has once again become the focus of world attention, with what has become a perpetual stalemate. The endless back and forth dance of death is no better exemplified than by the advances and retreats at Fleury, with French forces taking the town on 3 August, the day of Mr Casement's execution, German forces retaking it the very next day, and French soldiers taking it back again by the next morning. By 19 August, the Germans were able, once again, to make advances in Fleury, only to be repulsed by the French again later that same day. The inability of either side to make significant territorial advances has become the prevailing characteristic of this war of attrition; each side firmly dug in on opposite sides of a no-man's land with the only advances, of any significance, appearing in the catalogue of the dead, the maimed, and the captured.

Recognising the effects of the frustration, King George visited several units of the British army that have become bogged down in France, hoping to help rally the flagging morale of the troops; he returned to England two weeks ago on the 15 August. In an effort to rally the forces on the other side, Marshal Hindenburg was appointed Chief of the German Staff on the 29 August. Romania has now joined the madness, declaring war on Austria-Hungary just five days ago, with Germany and Turkey immediately responding by declaring war on Romania. The Battle of the Somme continues to rage after two months, with the death toll mounting into the thousands. And the battle at sea has claimed at least two more of His Majesty's light cruisers, with the sinking of the *Nottingham* and the *Falmouth*. One could easily conclude that the international furore over the Casement trial was nothing more than a diversion. The paralysing litany of reports from the various fronts on the continent and in the Middle East has once again reclaimed the headlines.

But for those of us who covered the trial, the life (and the death) of Roger Casement, formerly Sir Roger Casement, is more than a mere diversion, a transient blip in the turn-of-the-century history of western civilization. Trying to grasp the significance of a life that skyrocketed to the heights of fame, only to plummet to the depths of infamy is of more than passing interest. Implicit in the drama of this one man's rise and fall is an abiding import that touches both the highest and the lowest reaches of the human heart. The cumulative effect of his achievements and his failures, along with the forces that they unleashed transcends the passing political impact that he may have had over the course of these last thirty years.

Among those of us who have followed the proceedings against Mr Casement since the arraignment hearing at the Bow Street Police Court, there is still bafflement about why the Crown was so ferociously determined to execute its former hero. Personal animosities are perhaps understandable, specifically on the part of Mr Smith. In the case of Mr Smith, there may have also been the underlying fear that letting Mr Casement live would have allowed his most ardent adversary in the Home Rule conflict to recoup his forces for the civil war that will no doubt be in the offing, once the war with Germany is settled. But the positions taken by government, no matter how subject they might be to the pressures and influences of individual authorities, are ultimately taken for loftier political purposes. And while the allegations of sexual

perversion certainly dampened the clemency campaign, those allegations had no direct bearing on the charge of treason but simply made
it easier for the government to proceed with an execution to which it
was committed.

As many of those who spoke out for clemency noted, the execution
of Mr Casement, like the executions over which Sir John Maxwell presided in the aftermath of the Easter Rising, could only create another
martyr, while clemency in such a case was not unprecedented and
would have cast the government in a much more positive light among
the nations with which it has been attempting to curry favour for its
war with Germany (such as the United States) and among the peoples
of the world who still regard Mr Casement as a virtual saint. One can
only conclude that the authorities were so offended by this particular
case – a former knight who had renounced the very government that
had so honoured him, taken up arms on behalf of a group of people
who had been a thorn in the side of the Crown for centuries, and colluded with an enemy with whom the nation had been engaged in a war
of heinous proportions – that passion overwhelmed reason in the final
analysis. Whatever the real reasons for going against the tide of international opinion, the Crown has made no apologies for its decision.

Mr Casement's transformation from celebrated knight to excoriated
traitor is a tale that is not easily understood. In his experience in the
jungles of Africa and South America we can see a saga that is almost
archetypical in capturing the eternally recurring disillusionment that
we are all condemned to suffer, both individually and collectively, as an
inherent quality of our very existence as human beings. Like the Roger
Casement who embarked on a noble mission to bring the blessings of
western civilization to the indigenous populations of the underdevel-
oped world, we all begin, whatever our individual journey might be,
with the conviction that the human race is essentially good. At some
point along the way, we inevitably recognise that buried deep down in
some dark recess of the soul, there is a powerful force that beckons us
toward the edge of an abyss, that we never knew was there. And staring
into that abyss can rock the very foundation of our faith in the goodness and nobility of the human race.

Roger Casement found that abyss in King Leopold's Congo Free State and again in Julio César Arana's Putumayo rubber plantations, deep in the heart of the Amazon rainforest. The first experience was perhaps the more traumatic, given the untarnished idealism that he still possessed when he accepted the assignment to investigate the charges of atrocities that had been emerging from King Leopold's domain. Unfortunately, that idealistic sense of a civilizing mission, upon which the European nations had embarked, so eloquently articulated in the Berlin Accord that constituted the charter for Leopold's International Association of the Congo, left him unprepared for the reality that he discovered in those jungles during the fall of 1903.

The extent of his disillusionment is reflected in his report to the Foreign Office, the document that propelled him onto the world stage. The fact that he still clung to an underlying faith in the basic goodness of man is reflected in his expectation that the report would make a difference. That expectation may have been magnified by his overpowering ego, his perception of himself as the knight in shining armour, coming to the rescue of the dispossessed and the downtrodden of the earth. But no matter how much confidence he might have had in his own ability to sway world opinion, he could not have nurtured any realistic expectation of success, unless he still believed in the capacity of his fellow man to react with the same horror that had so overwhelmed him in the Congo.

The disillusionment could only have been intensified by his perception of the response. Again, his ego may have suffered from the fact that his report did not generate an immediate intervention by the Foreign Office and by the signatories to the Berlin Accord, but it had to have been his wounded sense of idealism that suffered the greatest damage by what he perceived to be at best a tepid response. Rhetorical outrage without concrete action is nothing more than empty posturing, and given the extent of his own disillusionment and his expectation of a more forceful response, Casement had to have concluded that the posturing of his colleagues was simply a way to deflect attention from their calloused lack of concern about the evil that he had so clearly unveiled. The loss of confidence in the Foreign Office to be a force for good in the world, more than any egotistical affront with the reception accorded his report, had to have marked the beginning of his estrangement from the government to which he had devoted his professional life. After all, he had entered government service with the conviction that the Crown, through its commercial and imperial interests around the globe, was indeed motivated by the same sense of mission that had guided him in his African ventures.

The international response that ultimately materialised, albeit belatedly from his perspective, had to have restored at least some degree of faith in man's capacity to be outraged by the existence of evil. And while his subsequent responsibilities with the Foreign Office precluded him from personally witnessing the ultimate outcome of that international furore, he could only assume that Belgium's formal assumption of responsibility for the administration of the Congo was a step in the right direction. Even so, he surely never recovered from the profound impact of those atrocities on his worldview, nor from the perceived dawdling of his British brethren in pressing the case against a clear evil perversion of the colonial mission. He could only rationalise the former by assuming that what he unearthed in the Congo Free State was an aberration in an otherwise noble quest to bring the benefits of western civilization to the less fortunate of the world. His faith in the government that he served had to have been permanently shaken by the latter.

His subsequent experience in the Amazon was undoubtedly the *coup de grace* to his faith in the civilizing mission of the colonial enterprise. While he might have been able to rationalise away the Congo as an aberration, the repetition of those horrors, once again at the expense of indigenous peoples being exploited by ruthless opportunists, suggested that there was a basic flaw in 'the system' that made innocent and unsuspecting people vulnerable to the more powerful of the world; a 'system' that lacked any inherent constraint against the abuses that follow when that evil force that lies deep in the human heart simmers to the surface and erupts upon the land. The colonial 'system', based on commercial endeavours that would, in an ideal world, benefit all parties, was itself a curse, for the disparity in power between the parties, reinforced by the allure of wealth and privilege, actually promoted the emergence of that deep, dark force that leads to the abyss. While individuals can be policed, as Casement himself was attempting to accomplish through the revelations of his investigative reports, the colonial 'system' and its imperialistic support structure could only be eliminated if the world were ever to be free of the evils attendant upon economic exploitation. Depending upon the innate goodness of man was simply not an option when the temptations inherent in 'the system' were too great. Casement's faith in the civilizing benefits of the colonial enterprise was probably interred forever in the Amazon jungle.

Parallel to the disillusioning process that led to his profound loss of faith in the British colonial enterprise, there appears to have been a kindling process that led to his equally profound commitment to the Irish nationalistic enterprise. The two are not unrelated, of course: Mr Casement's interpretation of Irish history would have ultimately led him to see the relationship between Britain and Ireland through the prism of the colonial system. Suppressed and exploited, the Irish, in Mr Casement's view, were not all that different from the Congolese natives or the Witoto tribes people. By the time he returned to his homeland after the Amazon expedition, his worldview had no doubt been drastically altered by the convergence of three long-term processes: the effects of his disillusioning exposure to the atrocities bred by commercial exploitation within the colonial system and to the less-than-enthusiastic response of his Foreign Office superiors; his long-standing interest in Irish history and culture, which made him especially sympathetic to, and supportive of, the cultural renaissance in his homeland; and the conviction, born of the interaction between these two evolving influences, that Ireland was as much a victim of colonial exploitation as the Congo Free State and the Putumayo. Upon returning to Ireland after his foray into the Amazon, he had to have been fully primed for full immersion in the cause of Irish nationalism.

History and personality obviously intersected at that fateful turning point in Anglo-Irish relations. At the very moment when Mr Casement's humanitarian proclivities led him to take up the cause of Ireland, with the same zeal that had led him into the Congo and the

Amazon, the threat of civil war between the unionists and the national-ists had reached its peak, and the relations between the nationalists and the Crown were at their nadir. The incendiary political situation had set the stage for the final act of the drama in which Mr Casement was to play such a tragic role.

The evidence presented to the court during his trial concluded just two months ago and the testimony of sources who were close to him in the IRB suggest that he played that role with the same degree of enthusiasm and commitment that characterised all the causes that he undertook during the course of his career. Given the outrage of those who presided over his trial and the ferocity of their campaign to impose the ultimate justice upon him, his opponents must surely have shared that opinion. The vilifications directed at him over these past several months have matched if not exceeded the celebrations heaped upon him over the course of his twenty years in the Foreign Office. Justice Isaacs, Justice Darling, Attorney General Smith, the Home Secretary Mr Samuel, the Prime Minister Mr Asquith, even King George himself, have all concurred in the judgement that Mr Casement's accomplish-ments during those celebrated twenty years have been more than offset by the calumny of the last two. And that judgement has certainly been endorsed by the British court of public opinion.

The Irish court of public opinion seems still to be out. The IRB and those associated with the recent rebellion naturally applaud his actions: their initial suspicions, bred of his long and celebrated service to the Crown, have been laid to rest by his trial and execution. As for the gen-eral public, they seem initially to have been as mystified by Casement as they were by the insurrection itself: what little they know about him relates to his long career as a British diplomat, leaving them puzzled by his involvement in what many first perceived to be nothing more than another in a long history of quixotic adventures by noble-minded but misdirected Irish romantics. And just as the public's initially tepid support of the rising has been galvanised by the violent reaction of the British under Sir John Maxwell, their knowledge about and regard for Mr Casement may have both been heightened enormously by the very public display orchestrated by the Crown over the course of this past summer. The relationship between Britain and Ireland remains tense and will probably not abate until the resolution of the Home Rule issue, still on hold for the duration of hostilities with Germany. How the Irish will ultimately regard Mr Casement, as well as the participants in the recent Easter Rising could well depend on the final resolution of that issue.

British and Irish opinion, indeed world opinion, can converge in honouring Mr Casement's humanitarian achievements in the Congo and the Amazon. Whatever the shared perception might be of those efforts, however, the perception of his role in the recent insurrection could not be more polarised. As it has often been said, one man's revolutionary is another man's freedom fighter. Which of the two judgements prevails depends simply on the side from which one views the events. My American readers will surely appreciate that: our own declaration of independence articulated the justification for the rebellion of the American colonies against the same Crown from which Ireland is seeking independence. Had that revolution failed, George Washington and his colleagues would have faced the same fate that has befallen Roger Casement and the others associated with the recent Irish rebellion. Those same readers can equally appreciate the view from the other side: had the followers of Jefferson Davis prevailed in their demands for independence, the union that has become the United States would have been torn asunder, fewer than a hundred years after its formation. To quote the nineteenth-century English historian James Anthony Froude, treason can be either 'the greatest of crimes or the noblest of virtues'.[105]

Whether a crime or a virtue, when seen in the context of his experience over the course of his career, Mr Casement's 'treason' was the inevitable climax of the humanitarian qualities that defined his character. Those qualities took him far from home, waging battles that often must have seemed futile on behalf of indigenous peoples who had become the victims, rather than the beneficiaries, of western expansion and economic globalisation. As he became increasingly disillusioned with the colonial 'system' and with his government's willingness to combat the attendant evils that it bred, he gradually refocused the outrage engendered by those basic humanitarian concerns, becoming an advocate for those in his homeland, whom he finally grouped in the same category of victims as those who had suffered economic exploitation at the outer reaches of human civilization.

At that point, for Mr Casement, being a humanitarian meant becoming a revolutionary. He had always harboured illusions of grandeur, in his perception of the role for which he was destined. As early as 1900, in Lourenço Marques he had envisioned himself at the head of a paramilitary expedition to sever the rail link between the Transvaal and Delagoa Bay as a means of interrupting the flow of arms to the Boer republics. Landing on the coast of Kerry in anticipation of leading an armed insurrection against Britain was no less quixotic than the proposal that had received Lord Kitchener's endorsement in southern Africa. After a lifetime of frustrated efforts on behalf of the exploited and the downtrodden, he could go out in a blaze of glory, waging a true flesh-and-blood struggle with human combatants, rather than assailing the more elusive bureaucratic battlements of entrenched political and commercial interests.

As with anyone who plays such a prominent role on the world stage, Mr Casement's final reputation will be determined by the course of history. Perhaps his most lasting legacy will not be in the achievements for which he was honoured but in the quest, however frustrating, that underlay those achievements. In spite of the interventions that his investigative efforts ultimately galvanised in the Congo and the Amazon, the deprivations associated with colonialism and economic exploitation are still a hallmark of relations between the developed and the less developed nations of the earth. In spite of his investigative reports' cautionary revelations about the human capacity for evil, atrocities continue to occur on a shocking scale. And in spite of all efforts to revive a sense of shared identity that might unite Ireland in common cause, intractable differences still divide his homeland into separate political entities. One could arguably contend that Mr Casement's entire career was spent tilting at windmills and that the true essence of any Casement 'legacy' lies therein. In the end, after all, tilting at windmills may be all there is – and may, in fact, be enough.

ENDNOTES

1. *The Times* ('The Treason Charge: Sir R. Casement at Bow Street'), 16 May 1916, p.9.
2. *The Times* ('The Irish at Limburg: Ex-Prisoners' Evidence'), 16 May 1916, p.10.
3. *Ibid.*, p.10.
4. *Ibid.*, p.10.
5. *Ibid.*, p.10.
6. *The Times* ('Casement Sent for Trial: End of Police Court Hearing'), 18 May 1916, p.4.
7. *The Times* ("Mr. Birrell on Sinn Fein"), 20 May 1916, p.7.
8. General Act of the Conference of Berlin Concerning the Congo. *The American Journal of International Law*, vol. 3, no. 1, Supplement: Official Documents (American Society of International Law, January, 1909), p.12.
9. Casement's Congo Report. Séamas Ó Síocháin & Michael O'Sullivan, eds. *The Eyes of another Race: Roger Casement's Congo Report and 1903 Diary* (University College Dublin Press: Dublin, 2003), p.56.
10. *Ibid.*, p.59.
11. *Ibid.*, p.63.
12. *Ibid.*, p.67.
13. *Ibid.*, p.53.
14. *Ibid.*, p.53.
15. *Ibid.*, p.53.
16. *Ibid.*, p.52.
17. *Ibid.*, p.53.
18. *Ibid.*, p.53.
19. *Ibid.*, p.56.
20. *Ibid.*, p.61.
21. *Ibid.*, p.57.
22. *Ibid.*, p.60.
23. *Ibid.*, p.60.
24. *Ibid.*, p.66.
25. *Ibid.*, p.73.
26. *Ibid.*, p.97.
27. *Ibid.*, p.97.
28. *Ibid.*, p.62.
29. *Ibid.*, p.163.
30. *Ibid.*, p.163.
31. *Ibid.*, p.163.

32. Quoted in *The Eyes of another Race: Roger Casement's Congo Report and 1903 Diary* edited by Séamas Ó Síocháin & Michael O'Sullivan (University College Dublin Press: Dublin, 2003), p.28.

33. From the Treason Act of 1351 (25 Edward III, Statute 5). The UK Statute Law Database, Office of Public Sector Information of the National Archives. Available online at: www.statutelaw.gov.uk/content.aspx?activeTextDocID=1517663

34. *The Times* ('Treason Charge: True Bill against Casement'), 26 May 1916, p.3.

35. First count of the indictment. George H. Knott, ed., *The Trial of Sir Roger Casement* (Cromarty Law Book Company: Philadelphia, 1917), p.2.

36. *Ibid.*, 2-3.

37. Fourth count of the indictment. *Ibid.*, p.3.

38. Casement's appeal to the Prisoners of War. *Ibid.*, p.3.

39. Fifth count of the indictment. *Ibid.*, p.3-4.

40. Sixth count of the indictment. *Ibid.*, p.4.

41. From St. Patrick's letter to Coroticus. Seumas MacManus, *The Story of the Irish Race* (Konecky and Konecky: Old Saybrook, Connecticut, 1921), p.119.

42. Knott, *The Trial of Sir Roger Casement*, p.7.

43. *Ibid.*, p.7.

44. *Ibid.*, p.7.

45. *Ibid.*, p.10.

46. *Ibid.*, p.12.

47. *Ibid.*, p.15.

48. Roger Casement, *The Crime against Europe* (Teddington, England, The Echo Library, 2007), p.7.

49. *Ibid.*, p.7.

50. *Ibid.*, p.16.

51. *Ibid.*, p.11.

52. *Ibid.*, p.15.

53. *Ibid.*, p.11.

54. *Ibid.*, p.16.

55. *Ibid.*, p.16.

56. *Ibid.*, p.16.

57. *Ibid.*, p.16.

58. *Ibid.*, p.53.

59. *Ibid.*, p.22.

60. Knott, *The Trial of Sir Roger Casement,* p.66-67.

61. *Ibid.*, p.67.

62. *Ibid.*, p.92.

63. *Ibid.*, p.92.

64. *Ibid.*, p.92.

65. Casement, *The Crime against Europe*, p.31.

66. *Ibid.*, p.32.

67. *Ibid.*, p.24.

68. *Ibid.*, p.36.

69. *Ibid.*, p.38.

70. *Ibid.*, p.43.

71. *Ibid.*, p.43.

72. Knott, *The Trial of Sir Roger Casement*, p.93.

73. *Ibid.*, p.104.

74. *Ibid.*, p.108.

75. *Ibid.*, p.141.

76. *Ibid.*, p.150-151.

77. *Ibid.*, p.151.

78. *Ibid.*, p.155.

79. Brian Inglis, *Roger Casement* (New York: Harcourt Brace Jovanovich, Inc., 1973), 282.

80. Knott, *The Trial of Sir Roger Casement*, p.160.

81. *Ibid.*, p.160.

82. *Ibid.*, p.181.

83. *Ibid.*, p.196.

84. *Ibid.*, p.205.

85. *Ibid.*, p.205.

86. *Ibid.*, p.197-205.

87. *Ibid.*, p.218.

88. *Ibid.*, p.218.

89. *Ibid.*, p.219.

90. *Ibid.*, p.233.

91. *Ibid.*, p.233.

92. *Ibid.*, p.287.

93. From a letter to the editor by George Bernard Shaw, *Manchester Guardian* ('Shall Roger Casement Hang?'), 22 July 1916, p.4.

94. *Ibid.*, p.4.

95. *Ibid.*, p.4.

96. *Ibid.*, p.4.

97. *The New York Times* ('Casement Pleas in Senate'), 26 July 1916, p.3.

98. *Ibid.*, p.3.

99. From a letter to the editor by Henry Nevinson. *Manchester Guardian* ('For Casement's Reprieve'), 25 July 1916, p.10.

100. *Ibid.*, p.10.

101. *Ibid.*, p.10.

102. *Ibid.*, p.10.

103. Inglis, *Roger Casement*, 360.

104. *The Times* ('A Willing Agent of Germany: Fresh Evidence of Treachery'), 4 August 1916, p.3.

105. Quoted in a column by John Quinn ('Roger Casement, Martyr') in the *New York Times* Magazine Section for Sunday, 13 August 1916.

BIBLIOGRAPHY

Broeker, G., 'Roger Casement: Background to Treason.' *The Journal of Modern History*, 29, 3 (September 1957), 237-245.

Campbell, J., 'Give a Dog a Bad Name: The Curious Case of F.E. Smith and the "Black Diaries' of Roger Casement" *History Today* 34, 9 (September 1984), 14-19.

Casement, R., *The Crime against Europe* (The Echo Library: Teddington, England, 2007).

Coogan, T.P., *1916: The Easter Rising* (Phoenix Paperbacks: London, 2005).

Costigan, G., 'The Treason of Sir Roger Casement', *The American Historical Review* 60, 2 (January 1955), 283-302.

Daly, M.E., ed. *Roger Casement in Irish and World History* (Royal Irish Academy: Dublin, 2005).

Desmond, S., *The Drama of Sinn Féin* (Charles Scribner's Sons: New York, 1923).

Edwards, O.D., 'Divided Treasons and Divided Loyalties: Roger Casement and Others' *Transactions of the Royal Historical Society* 5, 32 (1982),153-174.

Edwards, O.D., 'The Trial of Roger Casement: A Study in Theatre Management', *Roger Casement in Irish and World History*, ed. Mary E. Daly (Royal Irish Academy: Dublin, 2005).

Gearty, C., 'The Casement Treason Trial in Its Legal Context' *Roger Casement in Irish and World History*, ed. Mary E. Daly (Royal Irish Academy: Dublin, 2005).

Grant, K., 'Bones of Contention: The Repatriation of the Remains of Roger Casement' *The Journal of British Studies* 41, 3 (July, 2002), 329-353.

Harris, P.J., 'From the Putumayo to Connemara: Roger Casement's Amazonian Voyage of Discovery', *Irish Migration Studies in Latin America* 4, 3 (July 2006), *The Journal of the Society for Irish Latin American Studies*. Available online at www.irlandeses.org.

Hemming, J., 'Roger Casement's Putumayo Investigation', *Roger Casement in Irish and World History*, ed. Mary E. Daly (Royal Irish Academy: Dublin, 2005).

Inglis, B. *Roger Casement* (Harcourt Brace Jovanovich, Inc.: New York, 1973).

Knott, G.H., ed. *The Trial of Sir Roger Casement. Notable Trials Series* (Cromarty Law Book Company: Philadelphia 1917).

The London Times digital archives.

Louis, W.R., 'Roger Casement and the Congo', *Journal of African History* 5, 1 (1964), 99-120.

MacManus, S., *The Story of the Irish Race* (Konecky and Konecky: Old Saybrook, Connecticut, 1921).

McCaffrey, C., & Eaton L., *In Search of Ancient Ireland: The Origins of the Irish from Neolithic Times to the Coming of the English* (Ivan R. Dee, Publisher: Chicago, 2002).

McCaffrey, C., *In Search of Ireland's Heroes: The Story of the Irish from the English Invasion to the Present Day* (Ivan R. Dee, Publisher: Chicago, 2006).

McCormack, W. J., *Roger Casement in Death, or Haunting the Free State* (University College Dublin Press: Dublin, 2002).

Mitchell, A., 'An Irish Putumayo: Roger Casement's Humanitarian Relief Campaign in Connemara (1913-14)', *Irish Economic and Social History* 31 (2004).

Mitchell, A., *Casement. Life and Times Series.* (Haus Publishing: London, 2003).

The New York Times digital archives.

O'Síocháin, S., 'Evolution and degeneration in the thought of Roger Casement' *Irish Journal of Anthropology* 2 (1997), 45-62.

O'Síocháin, S., & O'Sullivan, M., *The Eyes of another Race: Roger Casement's Congo Report and 1903 Diary.* Edited with an introduction and notes by Séamas O'Síocháin and Michael O'Sullivan. (Dublin: University College Dublin Press, 2003).

Reid, B.L., *The Lives of Roger Casement* (Yale University Press: New Haven, 1976).

Sawyer, R., *Casement: The Flawed Hero* (Routledge & Kegan Paul: Boston, 1984).

Steele, E.D., 'J.S. Mill and the Irish Question: The Principles of Political Economy, 1848-1865.' *The Historical Journal* 13, 2 (June 1970), 216-236.